Salvation from Cinema

Salvation from Cinema offers something new to the burgeoning field of "religion and film": the religious significance of film technique. Discussing the history of both cinematic devices and film theory, Crystal Downing argues that attention to the material medium echoes Christian doctrine about the materiality of Christ's body as the medium of salvation. Downing cites Jewish, Muslim, Buddhist, and Hindu perspectives on film in order to compare and clarify the significance of medium within the frameworks of multiple traditions. This book will be useful to professors and students interested in the relationship between religion and film.

Crystal Downing teaches film adaptation, critical theory, and nineteenth-century British literature at Messiah College in Pennsylvania, USA. In addition to her first three books, which apply poststructuralist insight to issues of faith, Downing has published numerous essays on film in journals such as *Religion and the Arts*, *Film and History*, *Books and Culture*, *Literature/Film Quarterly*, and *The Cresset*.

Salvation from Cinema
The Medium is the Message

Crystal Downing

LONDON AND NEW YORK

First published 2016
by Routledge
711 Third Avenue, New York, NY 10017

and by Routledge
2 Park Square, Milton Park, Abingdon, Oxon, OX14 4RN

Routledge is an imprint of the Taylor & Francis Group, an informa business

© 2016 Taylor & Francis

The right of Crystal Downing to be identified as author of this work has been asserted by her in accordance with sections 77 and 78 of the Copyright, Designs and Patents Act 1988.

All rights reserved. No part of this book may be reprinted or reproduced or utilized in any form or by any electronic, mechanical, or other means, now known or hereafter invented, including photocopying and recording, or in any information storage or retrieval system, without permission in writing from the publishers.

Trademark notice: Product or corporate names may be trademarks or registered trademarks, and are used only for identification and explanation without intent to infringe.

Library of Congress Cataloging in Publication Data
Downing, Crystal.
Salvation from cinema : the medium is the message / Crystal Downing. -- 1st ed.
pages cm
1. Motion pictures--Religious aspects. 2. Religion in motion pictures. I. Title.
PN1995.9.R4D69 2015
791.43'682--dc23
2015016299

ISBN: 978-1-138-91393-6 (hbk)
ISBN: 978-1-138-91394-3 (pbk)
ISBN: 978-1-315-69113-8 (ebk)

Typeset in Goudy
by GreenGate Publishing Services, Tonbridge, Kent

For the Odd Men Out

Contents

Acknowledgments — viii

Introduction: Toward a Union of Medium and Message — 1

PART I
Theories of Film Salvation — 15

1 Let There Be Enlightenment: Salvation from Religion and Film — 17

2 Light from Light: Seeing Cinema Constellations — 38

3 Gazing at the Stars: Nudity on the Screen — 55

4 Breaking the Fourth Wall: Salvation from the Screen — 74

PART II
Salvation from Film Theory — 93

5 Enlightenment as Mass Deception: Certain Tendencies in Film Theory — 95

6 The Gift of Salvation: Derrida and Holocaust Cinema — 121

7 Seeing Cinema Differently: Salvation from Charles Sanders Peirce — 144

8 From Delusion to Deleuzean Cinema: Salvation from Hugo — 163

Bibliography — 179
Index — 191

Acknowledgments

This book was made possible by several grants from Messiah College, which not only provided me with a sabbatical but also named me Distinguished Professor of English and Film Studies, an honor that included a teaching load reduction in order to work on my scholarship. The college funded several superb research assistants as well: Alison Williams, Mary Finch, Sarah Kistler, and Elena Patton. My thoughts about cinema preceded these privileges by decades, however, due to a group of friends in Santa Barbara who gathered to watch and discuss avant-garde film: David, Bill, Anita, Jim, Doreen, Paul, and Andrea. At the same time, Garrett Stewart, the director of my doctoral dissertation, was igniting the "spiritual automaton" in me, deserving recognition that far exceeds his work on film that is cited in these pages. Equally important is John Wilson, editor of *Books and Culture*, who published many of my earliest efforts, encouraging me to view film through the lens of faith. More recently, two extraordinary conferences gave me the motivation and energy to finish *Salvation from Cinema*. In April of 2014, I presented an abstract from the book at an international conference sponsored by the *Journal of Religion and Film*, where I benefited from conversations with many superb scholars, several of whom I cite in the pages that follow: M. Gail Hamner, Alyda Faber, Terry Lindvall, John Lyden, and Bill Blizek. They have made this a better book. Several months later, I participated in a national conference on Christianity and Film sponsored by Baylor University, where I met Joseph Kickasola, Rebecca Ver Straten-McSparran, Jen Letherer, and William Romanowski, all of whom energized my thought.

Colleagues who read various parts of the manuscript were indispensable: Valerie Weaver-Zercher, Cynthia Wells, Jenell Paris, Meg Ramey, Kate Simcox, Leah Clarke, Jennifer McFarlane-Harris, Valerie Flower, and Lijuan Ye. I also thank Fabrizio Cilento for drawing my attention to the work of Johannes Ehrat, whose scholarship reinforced my thesis about the importance of Charles Sanders Peirce to film theory. Finally, I must acknowledge my best friend and film-viewing companion, David C. Downing, who helped me to understand the power of the medium, not only in cinema but also in love.

Introduction
Toward a Union of Medium and Message

For many twentieth-century Christians, "salvation from cinema" was tantamount to salvation from sin. I discovered this in elementary school when a friend invited me to join her family to watch the Richard Burton / Elizabeth Taylor *Cleopatra*. My parents refused to let me go, not because I was too young to sit through Joseph Mankiewicz's four-hour extravaganza, but because I was old enough to take a stand for my faith. After all, Taylor and Burton had become adulterous bedfellows, both on- and off-screen. Movies, my parents warned, bred a multitude of sinners.

Demonstrated by a multitude of cinema books since then, the word *from* in "salvation from cinema" has changed meaning. Christian pastors and professors mine movies for insight, extracting salvation messages from cinema. In addition to a plethora of work on Jesus films, they write books about biblical themes in cinema, with telling titles like *Saint Paul at the Movies* (1993), *Hollywood Dreams and Biblical Stories* (1994), *The Old Testament in Fiction and Film* (1994), *Pauline Images in Fiction and Film* (1999), *Screening Scripture* (2002), *Gospel Images in Fiction and Film* (2002), *Reading the Gospels in the Dark* (2003), *Scripture on the Silver Screen* (2003), *Finding St. Paul in Film* (2005), and *The Bible on the Big Screen* (2007).[1]

Pushing beyond biblical themes, some theologians address the sacramental implications of film images, while others focus on cinema "as a fertile site of redemptive activity," movie protagonists illustrating how to transcend the traumatizing exigencies of life.[2] And, of course, religious studies specialists discuss salvation from cinema in ways that exceed the particularity of Christianity. Some, in fact, celebrate film itself as a form of salvation, cinema offering myths and rituals that give meaning to existence. In the aptly titled *Film as Religion*, John C. Lyden takes an anthropological approach to belief, invoking theorists such as Clifford Geertz and Mircea Eliade to argue that cinema provides "a vision of what the world really is, and what it should be," paralleling what S. Brent Plate calls the religious "world-making" of cinema. Similar to Clive Marsh, who considers film-watching as a "life practice" that "helps shape a 'spirituality,'" Kutter Callaway asserts that "the practice of filmgoing has the capacity to function in a religious-like manner." Summarizing such views, Melanie J. Wright states that "film can at times be not simply a descriptor of, or a vehicle for, religious experience, but religion itself."[3] Rather than renouncing cinema in the name of salvation, such scholars argue that salvation comes *from* cinema.

It would be disingenuous, however, to argue that the semantic change to "salvation from cinema" proves increased intellectual sophistication. As suggested by poststructuralist thinkers, it is an Enlightenment fiction to assume that civilization has evolved from benighted religious superstition to free-thinking rationality. Michel Foucault implied throughout his work that medieval Christianity and modernist scientism, similarly embedded in discourse, are merely different kinds of rationality, both reflecting assumptions taken by faith.[4] Furthermore, and more to the point, historical data does not support an evolutionary model by which American Christians, once considering cinema as sin, eventually developed a more theologically astute understanding of salvation from cinema. Having researched the early decades of the movie industry, Terry Lindvall in *Sanctuary Cinema* (2007) and William D. Romanowski in *Reforming Hollywood* (2012) demonstrate that "salvation from cinema" had opposite meanings from the very start. As early as 1899, Salvation Army leader Herbert Booth used moving pictures for Christian evangelism, proclaiming "What photography has accomplished in the way of animated pictures has been adapted to the purposes of *salvation*."[5]

Rather than naively celebrate the evolution of "salvation from cinema," I am concerned with that pesky preposition "from." No matter how one reads the phrase "salvation from cinema," the preposition tends to signal a retreat *from* the cinematic medium. While some devout people extract themselves from cinema seats, others extract salvation messages—if not salvation itself—from cinema. Relevant to any theologian or religion scholar who teaches and/or writes about film, this book addresses the many professors and students who, in their enthusiastic endorsement of salvation from cinema, tend to ignore the artistry of the medium itself. *Salvation from Cinema* argues, in contrast, that the medium is the message.[6]

The Message of Marshall McLuhan

In 1964 Marshall McLuhan coined the phrase "the medium is the message" in a book so influential that it was republished in 1994 and again in 2003. *Understanding Media: The Extensions of Man* argues that human psychology is shaped more by the *way* media (like books, radio, television, and film) communicate than by their content. He gives the example of the printing press, which radically altered human behavior totally apart from the content of what presses produced: "Print created individualism and nationalism in the sixteenth century."[7]

McLuhan also gives the example of a lightbulb: a medium that transmits light but has no message. Nevertheless, by altering human environments, a lightbulb affects not only human perception but also behavior: eating, sleeping and working patterns changed as light became available at the flick of a switch. McLuhan goes so far as to argue that television functions similarly: children's behavior is affected more thoroughly by the placement of televisions in their homes than by any of the broadcasts they see *on* television—whether sacred or profane. The medium is more powerful than any story it presents.

Not surprisingly, McLuhan's claims have generated controversy, and many scholars consider his emphasis on medium alone as limited.[8] Any theory, of course, that attributes all of human behavior to a single cause is reductive, as when Marxists reduce human behavior to economic inequities and Freudians reduce human psychology to repressed impulses. Nevertheless, like Freud and Marx, McLuhan brought to light a powerful influence on human perception and behavior. He, in fact, not only predicted the development of VCRs and DVRs, but also foresaw a world-wide medium—what we now call the internet—anticipating decades in advance a "global village": another phrase he coined.[9]

In 2010, Nicholas Carr invoked McLuhan in his Pulitzer Prize-nominated book *The Shallows: What the Internet is Doing to our Brains*. Citing data from numerous scientific studies, Carr establishes that the internet, as a medium, "strains our cognitive abilities, diminishing our learning and weakening our understanding."[10] Like McLuhan, he therefore wants us to actively *think about* the medium itself rather than passively allow it to control our thought-processes. The same point, of course, applies to cinema, which sends unreflective audience members into what McLuhan calls a "subliminal state of Narcissus trance."[11]

The Narcissus Trance

According to the well-known Greek myth, Narcissus was a hunter famous for excessive pride about his extraordinary good looks. Nemesis, the spirit of divine retribution, therefore led Narcissus to a pool where he fell in love with his reflection in the water. Not able to take his eyes off of his mirrored image, Narcissus became oblivious to the world around him and, according to some renditions, fell into the pool and drowned.

Like Narcissus staring into a pool, we as moviegoers stare into a screen, subliminally falling in love with the protagonists we see there even as we identify with them. This "identification," as Richard Dyer calls it, explains why we feel tension during a chase scene, why we long for the male or female protagonist to take that first kiss—and more.[12] Under the Narcissus trance we don't think about how the medium manipulates us to identify with the screen heroes through extreme close-ups on their faces as well as through repeated point-of-view shots, as though we were seeing reality through their eyes. These, along with other techniques discussed in this book, lead us to desire what the protagonist desires, whether to incarcerate a law-breaking detective or to cheat on a despicable spouse. Other movies, however, may encourage us to do the exact opposite: to root for detectives who don't play by the rules and to despise cheating spouses. The message differs according to techniques employed by the medium. As film theorist André Bazin explained in 1951, "A member of a film audience tends to identify himself with the film's hero by a psychological process, the result of which is to turn the audience into a 'mass' and to render emotion uniform."[13] Audience members sit side by side with Narcissus, staring into the screen.

My Difference from McLuhan and Medium Essentialism

While McLuhan talked about the cultural and psychological impact of the technology itself, I focus on *techniques that constitute the medium*: visual elements that make a movie experience radically different from a reading experience—even when (or perhaps especially when) a movie is based on a novel or alludes to a religious myth. As McLuhan demonstrated with the assistance of graphic designer Quentin Fiore, we read a photographic image differently than we read typographic print. In their best-selling *The Medium is the Massage*, McLuhan and Fiore juxtapose visual images with textual descriptions in order to demonstrate that each medium "massages" our senses in different ways. At the same time, however, I seek to avoid what film scholar Noël Carroll has dubbed "medium essentialism," wherein particular pre-established techniques distinguish cinematic art from all other art forms.[14] Instead, I celebrate a pluralism of screen devices that differ from movie to movie, a pluralism that encourages new possibilities for filmic art. As Robert Sinnerbrink puts it, "The 'medium' of film is what remains to be invented by putting to work the inherited traditions, conventions and aesthetic possibilities of film in an open-ended manner."[15]

Finally, even though twenty-first-century scholars have been theorizing how changes to the cinematic medium—from celluloid to digitized images—shape viewer perception, that is not my focus.[16] Like many film scholars, I continue to describe movies as "films" even though more and more theaters no longer use film. Rather than taking huge rolls of celluloid out of metal canisters and then threading them through mechanical projectors, theaters are downloading their movies. I therefore talk about the beauty of "a film" the same way I talk about the beauty of "a sunrise." I know the sun does not literally move through the sky, just as I know digitized movies are not strips of celluloid that move through film-projectors. Nevertheless "sunrise" and "film" are useful metaphors about bringing light into dark places.[17]

Salvation, as well, is about bringing light into dark places, illuminating a problem with cinema.

Seeing the Light, Seeing the Art

Cinema is like the day star accompanying a sunrise: a phenomenon with opposite connotations. It can be the "light that shineth in a dark place, … the day star" that the Revelation of St. John aligns with Jesus. Or it can be Lucifer, whose name means "bearer of light": "How you are fallen from heaven, / O Day Star, son of Dawn! / How you are cut down to the ground, / you who laid the nations low!"[18]

Indeed, while sometimes cinema bears the light of truth, other times it brings the nations to a raunchy low. As Marxist cultural critics Max Horkheimer and Theodor Adorno argued in 1944, the cinematic "pleasure industry" can pander to viewers' basest desires. Using language reminiscent of Lucifer "cut down to the ground," they say of cinema, "after the descent, much is permitted; even license as a marketable specialty has its quota bearing the trade description 'daring'."[19] No doubt they have a point. A theater, for many moviegoers, is like Dante's Hell, filled with amazing images of lust and terror. It's just that, while Dante's Inferno bears the inscription "Abandon all hope, ye who enter here," movie theaters bear the sentiment, for many, "abandon all thought, ye who enter here." As Horkheimer and Adorno put it, "Pleasure [in cinema] always means not to think about anything, to forget suffering even where it is shown … It is flight; not, as is asserted, flight from a wretched reality, but from the last remaining thought of resistance."[20]

Whereas Horkheimer and Adorno assume that the angelic shimmers on movie screens are actually the flutters of capitalist devils in disguise, *Salvation from Cinema* argues that shimmering angels, though never divine, often point to the divine. Like angels depicted in Renaissance paintings who point to sacred subjects that share the canvas with them, so elements placed upon movie screens can point to subjects that have a place in religious faith. Unfortunately, many people fail to notice the angelic pointers, responding to film the same way many visitors respond to angel-graced paintings in Paris's Louvre. People wanting to see Leonardo da Vinci's *Mona Lisa* in the museum often discover a map is unnecessary: they merely need to follow the crowds. Barely noticing beautiful art on the walls surrounding them, masses head toward the *Mona Lisa* because it is famous—like moviegoers heading out to see films because they are hyped. In both cases, viewers are not conscious of *what* they see—shape, color, pattern—but only of their *act* of seeing. The medium is ignored in favor of an extrapolated message: either "I saw what everyone else is talking about" or "That picture is about a woman with a secret." Many books on religion and film merely combine the two responses, extracting religious messages from box-office hits. Ironically, their attempts to extract salvation from cinema echo a cautionary scene from a film they sometimes cite: *Raging Bull* (Martin Scorsese, 1980).

Raging for Salvation

Near the end of *Raging Bull*, Jake LaMotta (Robert De Niro) hammers away at the championship belt he won in the boxing ring years before, seeking to extract gems embedded within it. When he takes the gems to a jeweler, however, he discovers they have little value, whereas the rare championship belt he just destroyed might have supplied him with funds to bribe his way out of jail.

Like LaMotta, many theologians and religion scholars extract gems of insight from movies, not realizing that the brilliant objects are more valuable when seen as part of the film's entire visual structure. Ignoring visual artistry, they tend to discuss the implications of cinema in terms of story. But if it's all about the profundity of a carefully crafted story, why not simply read the screenplay?

The answer, of course, is obvious: reading the screenplay rather than seeing the film would eliminate pleasure in the movie-viewing experience. But what makes it pleasurable? Must we cede all pleasure to "freedom from thought," as do Horkheimer and Adorno?[21] Doesn't pleasure come from *how* cinematic images

6 *Introduction*

appear on the screen: an artistry worthy of contemplation? As noted by Martin Scorsese, the director of *Raging Bull*, "visual literacy is just as important as verbal literacy":

> What the film pioneers were exploring was the medium's specific techniques. In the process, they invented a new language based on images rather than words, a visual grammar you might say: close-ups, irises, dissolves, masking part of the frame for emphasis, dolly shots, tracking shots.[22]

Unfortunately, most who extract religious and theological insights from movies ignore such techniques, only rarely employing the basic cinematic vocabulary that identifies *how* viewers see what they see: *long take, long shot, graphic match, crosscutting, swish pan, high-angle lens, low-key lighting, crane shot*, etc. That's like writing a book on Buddhism without using key terms such as *bodhisattva* and *dharma*. It can be done, of course, but much is left out about the *medium* of salvation.

Similarly, theologians who would disdain any scholarly book about the Trinity that does not mention Christian theorists such as Tertullian or Augustine often ignore influential film theorists when writing about theology incarnated in film. Just as an understanding of Judeo-Christian theology necessitates knowledge of more than stories told in the Bible, an understanding of cinema necessitates appreciation for more than the stories told on celluloid. This is not to derogate story. As with many religions, Christian belief arises from story. But it also focuses on much more: Jesus as the flesh-and-blood *medium* of salvation. As media specialist Michael Wetzel puts it, "McLuhan's 'The medium is the message' is as Christian as you can get." Nevertheless, it is important to note that Wetzel makes this statement in conversation with the famous father of deconstruction, Jacques Derrida. Though having famously proclaimed "I rightly pass for an atheist," Derrida comments during the interview with Wetzel that "religious tolerance" arises from "the space of a Christian semantics."[23] Inspired by Derrida, then, *Salvation from Cinema* argues that McLuhan's famous phrase should inform all discussions of religion and film, no matter the religion, no matter the film. Indeed, attention to the medium can help viewers determine which films deserve analysis and which deserve dismissal. To exemplify how this might work, I return to *Raging Bull*, which instructs viewers about the importance of seeing.

Seeing Salvation in the Medium

Multiple reviewers and scholars have extracted a salvation message from *Raging Bull*. Christopher Deacy, in fact, quotes seven different people in less than three pages to demonstrate that the film is "perceived as a site of comprehensive redemptive significance." He even includes the voice of Martin Scorsese, the director, who hopes that viewers of the film might "see the beginning trajectory up to some kind of salvation."[24]

Scorsese's word "see" is telling, for he ends *Raging Bull* with a biblical quotation about seeing. The white words appear on a black screen as follows, the separate verses lit up one at a time:

> So, for the second time, [the Pharisees]
> Summoned the man who had been blind and said:
>
> "Speak the truth before God.
> We know this fellow is a sinner."
>
> "Whether or not he is a sinner, I do not know"
> the man replied.
>
> "All I know is this:
> once I was blind and now I can see."
>
> John IX, 24–6
the New English Bible
>
> Remembering Haig P. Manoogian, teacher.
> May 23, 1916 – May 26, 1980.
> With love and resolution, Marty.

Ironically, scholars interested in salvation from cinema often quote only the last verse above, failing to describe what they *see* on screen. They thus remain blind to the message of the medium itself. For, by including the dedication to his film professor, Scorsese implies that the biblical coda alludes to himself as much as to Jake LaMotta.[25] If Manoogian taught Scorsese how to see, the biblical passage implies that seeing the light is about the seeing the *medium* of salvation, which might include cinema itself.

Indeed, before the Bible passage appears on screen, the last scene of *Raging Bull* alludes to cinema. It begins with an analytic montage of extreme close-ups: a marquee announcing a performance by Jake LaMotta, followed by a full-frame bare lightbulb, cutting to a grimy light switch adjacent to empty bottles. As with Marshall McLuhan's lightbulb, the medium is the message: Jake has finally seen the light and gotten control of his life.

After the montage, we see Jake sitting before a backstage mirror practicing Terry Malloy's famous "I coulda been a contendah" speech from *On the Waterfront* (1954).[26] By filming Jake's recitation from *On the Waterfront* in a framed mirror, Scorsese gestures toward the cinema screen that framed Terry's original cinematic speech. As Charles Affron notes of mirrors framed by the movie screen, "The reflection of feeling in the faithful, impassive mirrors blurs conventional boundaries between what we call reality and what we call art."[27] In this case, *On the Waterfront* as a work of art helps Jake face, as in a mirror, the reality of his own personal demons. Indeed, the parallels are striking: Jake, like Terry (Marlon Brando), is a former 168-pound boxer who develops vexed relationships not only with his brother, but also with a beautiful platinum blonde.

Furthermore, the boxers in both movies make overtures to the female protagonist while looking at her through a metal fence. Finally, in order to reinforce *Raging Bull*'s closing allusion to cinema, Scorsese himself enters the shot—in the role of a stage manager directing Jake to get onstage. Significantly, we only see Scorsese's arm reflected in the mirror, as though alluding to the unseen presence of a director in any film.[28]

Shot in high-key lighting, the scene thus implies that *On the Waterfront*—iconic in film history—has helped Jake see the light about his own dark nature: the medium is the message. People who write about *Raging Bull* miss this message, however, when they ignore the medium. Like Jake wrenching jewels out of his championship belt, they extract salvation from cinema without seeing that salvation is more valuable when *seen* in the context of the medium (the belt) itself. In other words, the artistry of *Raging Bull* lies not in the story or in the dialogue (which was often improvised on the spot), but in the attention to visual details—like gems arranged in a belt. Indeed, Scorsese spent arduous hours story-boarding every single image for the boxing scenes, giving different matches different visual valences. For example, the establishing shot of the ring in which Jake wins a match is captured with a wide-angle lens, such that its welcoming white floor opens toward the viewer. In contrast, for a brutally hellish loss, Scorsese had fires set immediately underneath the camera so that the heat and smoke might distort viewers' perception of the ring, much as Jake's boxing opponent distorts his face.

Some might protest, quite rightly, that it takes a practiced eye (and a bit of research) to recognize such techniques. But that is the point of this book: to exercise the eye while explaining the ophthalmology of film theory. And we might start with an easy exercise, asking why Scorsese shot *Raging Bull* in black and white during a time when almost all movies were in color.

Theology/Religion in Black and White

As many film theorists note, black-and-white cinema captures radical contrasts between light and shadow—chiaroscuro effects—far better than color can. In *Raging Bull*, then, the black-and-white cinematography reflects the black-and-white thinking that dictates Jake's LaMotta's violent behavior, not only in the boxing ring but also toward his wife and brother. In contrast, interpolated scenes showing feel-good conventional behavior—weddings and cheery family life—are shot in home-movie grainy color.

Black and white is also appropriate for the era in which *Raging Bull* is set. Matches fought by the real-life Jake LaMotta in the 1940s and 1950s were, of course, televised in black and white. Not only does Scorsese show characters in the film watching Jake on their small television screens, he also frames Jake's unjustified suspicions about adultery between his brother Joey (Joe Pesci) and wife Vickie (Cathy Moriarty) with images of a television. When Jake first queries Joey about adultery, he sits to the side of a snow-filled tiny television he is attempting to hook up. Then, after succeeding scenes of violence toward both Joey and Vickie, we see Jake staring into the same television, which still delivers

Introduction 9

no picture. The point, unlike the television, is clear: due to his irrational jealousy, Jake's vision is as cloudy as the reception on his TV.

The size of the small 1940s televisions, purposively dwarfed by the film screen that frames them, also bears significance. Representing Jake's rages both inside and outside the ring, the small sets contribute to images of confined spaces throughout the film. When Jake hammers jewels out of his championship belt, we see him framed by a glass-free window opening onto a larger dining room space surrounding it. Adjacent to the opening is a dining room shelf with dishes on display, such that, once Jake starts hammering, the dishes fall and break—as though to say Jake's domestic life, like his boxing career, has been destroyed by misguided rage.

The shot then cuts to the scene with the jeweler, the lighting a bit dimmer as Jake discovers his misguided extraction of gems. We next see Jake confined outside the jewelry store in a phone booth, a low-angle lens emphasizing the claustrophobia of the space. The camera then takes us to a dimmer, more claustrophobic space: behind bars where prison guards wrestle Jake into an even more confining space. Here the chiaroscuro is so intense that we cannot see Jake at all, except for a few moments when he steps into a ray of light to hit his head and fists against the wall. The scene ends with Jake sitting in such impenetrable darkness that all we see is a sliver of his arm as he despairs, "I'm not an animal" and "I'm not that guy." Indeed, we can see no "guy" at all; Jake's dark demons have entirely swallowed him, leaving only a sliver of humanity: the chiaroscuro delivers the message.[29]

Once Jake recognizes his blindness, he can begin his journey back to the light. The next scene, therefore, is a bit brighter, though still shot with low-key lighting. This time Jake is framed by a stage, where he does stand-up comedy in a seedy stripper's joint. At one point the camera shoots over his shoulder, capturing in deep focus a handful of patrons heckling him. The scene echoes one earlier, when Jake jokes from the much larger stage of a glamorous club he owns, the camera shooting over his shoulder to show scores of well-dressed laughing patrons. The echo not only comments on how far Jake has fallen—from a huge glitzy stage to a tiny dark stage—but also alludes to a famous deep-focus shot from *Citizen Kane* (1941). In Orson Welles's black-and-white film—also about a talented man battling his demons—the camera shoots over Kane's shoulders to show well-dressed listeners laughing at his words. Kane, like Jake, eventually falls from this position of control.[30]

Jake, however, returns to the light. After leaving the dingy stripper's club, he sees his alienated brother on the street. Following Joey through the low-key lighting of the pre-dawn streets, Jake attempts reconciliation—which occurs when the two enter the high-key lighting of a parking garage. The film then ends with the closing montage, when Jake rehearses lines from *On the Waterfront*. Cinematic devices of the medium itself thus deliver a message about journeying out of darkness toward the light.[31]

Significantly, in the last shots before the Bible verse, we see Jake walk away from the mirror, and hence out of its frame, and then walk out of the frame of our screen, the final shot lingering on a well-lit empty room. The medium is the message: upon seeing the light about his imprisoning blindness, Jake can escape what has trapped him—including the film itself. Scorsese reinforces this message by having the entire film begin with a shot of Jake practicing his routine in the same well-lit room that closes the film, thus establishing that the intervening diegesis is a flashback on his life.[32] By creating this framing device, Scorsese communicates that the entire film—focusing on a boxer's rage—is a frame that imprisons Jake until he sees the light.

This message of the medium gives special resonance to the biblical story from which Scorsese quotes after Jake walks out of *Raging Bull*. In the account from John 9, Jesus ministers to the man born blind immediately after calling himself "the light of the world" (v. 5). Later he seeks out the healed man, identifying himself as "the Son of Man": "You have seen him, and the one speaking with you is he" (v. 37). The medium, in other words—"the one speaking with you"—is the message of salvation.

This assumption—solidified in the early centuries of Christianity by the first four ecumenical councils—reinforces a basic assumption of film theory. As cinema scholar Marc Furstenau summarizes, "the unique *material basis* of the *medium* has continued to guide theorists, and has led to theoretical accounts that, while differing in many respects, share a fundamental assumption about the relation between *form* and effect, between the *material* basis of film and the cinematic experience."[33] To ignore the medium is to remain blind to the *source* of the message. It is a failure to see the light that illuminates visual codes on screen. As film specialist James Monaco puts it, cinematic "codes are the *medium* through which the '*message*' of [a] scene is transmitted."[34] Though failure to value the medium is especially ironic for Christians, assessing the medium is relevant to any scholar who writes about religion and film. Buddhism scholar Francisca Cho, for example, integrates devices of the medium to emphasize that, "Like the sensory apparition of a Buddha, the illusion of film can lure us into a better practice of seeing."[35]

The Methodology of *Salvation from Cinema*

Seeking to lure religious cinephiles into a better practice of seeing, *Salvation from Cinema* is organized as follows. Part I focuses on what to look for and how to look. Chapter 1 takes a brief look at the history of cinema before surveying scholarship in the burgeoning field known as "religion and film" in order to establish the distinctiveness of *Salvation from Cinema*.[36] While praising theologians and religion scholars for resisting Hollywood materialism, the chapter illustrates their equal but opposite tendency to ignore the material basis of film. Chapter 2 therefore seeks to inculcate receptivity to the distinctive beauty of cinema, discussing films from Muslim, Buddhist, and Christian cultures to demonstrate how creativity through cinematic devices (not merely of the story being dramatized) might be creatively analyzed. Chapter 3 focuses on another aspect of seeing: how we look at naked bodies on the screen. Employing paradigms suggested by famous film theorist Laura Mulvey, this chapter offers insights that might help people of faith adjudicate the difference between gratuitous and artistic nudity in film: an issue under-theorized in the field of religion and film. The final chapter in

Part I narrows its focus to one particular cinematic device that has profound religious implications. Known as "breaking the fourth wall," the technique illustrates how creativity in the cinematic medium can generate religious messages that far exceed the significance of story.

Though film theorists are quoted throughout Part I of *Salvation from Cinema*, Part II takes an intense look at film theory itself, explaining how it speaks to the concerns of scholars interested in religion and film. Clarifying arcane writings with examples from multiple films, Chapter 5 discusses how secular scholars have theorized "salvation from cinema." Chapter 6 focuses on a theorist mentioned earlier in this introduction: Jacques Derrida, who helped incite "the religious turn" in philosophy. Applying his insights to Holocaust films, this chapter demonstrates Derrida's significance for the field of religion and film. Chapter 7 follows a clue suggested by Derrida in order to explore a theory of perception that has been especially helpful for feminist film scholars: the sign theory, or "semiotic," of Charles Sanders Peirce. Discussing classical Hollywood films as well as post-classical cinema, this chapter illustrates how Peirce's theory of perception illuminates issues presented in earlier chapters, addressing problems in both secular and religious film scholarship. The final chapter returns to the work of Martin Scorsese in order to tie together the many threads introduced in previous chapters. To verify the importance of Derrida and Peirce to the field of religion and film, this concluding chapter demonstrates how their work parallels that of a philosopher who revolutionized film theory: Gilles Deleuze.

If one were to inquire further about the methodology employed in *Salvation from Cinema*, I would have to respond that *the medium is the method*. As multiple film scholars have asserted, commitment to "methodology" imposes external constraints on cinema that obscure the distinctive artistry of individual films. Gilles Deleuze, in fact, believes that "art is the very opposite of method." As Claire Colebrook summarizes, "If Deleuze has a method it is that we should never have *a* method, but should allow ourselves to *become* in relation to what we are seeking to understand." And neoformalist Kristin Thompson, though significantly different from Deleuze in her approach to cinema, similarly defies "methodology," arguing that viewers who value the medium "construct a method specific to the problems raised by each film."[37] Concurring with these widespread views, *Salvation from Cinema* provides detailed analysis of artistic devices employed by individual films: the medium is the method. Furthermore, by discussing films made outside the USA that include Jewish, Muslim, and Buddhist perspectives, it seeks to avoid what S. Brent Plate rightly indicts as the "Hollywoodcentrism" of much religious film scholarship.[38]

The impetus behind this book might be summarized by a movie character in the famous French New Wave film *Hiroshima, mon amour* (Alain Resnais, 1959): "Looking closely at things is something that has to be learned." By looking closely at individual films as well as film theory, I hope to infuse the "from" in *Salvation from Cinema* with new meaning, encouraging students of religion to approach cinema with this question in mind: *from where* on the screen and *from what* cinematic devices does enlightenment come?

Notes

1 These books run the gamut from critically naive extraction of biblical messages to heady application of psychoanalytic theory, which will be discussed in Chapters 1 and 5. Publication data can be found in the Bibliography at the end of this book. Publication data can be found in the Bibliography at the end of this book under the author names Aichele and Walsh, Jewett, Kreitzer, Lang, Reinhartz, Scott, and Walsh.
2 Christopher Deacy, *Screen Christologies: Redemption and the Medium of Film* (Cardiff: University of Wales Press, 2001), 76.
3 John C. Lyden, *Film as Religion: Myths, Morals, and Rituals* (New York: New York University Press, 2003), 52; S. Brent Plate, *Religion and Film: Cinema and the Re-Creation of the World* (London: Wallflower, 2008), 3, 7; Clive Marsh, *Cinema and Sentiment: Film's Challenge to Theology* (Milton Keynes: Paternoster, 2004), 72; Kutter Callaway, *Scoring Transcendence: Contemporary Film Music as Religious Experience* (Waco: Baylor University Press, 2013); Melanie J. Wright, *Religion and Film: An Introduction* (New York: I.B.Tauris, 2007), 173.
4 See, for example, Michel Foucault, *The Archaeology of Knowledge and The Discourse on Language*, trans. A. M. Sheridan Smith (New York: Pantheon, 1972).
5 Quoted in Terry Lindvall, *Sanctuary Cinema: Origins of the Christian Film Industry* (New York: New York University Press, 2007), 57, emphasis mine; William D. Romanowski, *Reforming Hollywood: How American Protestants Fought for Freedom at the Movies* (New York: Oxford University Press, 2012). See also Terry Lindvall, "Silent Cinema and Religion: An Overview (1895–1930)" in *The Routledge Companion to Religion and Film*, ed. John Lyden (New York: Routledge, 2009), 13–31.
6 Gregory Watkins similarly argues that, in "the vast majority of work on film and religion," cinema is "made the object of [a] particular theoretical or theological point of view without careful consideration of the distinctive nature of the medium." See "Religion, Film and Film Theory," in *The Bloomsbury Companion to Religion and Film*, ed. William L. Blizek (New York: Bloomsbury, 2009), 82.
7 Marshall McLuhan, *Understanding Media: The Extensions of Man* (New York: McGraw-Hill, 1964), 19–20.
8 See, for example, Umberto Eco, *Travels in Hyperreality* (New York: Harcourt Brace, 1986), 136–8; and Raymond Williams, *Television: Technology and the Cultural Form* (London: Routledge Classics, 2003), 129–31. In contrast, Plate writes, "To say, with Marshall McLuhan (1964), that 'the medium is the message', may be slightly hyperbolic, but not by much" (*Religion and Film*, 62).
9 McLuhan, *Understanding Media*, 291. In *The Gutenberg Galaxy: The Making of Typographic Man* (Toronto: University of Toronto Press, 1962), McLuhan conceptualized the internet as a combination of a television and a computer, and he even coined the term "surfing" to describe employment of the not-yet-invented medium.
10 Nicholas Carr, *The Shallows: What the Internet is Doing to our Brains* (New York: Norton, 2011), 129.
11 McLuhan, *Understanding Media*, 15.
12 In his famous study of cinema stars, Richard Dyer states that "stars are supremely figures of identification." See *Stars*, 2nd edn (London: British Film Institute, 1998), 99.
13 André Bazin, "Theater and Cinema—Part Two" in *What Is Cinema?*, essays selected and trans. by Hugh Gray, vol. 1 (Berkeley: University of California Press, 1974), 99.
14 Marshall McLuhan and Quentin Fiore, *The Medium is the Massage: An Inventory of Effects* (Berkeley: Ginko Press, 2005); Noël Carroll, "Defining the Moving Image," in *Philosophy of Film and Motion Pictures: An Anthology* (Malden: Blackwell, 2006), 113–14. Carroll problematizes essentialism more thoroughly in *Theorizing the Moving Image* (Cambridge: Cambridge University Press, 1996).
15 Robert Sinnerbrink, *New Philosophies of Film: Thinking Images* (New York: Continuum International, 2011), 23.

16 See Garrett Stewart, *Framed Time: Toward a Postfilmic Cinema* (Chicago: University of Chicago Press, 2007); Costas Constandinides, *From Film Adaptation to Post-Celluloid Adaptation: Rethinking the Transition of Popular Narratives and Characters across Old and New Media* (New York: Continuum, 2010); and J. Hoberman, *Film After Film: Or, What Became of 21st Century Cinema?* (New York: Verso, 2012).
17 Since cinema does not have a "unique medium," Noël Carroll goes so far as to suggest we use the term "moving image" instead of "film." See "Forget the Medium!" in Noël Carroll, *Engaging the Moving Image* (New Haven: Yale University Press, 2003), 2, 9.
18 2 Peter 1:19 (KJV); Revelation 22:16; Isaiah 14:12 (NRSV).
19 Max Horkheimer and Theodor W. Adorno, *Dialectic of Enlightenment*, trans. John Cumming (New York: Continuum, 1972), 140.
20 Ibid., 144.
21 Ibid., 144. In contrast, Craig Detweiler quite rightly invokes theologian Hans Urs von Balthasar to argue that the recognition of beauty in cinema "can lead us to goodness and truth." His book takes a different approach to beauty than does mine, however. See *Into the Dark: Seeing the Sacred in the Top Films of the 21st Century* (Grand Rapids: Baker Academic, 2008), 161.
22 Quoted in Robert K. Johnston, *Reel Spirituality: Theology and Film in Dialogue* (Grand Rapids: Baker Academic, 2006), 163.
23 Jacques Derrida, "Above All, No Journalists!" in *Religion and Media*, ed. Hent de Vries and Samuel Weber (Stanford: Stanford University Press, 2001). Wetzel was one among several interviewers in the piece. For his question, see p. 86; for Derrida's perspective on the Christian foundations of religious tolerance, see pp. 73–4. For Derrida's statement about his atheism, see Jacques Derrida, "Circumfession," in Geoffrey Bennington and Jacques Derrida, eds, *Jacques Derrida*, trans. Geoffrey Bennington (Chicago: University of Chicago Press, 1993), 155.
24 Deacy, *Screen Christologies*, 124.
25 Deacy (ibid.) establishes that Scorsese identified with LaMotta.
26 *On the Waterfront* (d. Elia Kazan) won eight Oscars, including Best Picture, Best Director, and Best Actor. In a filmed conversation included with the Criterion Collection DVD of *On the Waterfront* (2013), Martin Scorsese testifies to the powerful effect the film has had on him.
27 Charles Affron, *Cinema and Sentiment* (Chicago: University of Chicago Press, 1982), 143.
28 I learned that the arm is Scorsese's in a "Behind-the-Scenes" feature included in the "MGM Martin Scorsese Film Collection Special Edition Collector's Set" DVD of *Raging Bull*. Other background information for the film, unless otherwise noted, comes from the DVD interviews and commentaries.
29 Paul Schrader, who wrote the screenplay for *Raging Bull*, reports that he wanted the scene in the dark cell to be about Jake's unsuccessful attempt to masturbate. See *Schrader on Schrader*, ed. Kevin Jackson (Boston: Faber & Faber, 1990), 131, 133. Robert De Niro successfully protested that a masturbation scene did not fit Jake's character.
30 While explaining the influence of *On the Waterfront*, Scorsese briefly mentions that *Citizen Kane* also profoundly affected him.
31 The imprisonment motif is adumbrated by images of the first meeting between Vickie and Jake. Scorsese shoots each of them through the apertures of fences that separate them, as though each is behind bars. Then, when Jake takes Vickie to his apartment, he points out a birdcage, telling her that the bird is dead.
32 *Diegesis* refers to the world of a film story: the location in space and time created by the fictional narrative. The adjectives *diegetic* and *non-diegetic* are commonly applied to discussions of sound, designating whether the sound is part of the film world or outside it, as in the musical score.

33 Marc Furstenau, "Introduction," *The Film Theory Reader: Debates and Arguments* (New York: Routledge, 2010), 10, emphasis mine.
34 James Monaco, *How to Read a Film: The Art, Technology, Language, History, and Theory of Film and Media*, rev. ed. (New York: Oxford University Press, 1981), 148, emphasis mine.
35 Francisca Cho, "Buddhism, Film, and Religious Knowing: Challenging the Literary Approach to Film," *Teaching Religion and Film*, ed. Gregory J. Watkins (New York: Oxford University Press, 2008), 120, 121. See also Francisca Cho, "Imagining Nothing and Imagining Otherness in Buddhist Film," *The Religion and Film Reader*, ed. Jolyon Mitchell and S. Brent Plate (New York: Routledge, 2007), 398–406.
36 For a chronological list of books about "religion and film," starting with 1932 and projecting into 2009, see Steve Nolan, *Film, Lacan and the Subject of Religion: A Psychoanalytic Approach to Religious Film Analysis* (London: Continuum, 2009), 185–95.
37 Claire Colebrook, *Gilles Deleuze* (London: Routledge, 2002), 46, emphasis hers; Kristin Thompson, *Breaking the Glass Armor: Neoformalist Film Analysis* (Princeton: Princeton University Press, 1988), 6.
38 S. Brent Plate, ed., *Representing Religion in World Cinema: Filmmaking, Mythmaking, Culture Making* (New York: Palgrave Macmillan, 2003), 9.

Part I
Theories of Film Salvation

1   Let There Be Enlightenment
Salvation from Religion and Film

In the beginning was *cinema*. Related to *kinesis*, Greek for *movement*, the word *cinema* resonates with the beginnings cited at the start of the Hebrew Bible. In the first chapter of Genesis we read, "And the Spirit of God *moved upon* the face of the waters. And God *said*, 'Let there be light: and there was light.'"[1] The moment of creation combines movement, light, image, and the spoken word: basic components of narrative cinema. But that is not all: "God *saw* the light, that it was good" (v. 4a). God's act of *seeing*, repeated seven times in the first chapter of Genesis, is essential to the work of creation. Similarly, the act of seeing is essential to the creative work of cinema, to the recognition of what is good.

Ironically, the majority of books extracting salvation from cinema talk more about what movies *tell* us through well-crafted story lines than about the artistry one can *see* on screen. They discuss religious and philosophical implications of things people say and do in movies, while largely ignoring what cinematic techniques say and do. As a result, they miss much of what is *good* about cinema. This chapter therefore outlines the genesis of cinema in order to explain the importance of theological/religious responses to it.[2] The chapter ends suggesting how attention to the cinematic medium might enrich the burgeoning field known as "religion and film."

Let There Be the Lightbulb

As mentioned in the introduction, Marshall McLuhan singled out the lightbulb as a life-altering medium that changed the way people viewed reality. As well as inspiring McLuhan's aphorism "the medium is the message," the lightbulb made possible what McLuhan calls the "hot medium" of moving pictures.

In the nineteenth century, numerous inventors tinkered with primitive forms of an electric lamp, starting with British chemist Humphry Davy in 1802. In 1840 another British chemist, Warren de la Rue, actually created the first lightbulb, but it wasn't until 1880 that the first incandescent lightbulbs, developed by Joseph Swan, lit up homes in England. Meanwhile, in America Thomas Edison was also perfecting a lightbulb, seeking his first patent in 1878, the same year that Swan unveiled his bulb at a British chemical society meeting. Though the Edison and Swan electric companies joined forces for several years, it was Edison who saw a future in moving images projected in front of a lightbulb.

Film history owes much to Edison's visionary materialism. Edison realized that inventions needed structures of support to make them marketable. Hence, he is often credited with "the invention of the lightbulb" because he understood that electricity needed to be grounded not just physically, but also economically. Providing generators and distribution systems, Edison made the lightbulb a viable commodity for consumers. That was also his goal for moving pictures.

When Edison commissioned one of his lab assistants, William Dickson, to develop a moving picture camera, he did so in order to make money off an earlier invention: his 1877 phonograph. Intended to accompany phonographic sound, moving pictures would enable Edison to sell his device to a whole new generation. Dickson therefore developed a camera with a stop-motion device that exposed each frame in a roll of celluloid to light, pulling the roll through the camera via sprocket holes punched into the film. To enable viewing, the process went in reverse: light was projected through the film as it moved inside a viewing box. Unfortunately, Dickson and Edison failed to fully synchronize those moving images with phonographic sound.

Edison therefore conceptualized another way to make money, asking Dickson to perfect a device through which individuals might view the soundless moving pictures. While Dickson's machine for recording reality was called a Kinetograph, the machine through which the recording could be watched was called a Kinetoscope: a contraption about four feet high into which an individual looked through a peep-hole at a continuously running film loop.

The words Kinetograph and Kinetoscope, of course, return us to the Greek word for movement that began this chapter: *kinesis*. What Edison saw as "good," however, was not creation for its own sake. By 1894, he was successfully selling Kinetoscopes to viewing parlors all over the country. Convinced about the financial potential of moving images, Edison next sought to purchase competitors' patents for new inventions, hoping to monopolize the cinematic marketplace as film viewing transitioned from Kinetoscope peep-boxes to screen projection.

It was a losing battle. By 1908, at least twenty filmmaking companies had been established, all motivated by profit. Most people who worked for film "manufacturers" therefore saw themselves not as contributors to a creative medium but as assembly-line workers in a tawdry commercial enterprise. As Lewis Jacobs puts it in *The Rise of the American Film*,

> most of the directors, actors, and cameramen who had come to the movies were more or less ashamed of their connection with them; they stayed in their jobs because they needed work, and they gave little thought to the *medium's* possibilities or opportunities. Nearly everyone still regarded movie making as a shabby occupation.[3]

Even after production companies moved from the East Coast to Hollywood (between 1907 and 1913), studio chiefs "saw their business as basically a retailing operation modeled on the practice of Woolworth's and Sears."[4] It's just that, rather than mass-producing clothing, they were stitching together off-the-rack movies, some studios at the rate of three to four per week.

The Studio System: Block Booking and Screen Idols

Considering movies to be more like amusement park rides than works of art, early production companies often did not list actor names in the credits. Even Mary Pickford (1892–1979), considered the most powerful female celebrity during the silent era, initially appeared in over fifty films without credit, known only to adoring fans as "Little Mary," the name of a character she played. Lured to a new studio in 1911, she finally got screen credit, and when she switched to Paramount she became a superstar. After a 1918 popularity poll established her as one of Paramount's top six actors, the studio allowed theaters to show a Pickford film only if they simultaneously contracted for multiple mediocre movies. Paramount thus established financial obligations on both ends of production: stars were contractually obligated to only appear in its films, and theaters were contractually obligated to show dozens of second-rate Paramount movies in order to get one star vehicle.

By the 1920s, most American production companies had followed suit, instituting a system called "block booking." Studio heads told movie exhibitors that, in order to book one of the studio's star-studded high-cost films, theaters had to "book" in advance a whole "block" of low-cost movies sight-unseen. Theater owners were thus forced to show hundreds of quickly made sub-par products in order to make money on several blockbusters.[5] Money, not the medium, was their message.

Block booking also intensified what is known as the "star system." Because the celebrity vehicles were few and far between, greater and greater value accrued to the stars themselves. As a result, the material conditions of those stars off-screen—whom they married, where they lived, how they partied—became as important to viewers as (if not more so than) the movies in which the stars appeared. When Pickford and her Paramount co-star Douglas Fairbanks married in 1920, they were mobbed by rioting fans in London and Paris during their honeymoon. The "star system" thus became materialistic both economically and philosophically: garnering money for studios, the material bodies of actors drew more attention than either the artistry of the medium or the profundity of the message.[6]

Significantly, the same year Paramount initiated block booking, it distributed a Mack Sennett comedy called *Her Screen Idol*. It was 1918, a mere seven years after Pickford got her first screen credit. The word *idol*, of course, is revealing. Something becomes an idol when its material presence predominates over its spiritual or intellectual significance. For example, in the book that follows Genesis in the Hebrew Scriptures, Israelites set up a golden calf after they were told not to look at God on Mount Sinai (Exodus 19:21). Hence, even though the Israelites saw Aaron artificially construct the calf (Exodus 32:4), they found its materiality more comforting than the unseen God who enlightened Moses on Sinai.[7]

Something similar could be said about "screen idols." They are artificial constructions insofar as they became identified with the false fictions they portray on the screen. Indeed, fans sometimes address actors by their screen character names. And those same fans pay for the movies that cast their screen idols—just as the Israelites contributed their own gold so that Aaron might cast the golden calf (Exodus 32:3). Screen idols are false gods created by the worshippers themselves.[8] To this day, many news and social media outlets celebrate films not according to their artistic quality and/or level of insight but by the screen idols starring in them and/or the money they amass during opening weekend. And studios still show movies to preview audiences, hoping to make changes that might generate greater viewer satisfaction and hence profitability.[9]

From Idolatry to Gnosticism

Considering how economic materialism has long been at the heart of Hollywood, it should amaze us that many filmmakers value cinematic art, seemingly for its own sake. Since later chapters discuss such artistry, the remainder of this chapter assesses scholarship that intelligently defies the idolatry of Hollywood. Renouncing golden calves, numerous theologians and religion scholars write books directing our attention toward spiritual and intellectual enlightenment.[10] However, in the process, many end up reinforcing a controversial claim made by Harold Bloom in 1992: because religion in the USA is based upon right "knowing," or enlightenment, it has overwhelming gnostic tendencies.[11]

Gnosticism, which shuns the material world in favor of spiritual enlightenment, has been aligned with multiple religions. Manichaeism, founded by the Iranian prophet Mani in the third century CE, asserted an opposition between the dark material world and the spiritual realm of goodness and light: a dualism that influenced early Christian sects, with which gnosticism is usually aligned. And in her famous book *The Gnostic Gospels*, religion scholar Elaine Pagels suggests similarities between Christian gnosticism and Buddhism.[12]

In film studies, some scholars have noted a "gnostic" opposition in film noir between light and dark, good and evil, and others have identified gnosticism in the "Jesus-film tradition," wherein Jesus's material body is downplayed in favor of his spirituality.[13] I am more concerned, however, about gnosticism within the field of religion and film itself. My following assessment of scholarship in the field, however, should not be read as a dismissal of powerfully intelligent and insightful work. Instead, it justifies yet another book on religion and film. By focusing on religious implications of the material medium, *Salvation from Cinema* offers something that hasn't already been published in scores upon scores of books, books that often focus on the same movies in order to extract theological/religious insight.

I argue that, in their search for enlightenment, Anglo-American theologians and religion scholars often take one of three gnostic approaches to cinema.[14] The first privileges transcendence, the second story, the third viewer response. To visualize these approaches I borrow a metaphor from Plato, whose work influenced Christian gnosticism. In his famous allegory of the cave, from Book VII of *The Republic*, Plato has Socrates present a parable in which prisoners sit inside a "den" watching images projected on the cave wall. As multiple film scholars have noted, this image uncannily anticipates viewers seated inside theaters watching movies on cinema walls.[15] In both cases, the moving images are artificial, mere shadows of reality projected via a light-source above and behind the viewers' heads. Plato even mentions a "screen" over which "marionette players" direct the movement of puppets that create these false pictures. Furthermore, some of the moving images, projected via the light behind them, are "talking, others silent."[16]

As far as Plato is concerned, enthralled viewers must be encouraged to turn from artificial images of reality to seek the light of Truth. Such knowledge is painful at first, as when spectators chained to classic Hollywood entertainment are forced to watch an avant-garde or foreign film containing little story and less action. As Plato puts it,

> At first, when any of them is liberated and compelled suddenly to stand up and turn his neck round and walk and look towards the light, he will suffer sharp pains; … and he will be unable to see the realities of which in his former state he had seen the shadows.[17]

Nevertheless, turning toward the light is necessary in order to attain True Ideas that transcend material realities. Significantly, by emphasizing a similar kind of transcendence, theologians in the 1970s and 1980s helped ignite scholarly discourse about religion and film.

The First Gnostic Approach: Cinematic Transcendence

Melanie Wright notes that "serious writing on the religion–film interfaces began in the 1920s."[18] Such interfaces did not begin to take shape as a distinct scholarly discourse, however, until the 1970s, when theologians began to celebrate films that demonstrated the transcendence of mindless Hollywood entertainment. In *Theology through Film* (1970), Neil Hurley summarizes numerous film plots that portray "the vertical upward pull of transcendence," mentioning Plato's cave allegory to argue that transcendence is "the dynamic piston in man's movement toward truth." Asserting that "Whoever sees through something … is exercising transcendence," *Theology through Film* indeed sees *through* film rather than ever truly looking at it.[19] Similarly, theologian Joseph Marty alludes to Plato's allegory in order to argue that cinema makes us "love what is not immediately perceivable, what is *beyond appearance* and evidence," echoing Michael Bird's celebration of cinema's ability to "point *beyond* itself toward the transcendental dimension."[20] And when Ernest Ferlita attests, in *Religion in Film*, that the "most timorous journey can disclose the journey of the mind to God," he also echoes Plato, who interprets "the journey upwards to be the ascent of the soul into the intellectual world," which is "the immediate source of reason and truth."[21]

Emphasis on transcendence through cinema was influenced by two Pauls: Tillich (1886–1965) and Schrader (b. 1946). Like their namesake who saw a blinding light on the road to Damascus, both turn from false reality to what Plato calls "beatific vision."[22] Tillich, considered by many to be one of the most influential theologians of the twentieth century, argued for a "belief-ful realism" that can inculcate experiences of transcendence similar to a Damascus road experience:

> The power of a thing is, at the same time, affirmed and negated when it becomes *transparent* for the ground of its power, the ultimately real. It is as in a thunderstorm at night, when the lightning throws a blinding clarity over all things, leaving them in complete darkness the next moment.[23]

Bird quotes this passage to argue *against* artistry created by cinematic techniques, celebrating instead "the *transparency* of the celluloid medium as it attends to its *proper* function of 'laying bare the realities.'" For Bird, film should be filmy, offering "*translucence* to another world underlying surface appearances." He illustrates his point with a 1951 French classic: *Diary of a Country Priest* directed by Robert Bresson. Rather than draw attention to dramatic artistry, Bresson's actors "refrain from acting at all. Instead, they pose as *transparent* figures through or behind whom a spiritual significance is discerned"—reminding us of Plato's exhortation to discern the light "behind" the "players" in the cave.[24]

Significantly, Robert Bresson is also praised by Paul Schrader, a screenwriter who argues that a movie's "realistic surface is just that—a surface—and the raw material taken from real life is the raw material of the Transcendent": somewhat like the raw shadows on a cave wall before viewers turn toward the light.[25] In 1972 Paul Schrader published *Transcendental Style in Film: Ozu, Bresson, Dreyer*, considered by some to be "one of the most intelligent books on the theology of film."[26] It may also be one of the most gnostic books on the theology of film, encouraging, as S. Brent Plate puts it, "a wholly disembodied cinematic experience."[27]

Ironically, a superficial glance at Schrader's book seems to support the thesis of *Salvation from Cinema*, that the medium is the message. Taking what he calls a "formalist" approach, Schrader assesses "the nature of the film medium," drawing attention to "camera angles [and] editing." However, he does so in order to demonstrate how artistic filmmakers turn the sights of viewers *away* from dependence on screen images in order to direct them toward the light of "spiritual universality." The projection on the wall/screen "expresses something deeper than itself," asserts Schrader, "undermin[ing] the viewer's customarily rock-solid faith in his feelings," which "are only part of a universal form which expresses the inner unity of every phenomenon."[28]

Elevating "universal form" to the greatest good, Schrader expresses animus against dramatic stories, beautiful imagery, creative camerawork, forceful acting, and distinctive directing styles. He seems only one step removed from Plato, who dismissed *all* cinema-like arts: painting, poetry and drama. Regarding them as only imitations of imitations—shadows of cave shadows—Plato banned most of the arts from his conception of an ideal Republic.[29] Though Schrader obviously values movies, he sounds like Plato when he discusses cinematic artistry:

> A film-maker truly devoted to expressing the Transcendent on film must not only eschew the more superficial elements of his personality and culture, but he must also sacrifice the vicarious enjoyments that cinema seems uniquely able to provide, empathy for character, plot, and fast movement.[30]

Such austerity echoes the heresy that vexed early Christianity. Gnosticism, as Hans Urs von Balthasar notes,

> constantly devalues the sensible world, visible organization, the flesh, matter: these are mere "appearances," either a deception or something to be seen through and overcome. Concealed behind them lies the only truth, the spirit, which must be set free and brought out into the open.[31]

The phrase "set free and brought out" reminds us of the prisoners in Plato's allegory of the cave. Significantly, Schrader discusses how Robert Bresson, who "prefers the soul to the body," employs prison metaphors in his films to communicate "matter being transcended."[32] Hence, for those who continue to preach transcendence through film, enlightenment comes as one turns away from the medium: salvation *from* cinema in both senses of the phrase.[33]

The Second Gnostic Approach: The Supremacy of Story

Emphasis on "transcendence" continues to inform work on religion and film in the twenty-first century. In *Scoring Transcendence* (2013), Kutter Callaway discusses how film music "points to that which is not present," expressing "that which lies 'outside' or 'beyond' representation," thus turning prisoners in the cave away from visual "signification" in order to experience "the Divine Other."[34] Nevertheless, by focusing on music, Callaway's lucid book fills a significant gap in scholarship about religion and film. Far more problematic—and popular—is the second approach to cinema, especially among evangelical Christians. Rather than turning away from false realities projected on theater walls, they move closer, looking for glittering gems of truth hidden within cinematic stories. Stressing the power of well-crafted narratives, they echo Plato's pupil Aristotle, who believed that a story's ability to imitate reality can be both informative and cathartic.[35]

Whether discussing down-home "teachable moments" or "controversies that have marked thinking about the saints,"[36] those taking the second approach paraphrase movie stories in order to establish them as entertaining containers of profound messages. Some explicitly proclaim their intentions to "*use* the films to explain the concepts" they discuss, "*garnering* insights about human life, love and relationships," while seeking to extract "Christian truths that are *illustrated* in popular films."[37] Others teach world religions through film, encouraging students to "*extricate* the religious ideas" from film stories.[38] Ignoring the medium in favor of an illustrative message, these approaches reduce cinema to little more than a content delivery system. Furthermore, believing that "in film, story reigns supreme,"[39] most disregard the fact that significant filmmakers and theorists have challenged the supremacy of story for nearly a century:

- Groundbreaking Soviet filmmaker Sergei Eisenstein proclaimed "Down with the story and the plot!" in the 1920s.
- Germaine Dulac, who directed silent films in France, considered the emphasis on story a "criminal error."
- Celebrating Italian neorealism in the 1940s, film theorist André Bazin asserted that "pure cinema" has "no more story."
- Helping incite the French New Wave in the 1950s, François Truffaut proclaimed "From now on, films no longer need to tell stories."
- In the 1960s and 1970s structuralists privileged not the shaping of film stories but the shaping of signs—both on the screen and in viewers' psyches.
- Believing that time was the constitutive attribute of cinema, Gilles Deleuze argued in the 1980s that viewer obsession with story impeded thought-altering perceptions of time.
- Iranian filmmaker Abbas Kiarostami, whose *Taste of Cherry* won the 1997 Palme d'Or at Cannes, asserts "I do not like to engage in telling stories."[40]

These attitudes will be explained more fully in Part II of *Salvation from Cinema*. I present them here merely to emphasize a problem in the field of religion and film, a problem anticipated in the 1960s by film theorist Christian Metz: "The rule of the 'story' is so powerful that the image, which is said to be the major constituent of film, vanishes behind the plot it has woven."[41]

In 1999, two scholars indicted the "rule" of story in religion and film. Maria Consuelo Maisto lamented that "The conflation of story with film, or techniques of literary interpretation with approaches to film, is typical of many efforts in Religion and Film," while Steve Nolan dismissed a "literary approach" as "fundamentally unsympathetic to the nature of film."[42] Neither mentions, however, that this so-called "literary approach" is also fundamentally unsympathetic to the nature of literature, duplicating what one literary critic dubbed "the heresy of paraphrase."[43]

In 1947, Cleanth Brooks published "The Heresy of Paraphrase," an essay that influenced American literary criticism for decades. Its goal was to combat a problematic practice in poetry criticism, by which critics were "yielding to the temptation to take certain remarks which we make about the poem—statements about what it says or about what truth it gives or about what formulations it illustrates—for the essential core of the poem itself."[44] One could easily substitute the word "film" for the word "poem" in Brooks's statement, as when famous film scholar David Bordwell encourages attention to the "poetics" of film. Indeed, Bordwell would agree with Brooks that "form and content, or content and *medium*, are inseparable."[45]

The heresy of paraphrase, then, parallels the gnostic heresy, manifest when scholars ignore the medium in order to focus on spiritual and/or intellectual enlightenment.

The Third Gnostic Approach: Watching the Watcher

After indicting theologians who take a so-called "literary approach" to cinema, Steve Nolan turns his attention to spectatorship. Plato's allegory of the cave helps distinguish Nolan's approach from the other two paths taken by theologians and religion scholars.

As we have seen, the first approach focuses on the light of transcendence shining above and beyond the cinematic cave, while the second studies stories projected on the cave wall in search of insightful nuggets buried within.[46] Nolan, in contrast, focuses on the viewers in chains, assessing how projected images affect them. Indeed, one of the film theorists Nolan cites, Jean-Louis Baudry, invokes Plato's famous allegory to describe spectatorship. However, rather than drawing attention to transcendent truth beyond the cave, Baudry focuses on the "cinematic apparatus"—"film stock, the camera, developing, montage considered in its technical aspects, etc."—which, like the apparatus of Plato's cave, creates only "an illusion of reality."[47] The apparatus so enthralls viewers—in both senses of *enthrall*—that they naively view the illusions projected on the cave wall as "realistic," if not in a movie's fantastical story line then in the psychological and ethical "realism" of its characters' responses. Problematically, according to "apparatus theorists" like Baudry, such delusive "realism" chains viewers to the false consciousness of capitalist ideology.[48]

Nolan does not discuss Plato's cave—and perhaps for good reason. As film scholar Robert Stam puts it, "spectators were never the pathetically deluded, shackled captives of a high-tech version of Plato's cave decreed by apparatus theorists."[49] However, sharing Baudry's concern about the ideological manipulation of film, Nolan offers psychoanalytic film theory as a corrective: an approach to cinema that some film scholars critique for its platonic/gnostic privileging of mind over matter, an approach "grounded in the alienation of visuality from the body," as Laura Marks puts it.[50] Nevertheless, there is merit to Nolan's argument that "theological film criticism should comment on the way film affects its viewers."[51] Some scholars, in fact, take this approach in order to explore what Marks calls "*embodied* self-in-becoming." Paralleling regular moviegoing with "attendance at worship and the practice of religious rites," such scholars regard viewer experience as "a form of lived religion."[52]

Though helpfully drawing attention to an important component of cinema—the bodies of spectators—many who regard "film as religion" nevertheless have a tendency to be gnostic when it comes to techniques of the apparatus itself, committing the heresy of paraphrase when they discuss particular films.[53] As with scholars taking the second approach, they emphasize the "use" of cinema, as in the following laudatory summary of religious responses to film:

moviegoers engage in sufficient numbers with the practice of film-watching in a way which indicates how they *use* film for meaning-making purposes. The religion-likeness of the *use* of the film is sometimes very explicit [and sometimes not] ... But that the religion-like *use* occurs at all is clear.[54]

Rather than assessing or encouraging the "use" of film, *Salvation from Cinema* suggests that the medium be allowed to speak for itself. At the same time it refuses to endorse apparatus theorists who regard the ideological chains of Plato's cave as inescapable. Instead, this book encourages viewers, and viewers of viewers, to loosen their chains—not simply to rush toward the light of transcendence or to dig out gems of insight from stories projected on the cave wall. Instead, it exhorts theologians and religion scholars to freely turn toward the cinematic apparatus, to inspect what Plato calls the "screen" via which "marionette players" create compelling images.

Medium and Message: A Hypostatic Union

Failure to engage with and assess the visual medium is especially ironic for Christian scholars. Doctrine hammered out in the first five centuries of the church—often in defiance of gnosticism—emphasizes that salvation is mediated not through stories and insights spoken by Jesus, but through his material body hung upon the cross, a medium *seen* after the resurrection. During the third ecumenical council, held at Ephesus in 431 CE, church leaders therefore borrowed a Greek philosophical term, *hypostasis*, meaning underlying substance, to argue that Christ's human nature cannot be separated from his divine nature: it is a hypostatic union. Inspired by this ancient doctrine of Christianity, confirmed at Chalcedon in 451 CE, *Salvation from Cinema* argues for a hypostatic union of medium and message in film scholarship: an emphasis relevant not simply to Christian scholarship but also for the broader discourse of religion and film, as shall become evident in future chapters.

Of course, numerous scholars have avoided cinematic gnosticism. However, when they do assess artistry in the medium itself, all too many echo a theologian declared heretical at the same ecumenical council that confirmed the hypostatic union.[55] Nestorius, Patriarch of Constantinople in the years 428-31, inherited the Antiochene conception of Christ's two natures, human and divine, as entirely separate: a position that has been paralleled to the mixing of two liquids. While theologians influencing Nestorius regarded the divinity and humanity in Christ as comparable to the combination of water with oil, their Alexandrine opponents considered Christ's nature as comparable to the infusion of water with wine.[56] Though some may regard this analogy as simplistic, the metaphor takes on new meaning when applied to salvation from cinema. Scholars who acknowledge artistry in the cinematic medium tend to be Nestorian about it: separating out discussion about technique from discussion of spiritually enlightening message.

For example, in *Film Odyssey: The Art of Film as Search for Meaning*, Ernest Ferlita and John R. May argue that "the discussion of meaning is best carried out in terms of the language of film itself." However, their book describes cinematic techniques primarily in its conclusion, not when films are first discussed.[57] Similarly, *Savior on the Silver Screen*, though profoundly insightful, separates out visual technique as one of three lenses through which the authors view nine films. Hence, like Nestorius establishing separate natures in Jesus, the book establishes separate ways to view Jesus films.[58] More problematic are books that preach the importance of cinematic artistry but rarely practice it. Melanie Wright notes that *Explorations in Theology and Film* (1997) "includes an introduction to film language, but the issues raised are not really followed through into actual analysis."[59] Rather than considering how messages are shaped by cinematic devices, many books on film and theology/religion anoint readers with the oil of story while alluding to the medium as if it were as transparent as water.[60]

This is not to deny the value of story. However, like water from wine, it is inseparable from the devices that present it. Techniques of the apparatus—such as pull-backs and cutaways, tracking shots and tilts—can lead attentive viewers to more fully appreciate powerful film messages, not in order to revel in moments of transcendence but in order to recognize how the transcendent is made immanent through cinematic artistry. C. S. Lewis, who was a firm believer in the hypostatic union as well as familiar with "the heresy of paraphrase" identified by Cleanth Brooks, once said of literary art,

> It is both *Logos* (something said) and *Poiema* (something made). As Logos it tells a story … As Poiema, by its aural beauties and also by the balance and contrast and the unified multiplicity of its successive parts, it is an *objet d'art*, a thing shaped so as to give great satisfaction.[61]

The same, of course, could be said of cinematic art: it should be regarded as both Logos and Poiema, or, in the words of Christian Metz, both "rhetoric and poetics."[62] It is about both/and thinking.

To demonstrate how both Logos and Poiema, both rhetoric and poetics, both message and medium interpenetrate like water and wine, this Chapter ends discussing a film made in defiance of Christian gnosticism that, ironically enough, generated numerous gnostic responses: *The Last Temptation of Christ* (1988).

The (Last) Temptation of Gnosticism

Paul Schrader, whose *Transcendental Style in Film* perpetuates gnostic approaches to cinema, wrote the screenplay for *Last Temptation*, as he did for the film discussed in my introduction: *Raging Bull* (1980).[63] Though both films were directed by Martin Scorsese, *Raging Bull* regularly appears on lists of the best films of all time, while *Last Temptation* never does. Nevertheless, many more theological works discuss the latter than the former. Much of this is due to the plethora of books on Jesus and Christ-figures in film, which usually feel obligated to include *Last Temptation* in their discussion. In addition, the scandal surrounding *Last Temptation* provides ample fodder for studies of audience reception. As Jeffrey

Staley and Richard Walsh astutely argue, since "there is a tendency toward gnosticism in both American religion and in the Jesus-film tradition," Scorsese's film about Christ's ambivalence over his vocation provides a unique response to gnosticism. However, while Staley and Walsh regard Scorsese's character as "the first fully round Jesus character in film,"[64] many others think *Last Temptation*'s protagonist behaves more like a raging bull than a sacrificial lamb.[65]

Scorsese decided to make the film after he read a 1960 translation of Nikos Kazantzakis's 1953 novel *The Last Temptation*. Raised as a Roman Catholic,[66] Scorsese was struck by Kazantzakis's emphasis on the savior's humanity: an aspect of church orthodoxy often overlooked. Many Christians, though ostensibly affirming doctrine established by the first four ecumenical councils—that Jesus was both fully human and fully God—seem gnostic when it comes to Jesus, uncomfortable with any consideration of his bodily functions or human urges. When such Christians heard about a Scorsese movie in which Jesus (Willem Dafoe) comes down off the cross to sire children with multiple women, they responded like raging bulls. Without having seen the movie they mounted protests, believing the information they heard was sufficient reason to repudiate the film as "the most blasphemous, evil attack on the church and the cause of Christ in the history of entertainment."[67]

Ironically, if protesters had given attention to devices of the cinematic medium, they would have realized that *The Last Temptation of Christ* does not at all suggest that Jesus sired children. Various screen techniques make clear that the sex scenes are an internalized temptation of Jesus, not externalized actions. Nevertheless, even though nineteen books discussing *The Last Temptation* mention that Christ's escape from the cross was merely a dream or "fantasy sequence,"[68] only one briefly describes (in three sentences) *how* the medium communicates that message.[69]

The medium, in fact, *is* the message. Christ's last temptation begins soon after a scene common to crucifixion movies: we see Jesus hanging on the cross via a long shot that pans behind mocking crowds as thunder rumbles and wind roars. When the shot cuts to a full-frame image of Christ's entire body, however, crowd noises have entirely evaporated as the wind continues to blow. This subtle change in sound precedes a more radical visual change: the camera rotates, so that the vertical image of Jesus on the cross moves clockwise, until it looks as though Jesus is lying on the bottom of the screen frame, a much smaller image of a crucified thief hovering horizontally along the top left of the screen, as though ready to fall into the out-stretched arms of Jesus beneath: a powerful symbol in and of itself.

More importantly, the rotating camera's manipulation of viewer perception anticipates the manipulation of Christ's perception soon to follow. After the horizontal Jesus cries out "Father, why have you forsaken me?" the shot suddenly cuts to a vertical close-up on his face, all sound eliminated. Through eyeline match cuts (cutting from close-ups on his face to what he sees) we see Jesus quizzically look at the yelling crowds and the thieves groaning on adjacent crosses, baffled because he hears no noise. The film thus plays with the difference between diegetic sound (that which characters hear on screen) and non-diegetic sound (what film viewers hear that characters on screen do not, such as the musical score). Assuming the absence of sound was non-diegetic, attentive viewers are startled to discover that Jesus also hears no sound, transforming the non-diegetic into the diegetic. The strange manipulation of viewer perception thus signals something strange about the diegesis. Both sound and mise-en-scène (all that can be seen within the screen's frame) prepare us for the distortion of reality Jesus next experiences.

At the foot of the cross a young girl, claiming to be an angel, tells Jesus that he does not need to die. Because we first see the girl with a high-angle lens from Christ's point of view, we know how far beneath the cross she squats. So when a close-up soon shows the girl at the level of Christ's head pulling off his crown of thorns and extracting nails from his hands and feet, viewers should wonder what the crowds think of such superhuman activities. Then, when the girl leads Jesus through soundlessly shouting crowds and into a green landscape entirely different from the dusty Judea pictured in earlier scenes, the attentive viewer suspects that the next thirty minutes, when Jesus sires children and ages, is an alternate reality. Suspicion is confirmed by a radical visual contrast: at the end of the sequence we see, in low-key lighting, the graying Jesus pray that God will accept him as Messiah, followed by a match cut to the high-key lighting of the cross, zooming in to a close-up as Jesus says, with a smile, "It is accomplished."

Through the medium itself, then, Scorsese establishes that Jesus was tempted to experience what most humans desire: the satisfactions of sexual intimacy and the joys of family. To deny that Jesus may have been tempted is to deny, with the gnostics, that Jesus "in every respect has been tempted as we are."[70] The film thus affirms what Chalcedon affirmed: salvation depends on a fully human medium.[71] Furthermore, consonant with the Gospels, Scorsese's Jesus renounces temptation in order to die for the sins of humanity.

Some protested, however, that the film contains no resurrection scene, thus subverting the Christian doctrine of salvation.[72] The medium, however, undermines this critique. Take, for example, the Last Supper scene. Before Jesus passes the bread and wine to his disciples, we see shots of a simultaneous Passover celebration in Jerusalem's temple, where a priest lifts a bowl to catch the blood of the Paschal lamb: a bowl that matches the bowl Jesus lifts in the next scene while saying "This is my blood, shed for you." An intellectual connection is made between the actions of the juxtaposed scenes: just as the Last Supper follows the scene of lambs sacrificed in the temple, we sense that Jesus will supersede the need for animal sacrifice, becoming himself the lamb of God who takes away the sins of the world.[73] The medium is the message in more ways than one.

Indeed, after the final freeze-frame of Christ's smiling face upon the cross, the film ends with bright colors and brief images of sprocket holes one might see at the edges of celluloid, looking as though the film stock has been overexposed. Because excited ululation and resounding church bells accompany the bright colors, we cannot help thinking that something glorious has succeeded Christ's death, its brilliant light burning the celluloid. It is as though the first reel of history, traditionally subtitled "BC," has ended through exposure to a supernatural light, anticipating the doctrine first proclaimed at Nicaea—"Light of Light; Very God of very God"—a Light Bishops at Chalcedon declared inseparable from the human medium.[74]

This does not mean that *The Last Temptation* is a masterful film. Seeking to defy the gnosticism that marks other Jesus films, Scorsese employed "overwrought, almost drunken hyperbolism,"[75] as when Jesus pulls a beating heart out of his chest and Judas picks blood clots out of his mouth after drinking wine at the Last Supper. The film, in fact, seems more Nestorian than orthodox, for it radically separates the two natures of Jesus: when the oil of his God-nature is in ascendancy Jesus does miracles; when his man-nature dominates he waters the desert with anguished tears about his sins.[76] His rages against God make him seem more narcissistic than Messianic, the film implying, as Pamela Grace notes, that "it is primarily his own sins that this unusual Jesus pays for when he dies on the cross."[77]

Nevertheless, in its defiance of gnosticism, *The Last Temptation of Christ* might teach Christians to be less gnostic in their viewing of cinema: an issue relevant to all scholars who explore the relationship between religion and film, many of whom say nothing about a movie that couldn't have been ascertained simply by reading the screenplay. Filmmaker Nathaniel Dorsky argues the point well:

> Not to respect the screen as its own self-symbol is to treat film as a medium for information. It is to say that the whole absorbing mechanism of projected light—the shots, the cuts, the actors—is there only to represent a scripted idea. But film at its transformative best is not primarily a literary medium. The screen or the field of light on the wall must be alive as sculpture, while at the same time expressing the iconography within the frame.[78]

Rather than turning away from "the field of light on the wall"—and proving Harold Bloom correct about the inherent gnosticism of the American religion—scholars need to study and discuss the "iconography" created by cinematic devices. In the process, they might very well experience "light of light." As one film theorist puts it, "it is not the mind that sheds light on matter ... Instead, matter itself provides its own illumination."[79] The medium, in other words, is the message.

Notes

1 Genesis 1:2–3, KJV. According to Hebrew scholar Brian Smith, the verb translated as "moved" occurs only three times in the Hebrew Bible: Genesis 1:2, Deuteronomy 32:11, and Jeremiah 23:9. The word denotes "hovering": not a "big sweeping movement," but more like a "subtle, fluttering movement of a bird pulling up just as she is about to land on her nest" (Brian Smith, via email February 14, 2014). The idea of "fluttering" has special resonance with the "flickering" of celluloid through a projector.

2 I borrow the portmanteau terms *theology/religion* and *theological/religious* from Melanie J. Wright, who uses them repeatedly throughout her book *Religion and Film: An Introduction* (New York: I.B.Tauris, 2007).

3 Lewis Jacobs, *The Rise of the American Film: A Critical History* (New York: Harcourt, Brace, 1947), 59, emphasis mine.
4 David A. Cook, *A History of Narrative Film*, 2nd edn (New York: Norton, 1990), 44.
5 William D. Romanowski provides a detailed account of how mainline Protestants sought to rid Hollywood of block booking in *Reforming Hollywood: How American Protestants Fought for Freedom at the Movies* (New York: Oxford University Press, 2012). See especially 41–2, 51–2, 90–107.
6 Wryly commenting on the star system, Christopher Bray notes that "You could write everything Elizabeth Taylor knows about acting on a matchbox with a marker pen … but a star Liz certainly was, and is." Christopher Bray, "The Cat in Catatonia," *Times Literary Supplement* (Nov. 13, 2009), 22. Bray is reviewing William J. Mann, *How to Be a Movie Star: Elizabeth Taylor in Hollywood* (London: Faber, 2009). For a scholarly study of the ideology perpetuating the star system, see Richard Dyer and Paul McDonald, *Stars*, 2nd edn (London: British Film Institute, 1998).
7 Christopher Deacy argues that the worship of screen idols "is testimony that films have the potential to fulfill certain religious needs and requirements." See *Faith in Film: Religious Themes in Contemporary Cinema* (Burlington: Ashgate, 2005), 81.
8 Writing in the 1960s, film theorist André Bazin described film stars like Rudolph Valentino and Greta Garbo as "golden calves" that have disappeared: "the most characteristic disappearance is undoubtedly that of the star." Today, many would beg to differ. See André Bazin, "In Defense of Mixed Cinema" in *What Is Cinema?*, essays selected and trans. by Hugh Gray, vol. 1 (Berkeley: University Of California Press, 1974), 74.
9 Robert K. Johnston gives several helpful examples of changed endings to illustrate "creativity … coming into conflict with commerce." Robert K. Johnston, *Reel Spirituality: Theology and Film in Dialogue* (Grand Rapids: Baker Academic, 2006), 175.
10 In a superb essay that includes references to both film theory and cinematic devices (as well as to Marshall McLuhan), Jeffrey F. Keuss states, "Merely 'viewing' any image is ultimately a form of both idolatry (passively becoming the object rather than the subject) and iconoclasm (seeing only the surface and not into the depth of a thing is ultimately to destroy it)." See "Reading Stanley Kubrick" in *Cinéma Divinité: Religion, Theology and the Bible in Film*, ed. Eric S. Christianson, Peter Francis, and William R. Telford (London: SCM Press, 2005), 83.
11 Harold Bloom, *The American Religion: The Emergence of the Post-Christian Nation* (New York: Simon & Schuster, 1992), 30, 264.
12 Elaine Pagels, *The Gnostic Gospels* (New York: Random House, 1979), xxi, 146. Pagels does not capitalize *gnosticism* or *gnostic* in her book, and I follow her example.
13 Alan Woolfolk, "The Horizon of Disenchantment: Film Noir, Camus, and the Vicissitudes of Descent," in *The Philosophy of Film Noir*, ed. Mark T. Conard (Lexington: University Press of Kentucky, 2006), 108; Jeffrey L. Staley and Richard Walsh, *Jesus, the Gospels, and Cinematic Imagination: A Handbook to Jesus on DVD* (Louisville: Westminster John Knox, 2007), 113.
14 The approaches roughly correlate with the "three waves" of scholarship that S. Brent Plate briefly identifies in *Religion and Film: Cinema and the Re-Creation of the World* (London: Wallflower, 2008), n.p. His book pays attention to the medium better than most, as do the following: Wright, *Religion and Film*; Ulrike Vollmer, *Seeing Film and Reading Feminist Theology: A Dialogue* (New York: Palgrave Macmillan, 2007); M. Gail Hamner, *Imagining Religion in Film: The Politics of Nostalgia* (New York: Palgrave Macmillan, 2011); and, written for popular Christian audiences, Grant Horner, *Meaning at the Movies: Becoming a Discerning Viewer* (Wheaton: Crossway, 2010).
15 See, for example, Irving Singer, *Reality Transformed: Film as Meaning and Technique* (Cambridge: MIT Press, 1998), 19–21; and Carl Plantinga, "Moving Pictures and the Rhetoric of Nonfiction: Two Approaches," in *Post-Theory: Reconstructing Film Studies*, ed. David Bordwell and Noël Carroll (Madison: University of Wisconsin Press, 1996), 307. Gerard Loughlin uses Plato's allegory not only to explore the narrative

32 Theories of Film Salvation

of *A Clockwork Orange* (Stanley Kubrick, 1972), but also to make a parallel with the Church, astutely deconstructing a paradox that informs Plato's allegory. See *Alien Sex: The Body and Desire in Cinema and Theology* (Malden: Blackwell, 2004), 41–57, 75–9, 85. Other scholars invoking the allegory will appear in subsequent notes.

16 Plato, *The Republic*, Book VII, in *Dialogues of Plato*, trans. Benjamin Jowett, ed. J. D. Kaplan (New York: Washington Square Press, 1967), 357, 358.
17 Ibid., 358–9.
18 Wright, *Religion and Film*, 16.
19 Neil Hurley, *Theology through Film* (New York: Harper & Row, 1970), 74, 7–8; Michael Bird, "Film as Hierophany," in John R. May and Michael Bird, eds, *Religion in Film* (Knoxville: University of Tennessee Press, 1982), 3–4. Anticipating their approach was French priest Henri Agel, who published *Le cinéma et le sacré* in 1961. As Sheila L. Nayar notes, Agel favored "films capable of transporting a viewer *beyond* human reality," deeming as "transcendent" those which "lead their viewers to the realm of the absolute." See *The Sacred and the Cinema: Reconfiguring the "Genuinely" Religious Film* (London: Continuum, 2012), 41.
20 Joseph Marty, "Toward a Theological Interpretation and Reading of Film: Incarnation of the Word of God—Relation, Image, Word," in John R. May, ed., *New Image of Religious Film* (Kansas City: Sheed & Ward, 1997), 135, emphasis mine. Marty's brief reference to Plato's cave is three pages earlier (132).
21 Ernest Ferlita, "Film and the Quest for Meaning," *Religion in Film*, 131; Plato, *The Republic*, 361–2.
22 Plato, *The Republic*, 362. Paul Schrader actually celebrates "blinding moments" through cinema. See Kevin Jackson, ed., *Schrader on Schrader* (Boston: Faber & Faber, 1990), 29. Though Tillich is often cited by scholars interested in religion and film, Christopher Deacy notes that "cinema is not accommodated at all" in Tillich's discussions about art and religion. See Deacy, "From Bultmann to Burton, Demythologizing the Big Fish: The Contribution of Modern Christian Theologians to the Theology–Film Conversation," in *Reframing Theology and Film: New Focus for an Emerging Discipline*, ed. Robert K. Johnston (Grand Rapids: Baker Academic, 2007), 248.
23 Paul Tillich, *The Protestant Era* (Chicago: University of Chicago Press, 1957), 60, quoted in Bird, "Film as Hierophany," 6. For an astute critique of Tillich's privileging of transcendence see John C. Lyden, *Film as Religion: Myths, Morals, and Rituals* (New York: New York University Press, 2003), 38–40.
24 Bird, "Film as Hierophany," 19, 20, 17, emphasis mine. Robert Pope attributes emphasis on "transcendence" through cinema with the "theological tradition in the West during the nineteenth and twentieth centuries." See "Speaking of God and Donald Duck," in *Cinéma Divinité*, 169.
25 Paul Schrader, *Transcendental Style in Film: Ozu, Bresson, Dreyer* (Berkeley: University of California Press, 1972), 63. For a helpful summary of Schrader and his critics, see Nayar, *The Sacred and the Cinema*, 43–7.
26 Richard C. Stern, Clayton N. Jefford, and Guerric DeBona, *Savior on the Silver Screen* (New York: Paulist, 1999), 287.
27 S. Brent Plate, "Religion/Literature/Film: Toward a Religious Visuality of Film," *Literature & Theology* 12.1 (March 1998): 28.
28 Schrader, *Transcendental Style*, 3, 51.
29 For Plato, a fictional story not only distracts people from transcendent truths, but also "feeds and waters the passions" that "ought to be controlled." See *The Republic*, trans. Charles M. Bakewell (New York: Scribner's, 1928), 405.
30 Schrader, *Transcendental Style*, 112. Decades before Schrader's book, film theorist André Bazin celebrated the "transcendence" communicated through Bresson's film; however, he avoids the Platonism that interlards Schrader's rhetoric. See "*Le Journal d'un Curé de Campagne* and the Stylistics of Robert Bresson" in Bazin, *What Is Cinema?*, vol. 1, 125–43.

31 Hans Urs von Balthasar, *The Scandal of the Incarnation: Irenaeus against the Heresies*, trans. John Saward (San Francisco: Ignatius, 1981), 4.

32 Schrader, *Transcendental Style*, 90, 3. Richard A. Blake, SJ, attributes this renunciation of materiality to Schrader's Protestant background, arguing that Catholics, in contrast, recognize that "the material universe is sacred." See *AfterImage: The Indelible Catholic Imagination of Six American Filmmakers* (Chicago: Loyola Press, 2000), 13, 33–5. Nayar makes a similar point, aligning Schrader's transcendental style with the alphabetic literacy privileged by Protestants. She does so in order to valorize Jesus-film and Bollywood spectacles, which she aligns with ritualized orality. See *The Sacred and the Cinema*, 108–17.

33 Johnston takes a more complex approach to transcendence, identifying different varieties that cinema generates (*Reel Spirituality*, 240–5).

34 Kutter Callaway, *Scoring Transcendence: Contemporary Film Music as Religious Experience* (Waco: Baylor University Press, 2013), 73, 72, 74, 121.

35 Bernard Brandon Scott echoes Aristotle when he writes that stories "allow us to undergo a life experience without risk. We can seek in story to overcome death without dying and return to everyday life all the wiser for having learned our options from story." See *Hollywood Dreams and Biblical Stories* (Minneapolis: Fortress, 1994), 48.

36 Richard Leonard, SJ, *Movies that Matter: Reading Film through the Lens of Faith* (Chicago: Loyola Press, 2006), 169–70; Theresa Sanders, *Celluloid Saints: Images of Sanctity in Film* (Macon: Mercer University Press, 2002), xiv.

37 James S. Spiegel, "Introduction" to *Faith, Film and Philosophy: Big Ideas on the Big Screen*, ed. R. Douglas Geivett and James S. Spiegel (Downers Grove: IVP Academic, 2007), 14, 13, emphasis mine; James Hogan, *Reel Parables: Life Lessons from Popular Films* (Mahwah: Paulist, 2007), 1, emphasis mine. See also Robert Jewett, *St. Paul at the Movies: The Apostle's Dialogue with American Culture* (Louisville: Westminster John Knox, 1993). Jewett admits he is "not as much interested in evaluating films on the basis of aesthetic criteria as in discerning the message these interacting 'stories' disclose for our society" (8).

38 Julien R. Fielding, *Discovering World Religions at 24 Frames per Second* (Lanham: Scarecrow Press, 2008), xii, emphasis mine.

39 "In Film, Story Reigns Supreme" is a chapter title in Johnston's *Reel Spirituality*. For "the importance of story," also see Anthony J. Clarke and Paul S. Fiddes, eds, *Flickering Images: Theology and Film in Dialogue* (Macon: Smyth & Helwys, 2005), 2; and Robert Benne, *Seeing is Believing: Visions of Life through Film* (Lanham: University Press of America, 1998). My colleague Jennifer McFarlane-Harris suggested the descriptor "content delivery system."

40 Sergei Eisenstein, "Through Theater to Cinema," trans. Jay Leyda and Paya Haskelson, in *Theater and Film: A Comparative Anthology*, ed. Robert Knopf (New Haven: Yale University Press, 2005), 250; Germain Dulac, quoted in Robert Stam, *Film Theory: An Introduction* (Oxford: Blackwell, 2000), 37; André Bazin, *What Is Cinema?*, trans. Hugh Gray, vol. 2 (Berkeley: University of California Press, 1971), 60; "Interview with François Truffaut," in *The French New Wave: Critical Landmarks*, ed. Peter Graham with Ginette Vincendeau (New York: Palgrave Macmillan, 2009), 198; Kiarostami makes this statement during an interview included in the *Taste of Cherry* Criterion Collection DVD (1999).

41 Christian Metz, *Film Language: A Semiotics of the Cinema*, trans. Michael Taylor (Chicago: University of Chicago Press, 1974), 45. Metz's statement was first published in 1964.

42 Maria Consuelo Maisto, "Cinematic Communion? *Babette's Feast*, Transcendental Style, and Interdisciplinarity," *Imag(in)ing Otherness: Filmic Visions of Living Together*, ed. S. Brent Plate and David Jasper (Atlanta: Scholars Press, 1999), 86. Steve Nolan, "Understanding Films: Reading in the Gaps," in *Flickering Images*, 26. Nolan's alternative to a "literary approach" is psychoanalytic film theory (35), while Maisto's solution

is a return, albeit a qualified return, to Schrader's *Transcendental Style*. Preceding them both was Margaret R. Miles, *Seeing and Believing: Religion and Values in the Movies* (Boston: Beacon, 1996), whose "cultural studies" approach to cinema has been astutely critiqued by Lyden (*Film as Religion*, 28–31).

43 Attacks on the "literary approach" infiltrated subsequent discussions of religion and film. See, for example, "Section 1: Moving beyond a 'Literary' Paradigm," in Robert K. Johnston, ed., *Reframing Theology and Film*, 29–72; Francisca Cho, "Buddhism, Film, and Religious Knowing: Challenging the Literary Approach to Film," *Teaching Religion and Film*, ed. Gregory J. Watkins (New York: Oxford University Press, 2008), 117–28.

44 Cleanth Brooks, "The Heresy of Paraphrase," in *The Well Wrought Urn: Studies in the Structure of Poetry* (New York: Harcourt, Brace & Co., 1947), 199.

45 David Bordwell, *Narration in the Fiction Film* (Madison: University of Wisconsin Press, 1985), xiii; Brooks, "The Heresy of Paraphrase," 199, emphasis mine. In his valorizing of cinematic poetics, Bordwell acknowledges the influence of and limitations to the Russian Formalists, who in 1927 produced *Poetika Kino* [The Poetics of Cinema].

46 Making a bridge between the first two paths is Douglas E. Cowan in *Sacred Space: The Quest for Transcendence in Science Fiction Film and Television* (Waco: Baylor University Press, 2010).

47 Jean-Louis Baudry, "The Apparatus: Metapsychological Approaches to the Impression of Reality in Cinema," in *Film Theory and Criticism*, ed. Marshall Cohen, Gerald Mast, and Leo Braudy, 6th edn (New York: Oxford University Press, 2004), 209–10. See also Jean-Louis Baudry, "Ideological Effects of the Basic Cinematographic Apparatus," trans. Alan Williams, *Film Quarterly* 28.2 (Winter 1974/5): 45. John Lyden briefly cites Baudry's reference to Plato's cave (*Film as Religion*, 50–1).

48 Baudry is also discussed by Julie Kelso in "Gazing at Impotence in Henry King's David and Bathsheba," *Screening Scripture: Intertextual Connections between Scripture and Film*, ed. George Aichele and Richard Walsh (Harrisburg: Trinity, 2002), 159–62.

49 Robert Stam, *Film Theory: An Introduction* (Oxford: Blackwell, 2000), 139.

50 Laura U. Marks, *The Skin of the Film: Intercultural Cinema, Embodiment, and the Senses* (Durham: Duke University Press, 2000), 150. Marks is describing theories associated with Jacques Lacan, who has influenced the thought of Nolan, as in Steve Nolan, *Film, Lacan and the Subject of Religion: A Psychoanalytic Approach to Religious Film Analysis* (London: Continuum, 2009).

51 Nolan, "Understanding Films," 35. See also Steve Nolan, "Towards a New Religious Film Criticism: Using Film to Understand Religious Identity rather than Locate Cinematic Analogue," in *Mediating Religion: Conversations in Media, Religion and Culture*, ed. Jolyon Mitchell and Sophia Marriage (London: T&T Clark, 2003), 169–78.

52 Marks, *The Skin of the Film*, 151, emphasis mine. Craig Detweiler, *Into the Dark: Seeing the Sacred in the Top Films of the 21st Century* (Grand Rapids: Baker Academic, 2008), 45. In the first quotation, Detweiler summarizes Clive Marsh's "attempts to measure the religious responses of filmgoers" in *Cinema and Sentiment: Film's Challenge to Theology* (Milton Keynes: Paternoster, 2004). The second quotation refers to Detweiler's own experience.

53 Though acknowledging close parallels, Nolan establishes "three important differences" that distinguish "film as religion" scholarship and his own approach (*Film, Lacan and the Subject of Religion*, 36).

54 Clive Marsh, "Audience Reception," in *The Routledge Companion to Religion and Film*, ed. John Lyden (London: Routledge, 2009), 268, emphasis mine. Similarly, Deacy encourages "utilizing film as a resource" in *Faith in Film* (137). In contrast, Wright indicts the "sheer instrumentalism and seeming disregard for film per se" in *Religion and Film* (15).

55 Nestorius was initially denounced during the First Council of Ephesus (431 CE) and declared heretical at the Council of Chalcedon in 451 CE. Nevertheless, Nestorianism

thrived for well over a millennium in "The Church of the East." For more detail about the tension between Nestorian "Dyophysites" and Alexandrine "Miaphysites" see Diarmaid MacCullough, *Christianity: The First Three Thousand Years* (New York: Viking, 2010), 224–8.

56 MacCullough employs this analogy to explain the difference between the Antiochene assumptions influencing Nestorius, and the Alexandrine opposition (*Christianity*, 223). The Council at Chalcedon (451 CE) established a "compromise" between the two positions by emphasizing "the Union of Two Natures" in Christ (*Christianity*, 226–7).

57 Ernest Ferlita and John R. May, *Film Odyssey: The Art of Film as Search for Meaning* (New York: Paulist, 1976), 151. Their Nestorian approach is also evident in *Religion in Film*. In the book's preface, May argues that "the best analyses of film, attempt, as far as possible, to discover the harmony of the whole in terms of the language of film itself." But only rarely does he use the grammar of cinema to discuss film, placing various techniques in separate paragraphs (ix, 43). Though repeating the phrase "language of film itself," May never clarifies what it means for film to be "a language."

58 Explaining how visual techniques like camera angles, dissolves, and graphic matches contribute meaning to films, Stern, Jefford, and DeBona brilliantly practice what they preach, if even distinguishing oil from water. Another example is the handbook by Staley and Walsh, *Jesus, the Gospels, and Cinematic Imagination*, which begins with a brief section titled "Film Medium: Camera, Editing, Set, Lighting" (1–2), explaining that attention to cinematic artistry is key to "sophisticated" film viewing. But then the authors divide each film discussion into six or more discrete sections, occasionally including several sentences about visual techniques in the brief "Director" section. In most instances, the longest section covering each film is a list that names all the chapters, and their lengths, on the film's DVD. This reflects the book's stated purpose: to help professors select chapters from DVDs that they can use in the classroom. Given that goal, the book is successful as a type of "CliffsNotes" or "Spark Notes" on Jesus films.

59 Wright, *Religion and Film*, 20, 23, commenting on *Explorations in Theology and Film*, ed. Clive Marsh and Gaye Ortiz (Malden: Blackwell, 1998).

60 For example, Johnston adds a separate chapter titled "Image and Music" to his second edition of *Reel Spirituality* (163–84). Similarly, Peter Fraser and Vernon Edwin Neal separate out a chapter called "Learning the Language" in *ReViewing the Movies: A Christian Response to Contemporary Film* (Wheaton: Crossway, 2000), 39–62.

61 C. S. Lewis, *An Experiment in Criticism* (Cambridge: Cambridge University Press, 1965), 132.

62 Metz, *Film Language*, 81.

63 It must be noted that "though Paul Schrader has the on screen credit as scriptwriter of *The Last Temptation of Christ*, Scorsese, along with the New York film critic Jay Cocks, is responsible for most of its dialogue and much of its action." Lloyd Baugh, *Imaging the Divine: Jesus and Christ-Figures in Film* (Kansas City: Sheed & Ward, 1997), 53. For an intriguing exploration of the disjunction between Schrader's theory about transcendental style and his practice as a screenwriter, see Peter Fraser, *Images of the Passion: The Sacramental Mode in Film* (Westport: Praeger, 1998), 123–7. Both Fraser and Baugh draw attention to artistry of the medium more than many other Christian scholars.

64 Staley and Walsh, *Jesus, the Gospels, and Cinematic Imagination*, 113, 111. Stern, Jefford and DeBona also remark on the gnosticism that infects "the Hollywood tradition around Jesus" (*Savior on the Silver Screen*, 294). Arguing that *The Last Temptation* "rejects the gnostic Jesus of American popular religion," Richard Walsh attributes the many "Gnostic Jesuses" in cinema to gnosticism within the Gospel of John. See *Reading the Gospels in the Dark: Portrayals of Jesus in Film* (Harrisburg: Trinity Press International, 2007), 181, 162–5.

65 Some critics explicitly make a parallel between *Raging Bull*'s Jack LaMotta and *Last Temptation*'s Jesus. See, for example, Bruce Babington and Peter Williams Evans,

36 Theories of Film Salvation

    Biblical Epics: Sacred Narrative in the Hollywood Cinema (New York: Manchester University Press, 1993), 151; Christopher Deacy, *Screen Christologies: Redemption and the Medium of Film* (Cardiff: University of Wales Press, 2001), 123; and Baugh, *Imaging the Divine*, 69.

66 For Scorsese's spiritual biography and testimonials about his Roman Catholic faith, see Baugh, *Imaging the Divine*, 57, and Blake, *AfterImage*, 25–7, 31.

67 James Dobson, "Focus on the Family" radio broadcast, July 11, 1988. For helpful background on the making of and protests against the film, see W. Barnes Tatum, *Jesus at the Movies: A Guide to the First Hundred Years* (Santa Rosa: Polebridge, 1997), 162–3, 170–4; as well as Baugh, *Imaging the Divine*, 51–3; and Romanowski, *Reforming Hollywood*, 193–6. For an extended assessment of the cultural context in which the protests were embedded, see Gerald E. Forshey, *American Religious and Biblical Spectaculars* (Westport: Praeger, 1992), 171–6.

68 The number nineteen only reflects those books on Jesus films that I have read. The phrase "fantasy sequence" is from Roy Kinnard and Tim Davis, *Divine Images: A History of Jesus on the Screen* (New York: Carol, 1992), 207.

69 Baugh, *Imaging the Divine*, 67. Baugh's discussion of *Last Temptation* is admirable, exemplifying the integration of cinematic devices to exfoliate the film (56, 62–3). Two other discussions of *Last Temptation*, though overlooking how visual techniques establish the "dream sequence," nevertheless provide valuable insight to the way camera angles and POV shots create meaning in other parts of the film. See Stern, Jefford, and DeBona (*Savior on the Silver Screen*, 279–84) and Babington and Evans (*Biblical Epics*, 151–8). Also including occasional references to cinematic devices is Stephenson Humphries-Brooks, *Cinematic Savior: Hollywood's Making of the American Christ* (Westport: Praeger, 2006), 94–8. Humphries-Brooks, however, tends to emphasize deficiencies in cinematic portrayals of Christ rather than the artistic power of film.

70 Hebrews 4:15, NRSV. In his positive assessment of *Last Temptation*, Peter Malone alludes to the Hebrews passage. See *Screen Jesus: Portrayals of Christ in Television and Film* (Lanham: Scarecrow, 2012), 114. Bryon Stone also cites Hebrews 4:15, but concludes that Scorsese gives us a Jesus "who is really neither human nor divine." See *Faith and Film: Theological Themes at the Cinema* (St. Louis: Chalice, 2000), 74, 76.

71 As Baugh notes, "Scorsese knows and speaks intelligently" of the Council of Chalcedon (*Imaging the Divine*, 65).

72 Tatum suggests that the film, during the fantasy sequence, raises "the possibility that belief in the resurrection of Jesus had been fabricated," approvingly tracing the history of such suspicions (*Jesus at the Movies*, 166). Babington and Evans, failing to reference the concluding light display in *The Last Temptation*, argue that "this film refus[es] to gesture to a resurrection" (*Biblical Epics*, 168). Baugh describes how cinematic techniques suggest a resurrection but then ultimately undermine it (*Imaging the Divine*, 69).

73 Scorsese's intention behind this graphic match is confirmed in an interview: "I tried to show that the sacrifices of animals lead to the sacrifice of the Cross…. Sacrifices took place in the Temple, under the supervision of the priests. It must have looked like a slaughterhouse." See Richard Corliss, "… and Blood: An Interview with Martin Scorsese," *Film Comment* 24.5 (September–October 1988): 42.

74 The first ecumenical council, convened at Nicaea in 325, described Jesus as "Light of Light; Very God of very God; Begotten, not made; Being of one substance with the Father."

75 Hal Hinson, "The Last Temptation of Christ," *Washington Post*, August 12, 1988. For other secular critiques of the film, see Tatum, *Jesus at the Movies*, 171.

76 As Baugh notes, "Scorsese's Jesus shifts repeatedly in his understanding and acceptance of his divine identity, as if there were a *profound and unbridgeable gap* between his humanity and his being the Son of God" (*Imaging the Divine*, 71, emphasis mine).

Peter Fraser, noting the gnosticism that Scorsese seeks to avoid, aligns the "dichotomy between God and man" in Jesus with a different heresy, one "condemned by the Fifth Ecumenical Council in 553" (Fraser, *Images of the Passion*, 181n. 11). Deacy, who applies the Antiochene conception of a redeemer to film noir protagonists in *Screen Christologies*, mentions the difference between Alexandrine and "Antiochene Christological formulation" that informs *Last Temptation* (86–7).
77 Pamela Grace, *The Religious Film: Christianity and the Hagiopic* (Malden: Wiley-Blackwell, 2009), 151.
78 Nathaniel Dorsky, *Devotional Cinema*, rev. 2nd edn (Berkeley: Tuumba, 2005), 44.
79 Johannes Ehrat, *Cinema and Semiotic: Peirce and Film Aesthetics, Narration, and Representation* (Toronto: University of Toronto Press, 2005), 237. The quotation summarizes a premise in the famous film theory of Gilles Deleuze, which will be discussed in my conclusion.

2 Light from Light
Seeing Cinema Constellations

In the midst of the Hebrew Bible, the Psalms repeatedly present evidence of the divine in visual terms:

> The heavens are telling the glory of God;
>   And the firmament proclaims his handiwork.
> Day to day pours forth speech,
>   And night to night declares knowledge.
>
> (Psalm 19:1–2)

The Psalmist, here, may have been thinking of the constellations mentioned in the Book of Job (9:9; 38:31–2). Then as now, humans look to the heavens and see constellations of stars that make pictures: images that move across the screen of the night sky.

Significantly, when the Psalmist exults in the patterns of the skies, he notes they need "no speech" because beauty is its own "voice," one that "goes out through all the earth":

> There is no speech, nor are there words;
>   Their voice is not heard;
> Yet their voice goes out through all the earth,
>   And their words to the end of the world.
>
> (Psalm 19:3–4)

Something similar could be said about a well-crafted film: it goes out through all the earth, and its speech is much more than the mere "words" actors give "voice" to. Some theorists have suggested, in fact, that the beauty of cinema was undermined by the development of sound. Thirty years after the first feature-length "talkie" premiered in 1927 (*The Jazz Singer*), Rudolf Arnheim argued that film reached its apex as "an artistic medium" in the late silent period. And Marshall McLuhan, who coined "the medium is the message," similarly asserted the superiority of silent movies, believing that they elicit more mental activity from viewers.[1] Like the beauty of heavenly constellations, the "voice" of silent film can go out through all the earth, enjoyed by people of all nations and tongues.

Just as ancient viewers of the skies named constellations after religious stories from their own culture, so viewers of silent film were able to insert intertitles in their own language.

Artistic filmmakers, then, recognize the power of voiceless beauty, the visual medium presenting its own message. As Johannes Ehrat puts it, "film does not need to assert by means of a linguistic intermediary, because as a Sign it has its own power of argumentation."[2] An award-winning film from 1982 employs no words at all, neither in voice-overs, nor through subtitles or intertitles. Called *Koyaanisqatsi*, a Hopi word for "life out of balance," the film uses slow-motion and time-lapse photography, dissolves, fade-ins, fade-outs, long shots, graphic matches, aerial shots, and more: signs with their own power of argumentation. Directed by Godfrey Reggio, *Koyaanisqatsi* is thus beautiful even though its images are often ugly: power plants, parking lots, dilapidated houses, atomic bomb detonations, rush-hour traffic, etc. The beauty results from the way the images connect to each other as they flash across the screen in time with the rousing music of Philip Glass.[3] Through its splicing together of similar shapes set to non-diegetic music, *Koyaanisqatsi* causes us to *think about* the beauty humans have lost as they value industry and technology over nature.

Precisely because it has no story, *Koyaanisqatsi* teaches viewers to look for visual codes within the medium itself: constellations of meaning that enhance an entire film—but only when actively contemplated. Beauty in film, in other words, is most fully appreciated by the intellectual activity of a beautiful mind: one attentive to patterns on screen.

A Beautiful Mind: Recognizing Patterns in Black and White

The title of Academy Award-winning *A Beautiful Mind* (2001) refers to the ability of mathematician John Nash (Russell Crowe) to make connections that lead to new mathematical insights. Often used by mathematicians and scientists to describe a streamlined solution or code, the word "beautiful" refers to Nash's original pattern recognition. A problem arises only when Nash, later diagnosed with schizophrenia, becomes obsessed with codes, seeing constellations of meaning even where they don't exist.

Beauty in film is similar. Recognizing patterns on the screen can enhance our understanding of or appreciation for the plot, which is like a mathematical problem that takes time to work out. Sometimes, however, overzealous viewers impose patterns that don't fit the context, a problem that has led to the proliferating identification of Christ-figures in movies. As John Lyden aptly notes, "If every bloodied hero becomes a Christ figure … it will seem that we can find Christianity in every action film"—much as John Nash seems to find secret codes in every newspaper and magazine.[4]

To avoid arbitrary (or obsessive) pattern recognition, attentive viewers educate themselves in what film theorist Christian Metz calls "signifying figures": the devices and techniques that constitute "specialized codes" of film itself. Figures that enhance the aesthetics of film are never "tacked on," as Metz notes in *Film Language*:

we arrive at an observation that film aestheticians frequently make: Namely, that pre-existing symbols (whether social, psychoanalytic, etc.) that are artificially "tacked on" to filmic continuity represent a poor and simplistic approach, and that the essential part of cinematographic symbolism lies elsewhere (the symbol must be "born out of the film").[5]

Viewers, of course, are not the only ones guilty of tacking on pre-existing symbols. "Tacked on" is another way to talk about "gratuitous" elements filmmakers put into movies in order to sell tickets: humans coded "sexy" by their lack of clothes, or landscapes coded "idyllic" by their lack of civilization. In contrast, Metz argues, beauty should be "born out of the film," not arbitrarily inserted into it.

Take, for example, two devices that emphasize constellations of beauty on the screen: *graphic matches* and *graphic motifs*. Most people associate the word "graphic" with explicit (often gratuitous) sex or violence. But the word has another connotation for film specialists. Because "graphic" means "drawing or writing," film specialists apply the word to shapes written onto the screen, shapes often enhanced by editing. The word cinemato*graphy*, after all, means "movement writing."

By avoiding the distraction of color, black-and-white cinematography superbly illustrates graphic techniques, creating constellations of meaning that echo the black-and-white beauty of the night sky. Especially helpful are black-and-white films adapted from stage plays, because they demonstrate how codes *not in the play* might be "born out of the film" in order to enhance the original script, such that the medium is the message. I start with adaptations of stage plays because a key term in film analysis, mise-en-scène, was borrowed from the French stage. Translated as "the fact of putting into the scene,"[6] the mise-en-scène in both theater and film refers to everything a director has put on the stage or screen in a particular scene or shot. To emphasize mise-en-scène, then, is to emphasize the seeing of constellations.

Seeing Graphic Beauty: *A Raisin in the Sun* and *A Streetcar Named Desire*

The 1961 black-and-white film *A Raisin in the Sun* closely follows the scripted dialogue of Lorraine Hansberry's award-winning 1959 play. Both follow the frustrations of an African American family, three generations of the Youngers, living in a claustrophobic apartment in a 1950s Chicago ghetto. However, while Hansberry's play keeps all the visible action inside the Younger apartment, the movie periodically moves the action to other locations, where visual language communicates more than verbal language.

In one scene Walter Lee Younger, played by the stunning Sidney Poitier, leans against the car he chauffeurs for a rich white man. In disgust with his dead-end job he throws a folded up newspaper inside the car window. The shot then dissolves into another location, where we see an object the exact same size as the newspaper, located on the exact same spot on the screen, thrown in the exact same direction. It is a napkin tossed into a laundry basket by Walter's wife, Ruth (Ruby Dee), who irons linens for rich white folk. This "graphic match" between similarly shaped objects located on the same part of the screen is emphasized by the dissolve, establishing a parallel between Walter and Ruth: though both are intelligent and hard-working, their potential is tossed away, like the newspaper and the napkin, due to a racist system that makes it nearly impossible to escape the ghetto. The dissolve speaks, while Ruth and Walter do not: the medium is the message.[7]

Another graphic technique, later in the film, reinforces the limited mobility suggested by the graphic dissolve. As the frustrated Walter dances to African music in his apartment, he gets uncomfortably close to the camera, kicking toward the lens—and hence toward the viewer's screen—as though seeking to break it. Since Walter's actions pull him out of the well-lit set, attentive viewers notice a change in lighting as Walter nears the camera. This graphic breaking of boundaries between lit set and the darker space of the film crew becomes a metaphor for Walter's spirit, which wants to break free not only from the claustrophobic setting of his ghetto apartment, but also from the imprisoning limitations imposed on his race.

A Raisin in the Sun also employs various graphic motifs, like repeated shots of a plant barely able to survive in the ghetto apartment: a motif that appears in the original play. More interesting for cinema analysis, however, are visual motifs *added to* a film adaptation. Take, for example, a motif in one of the most spectacular films of all time: A *Streetcar Named Desire* (1951). Based on Tennessee Williams's 1947 play, *Streetcar* is about an aging Southern belle, Blanche DuBois (Vivien Leigh), who moves into a cramped New Orleans apartment with her sister and brother-in-law: Stella and Stanley Kowalski (Kim Hunter and Marlon Brando). The plot develops around Blanche's efforts to disguise both her age and her promiscuous past in order to attract an upright man into marriage. Hoping that the "magic" of romantic love might save her from pernicious memories, Blanche flirtatiously attempts to appear young and innocent.

To emphasize Blanche's desire to cover up her tawdry past, the filmmakers add a graphic motif that doesn't appear in the play: literal clouds of smoke, steam, and fog that suggest the figurative smoke screen she generates. The very first time we see Blanche in the film, she walks through a cloud of steam emitted by the engine of the train upon which she has just arrived. (Significantly, immediately before we see her, a wedding party runs through the steam.) Later, steam billows out of the bathroom in the Kowalski apartment, representing Blanche's attempts to wash away her compromised past, and several times we see cigarette smoke envelope her face. When Blanche finally manipulates a proposal out of the tender-hearted Mitch (Karl Malden), the two stand on a deck where fog moves across the adjacent water, enveloping their feet.

After Blanche's affair with one of her high school students is revealed by a traveling salesman, we see a street vendor walk out of the fog toward Blanche, crying "Flores por las muertes [Flowers for the dead]." Indeed, the death of Blanche's innocence has finally broken through her smoke screen. As a result, Mitch tries to molest her and Stanley successfully rapes her, undermining Blanche's psychological stability. When workers from a mental institution come to take her away, we first see them framed by a window, underneath which a boiling pot emits steam. This latter image is doubly significant, for Stanley has developed his own smoke screen, saying he "never touched" Blanche.

Through this graphic motif, *A Streetcar Named Desire* draws attention to *how* we see, not just *what* we see. Blanche's beauty does not change after her promiscuous past comes to light. Nevertheless, Mitch and Stanley *see* her beauty differently after her smoke screen dissipates. Rather than as a well-educated English-teacher, they regard her as a sex object: a superficial source of titillation, something that might be used for pleasure. They look at her beauty, in other words, the way many people look at film.

The *Bliss* of Beauty

A more recent film makes a similar point, this time in color. Turkish in both setting and language, *Mutluluk* (2007) shares a grammar with its black-and-white predecessors: a graphic grammar born of the medium itself.[8] Called *Bliss* in English, the award-winning film focuses on an adolescent girl, Meryem, who is found ravaged at the side of a lake in present-day Turkey. Condemned as a whore, she flees the village and eventually achieves salvation. Though most viewers will enjoy the film's amazing scenery and its surprise ending, they nevertheless might miss the beauty of the graphic matches and motifs that add constellations of meaning to the diegesis.

The opening long shot (the focal image a long distance from the camera) captures a smooth hill perfectly reflected in glass-smooth water. Beautiful in and of itself, this establishing shot initiates a water motif that eventually represents Meryem's baptism into a new life. But before we get there we see her degradation. The camera pans left from the establishing shot, showing sheep and shepherds in the far distance, and over to Meryem lying at the side of the lake. A crane shot (the camera looking down on her from above) shows that her rumpled form creates an arc on the dirt. As the seemingly dead body fills the mise-en-scène, the camera rotates above it, giving a sensation that the body is slowly spiraling clockwise. The shot then cuts to the circle of sheep, a crane shot capturing how they begin to spiral clockwise next to the lake. Next, a low-angle shot (as though the camera is on the ground) shows a shepherd, in close-up, looking down. Rather than giving us an eyeline match cut to show us what he sees (presumably the body of Meryem), the shot cuts to a reflection, in the water, of Meryem thrown over the shepherd's shoulders like a sheep. The graphic grammar is clear: Meryem is a sacrificial lamb.

In the next scene we discover that she is sacrificed to protect the honor of her village, whose imam tells Meryem's father that the sexually tainted girl must be killed.[9] After this pronouncement, a shot of some mill machinery fills the mise-en-scène, such that we see a wheel spinning clockwise. This all happens in the first several minutes of the film, setting up a constellation that foreshadows the film's denouement.

The clues are reinforced later with a high-angle shot of Cemal, the imam's son sent to track and kill Meryem. On a boat and hence adjacent to water, Cemal's body forms an arc. As the camera turns above the body, briefly giving the sensation of a slow spiral clockwise, the same music plays that accompanied the crane shot of Meryem's abused body spiraling clockwise. By paying attention to these parallel codes, we suspect that Cemal may also be a sacrificial lamb. Indeed, we later learn that he has been sacrificed to serve the selfish interests of the imam. Once Cemal catches up with Meryem, however, he renounces his duty to kill her, thus exercising the Third Pillar of Islam: charity. Furthermore, like Meryem, he is vindicated by the end of the film—but only after we once again see a close-up on the village mill wheel spinning clockwise, turning accuser into the accused. Like all effective motifs, then, images of spiraling and of water create a pattern that connects various parts of *Bliss* together: the medium encapsulates the message.

Graphic Grammar: The Framing Device of *Little Moth*

Repeated close-ups on a spinning wheel—one toward the beginning of *Bliss*, the other near the end—gesture toward another kind of screen constellation: a graphic match that frames a film. Reminiscent of a medieval triptych, where two images frame a primary religious image in the center, framing devices often speak louder than the words in a film. Take, for example, the triptych of *Little Moth* (2007), an independent Chinese film directed by Peng Tao.

Beginning with long takes of a couple riding noisy public transportation, the film eventually establishes that the two are on their way to purchase an eleven-year-old disabled girl from a father who no longer wants to tend her. Viewers feel hopeful that the sweet-faced child, called Little Moth, will finally experience parental love. Images on the screen abet this hope. As the couple once again travels on noisy public transportation, this time with their newly acquired daughter, the wife tenderly cradles the adorable pig-tailed girl, after which the husband gently carries her piggyback to a doctor's office.

After this sweet start, however, the film suddenly changes tone. In their squalid living-space, the husband violently knocks medicinal herbs from his wife's hands, deriding her for wanting to heal Little Moth's inert legs. The change in tone is followed by a change in imagery: next we see the tiny wife, Guihua, carrying the girl piggyback down the street while the husband, Luo, walks fifty paces ahead of them. Viewer bafflement is resolved when Guihua sits down with Little Moth at the side of the road, spreading out a blanket-sized inscription asking for handouts as her husband watches from afar. Evidently, Luo wants Little Moth healthy enough to beg but not healed of the crippling infection that makes her an object of charity. *Little Moth*, then, is about human trafficking, the long scenes of riding through traffic functioning as visual metaphors.

The film builds up viewer hopes again when a woman on the street takes interest in Little Moth, offering to provide medical attention for the adorable girl's ailment. Rebuffed because she threatens the couple's source of income, the wealthy woman (Zhong) has another chance later in the film after a one-armed beggar boy helps Little Moth escape. Zhong's interest in Little Moth thus frames the central piece of the film's triptych: a scene in which human traffickers—Luo and the beggar boy's owner—get drunk together, enabling the boy to surreptitiously carry Little Moth away. Upon discovering the girl begging with the boy, Zhong takes Little Moth to her posh apartment, where she and a younger woman shower the darling child with affection and clothes, promising that doctors will heal her condition. Viewers are elated as the film promises a happy Hollywood ending. However, once a doctor tells Zhong that the girl's infection necessitates amputation of both legs, the tone changes, much as it did at the start of the film.

Significantly, the scene with the doctor near the end of the film matches the visit to the doctor made by Luo and Guihua earlier in the film, the doctor telling the couple that if the girl's infection is not treated immediately, her legs must be amputated. A framing device is confirmed when the shot cuts, after the doctor visit, to the disgruntled Zhong walking down the street twenty paces ahead of the younger, smaller woman carrying Little Moth piggyback. Using the excuse that "nature calls," Zhong asks the smaller woman to sit with Little Moth at the side of the busy street—duplicating the way Luo had Guihua sit with Little Moth earlier in the film. The parallel implies that Zhong is no different than the greedy Luo, both using Little Moth to satisfy their desires—he for income, she to enjoy a walking, talking, living doll.

The film ends after the smaller woman walks away from Little Moth in search of Zhong. The final shot, a long take of Little Moth sitting alone at the side of the road watching noisy traffic, echoes the long take of noisy traffic that began the film. Turning her head back and forth, back and forth, back and forth, Little Moth seems to question, like viewers, "What next?" Hence, as with many foreign films, *Little Moth* refuses to provide a satisfying denouement, ending, instead, with no resolution to the issue repeatedly faced by the world's poor: abuse by those with power.

The film's framing device could be charted as follows:

>Traffic accompanying Little Moth's rescue
>Little Moth carried piggy-back
>Visit to doctor with remedy being rejected
>Rich woman approaches Little Moth to rescue her
>
>**Center: Slave-owners get drunk and trafficked children escape**
>
>Rich woman approaches Little Moth and rescues her
>Visit to doctor with remedy announced impossible
>Little Moth carried piggy-back
>Traffic accompanying Little Moth's abandonment

The symmetrical structure draws attention to the artistry of the medium itself while simultaneously alluding to cycles of abuse generated by human trafficking. The visual medium, in other words, reinforces its message.

The medium, however, also provides a faint glimmer of hope. Interpolated into Zhong's abandonment of Little Moth at the side of the road are short takes of Guihua pasting ideogram-inscribed posters on telephone poles. Ostensibly pleading for information about the missing girl, the posters look like smaller versions of the earlier plea for money laid on the ground in front of the crippled girl. The difference in display—one sign stretched out on the ground, the other on a vertical pole—suggests a different view of Little Moth. Guihua's desire, the medium suggests, has become upright: rather than use the girl, as did her husband and Zhong, she wants to love the girl, valuing Little Moth for who she is rather than for what benefits she might bring.

Nevertheless, viewers are not given the satisfaction of seeing a reunion between Guihua and the girl, implying that such Hollywood closure would mimic the gifts Zhong offers Little Moth. Like the wealthy Zhong who expects a happy ending in exchange for her gifts—a walking talking living doll—wealthy Hollywood producers expect something in exchange for their gifts of happy endings: abundant box-office receipts. Most independent filmmakers like Peng Tao, in contrast, recognize that the inherent value of the medium—like the inherent value of Little Moth—should be the message.

Little Moth may also be informed by Buddhist thought. The framing device, calling attention to a cycle of rescue and abandonment, brings to mind *samsara*, the Hindu cycle of birth, death, and rebirth appropriated by Buddhism. Little Moth, in fact, illustrates the First Noble Truth of Buddhism: that life is *dukkha*, or suffering. Luo and Zhong, who cause Little Moth's suffering, illustrate the Second Noble Truth of Buddhism: that "the drive for private fulfillment," or *tanha*, causes suffering—to the self as much as to others.[10] By closing the film with Little Moth turning her head back and forth watching vehicles speed by, Peng Tao may even gesture toward the Buddhist concept of Greater Vehicle (Mahayana) Buddhism versus the Lesser Vehicle of Salvation (Hinayana Buddhism). The film ends, however, with no sign of salvation—unless we remember the signs hung up by Guihua.

Salvation from the Bodhisattva: *The King of Masks*

Unlike *Little Moth*, Buddhist perspectives are explicit in *The King of Masks*, a 1996 Chinese film, directed by Wu Tianming, that includes a "Living Bodhisattva" in the diegesis. In early Indian Buddhism, *Bodhisattva* referred to the early lives of Siddhartha Gautama, before he reached enlightenment and became the Buddha. As the *Bodisat*, or "Buddha-to-be," Siddhartha was reincarnated in various forms, including a king and a monkey. Later, *bodhisattva* was used to describe enlightened *followers* of the Buddha. In Lesser Vehicle (Hinayana) Buddhism, especially after it was renamed *Theravada*, the term *bodhisattva* referred to individuals who, through solitary meditation, achieve wisdom (*bodhi*) and Nirvana on their own. Greater Vehicle (Mahayana) Buddhism, in contrast, celebrates a bodhisattva who touches the shore of Nirvana only to turn back to the watery flux of existence in order to help others reach Nirvana. As religion scholar Huston Smith explains, "Buddhism is a voyage across the river of life, a transport from the common-sense shore of nonenlightenment, spiritual ignorance, desire, and death, to the far-flung bank of wisdom which brings liberation from this prevailing bondage."[11] The suffix *yana* in *Hinayana* and *Mahayana* literally means *raft* or *ferry*: a vehicle that crosses foggy waters toward the shores of enlightenment.

Significantly, *The King of Masks* begins with a long take of white fog, images of dark land slowly appearing until an isolated raft becomes visible in the distance. The shot dissolves like the fog, revealing, in close-up, a man poling the raft, with a monkey behind him. Dissolving once again, the shot reveals village roofs encased in fog, until the camera tilts down to street level, where we see the same man with a bundle on his back. The filmmakers thus visually allude to the "Great Period" of Chinese art in the seventeenth century, when the male form was often depicted "climbing with his bundle ... or poling a boat—man with his journey to make, his burden to carry, his hill to climb, his glimpse of beauty through the parting mists."[12] The shot dissolves two more times, until we see the man, Wang, announce to a surrounding crowd that he is "the King of Masks," having come on his "solitary skiff" to perform an ancient Chinese craft known as *Bian Lian*. Significantly, as soon as the shot moves away from Wang, the camera cuts, rather than dissolves, from one scene to another—the montage of conventional cuts distinguishing a crowded street celebration from the unique, solitary man who has come out of the dissolving fog. In addition to showing masses of people, the montage displays fireworks, a colorful dragon parade, a float carrying a female Bodhisattva seated on a Lotus, and a general's family watching the activities from a café—all set in 1930s Sichuan. Only after the general's grandson follows promptings to say "Grandpa" does the camera return to the *Bian Lian* performer, the significance of which will soon become apparent.

Serving as the Chinese title of the film, *Bian Lian* is a process whereby a performer causes delicate hand-painted silk masks to appear and disappear over his face in the twinkling of an eye. Wang's performance is so amazing that Liang, the actor portraying the Bodhisattva, temporarily breaks his Buddha-like position on the Lotus float. A full-frame close-up registers his awe, followed by an eyeline match cut to what he sees. A visual connection is thus made between the Living Bodhisattva, as Liang is called throughout the film, and the King of Masks. Indeed, as "the hottest female impersonator in Sichuan opera," Liang is also a king of masks, colorfully painting his face to look female. However, while the wealthy Liang surrounds himself with creature comforts and servants, the impoverished Wang renounces money and ease, preferring his "solitary ways." The medium thus encourages attentive viewers to consider the following: if the Living Bodhisattva is really a king of masks, perhaps the King of Masks is really a living bodhisattva, guiding his solitary (c)raft away from desires and delusions of the world.

Multiple screen constellations, however, prove otherwise. Wang is wracked with desire, wishing to find a boy to whom he might transfer his ancient, and very secret, craft. Believing that only males can practice *Bian Lian*, Wang buys a shiny statue of "the Goddess of Mercy" to guarantee finding a "grandson." He thinks the charm has worked when an eight-year-old, tied with a rope around his neck in a marketplace, calls out to him "Grandpa." Purchasing the boy and calling him "Doggie," Wang lovingly takes him to his boat, rafting down the river to offer gratitude to a huge statue of Buddha carved into the side of a mountain. A low-angle shot captures the King of Masks dwarfed between the legs of the gigantic form, the full-frame static image contrasting with a juxtaposed full-frame shot of Doggie crawling over the Buddha's toes, like a monkey. The contrasting shots gesture toward Bodhisattva stories about Siddhartha's contrasting reincarnations as a king and a monkey, an allusion confirmed by connections between Doggie and Wang's monkey. Not only is the monkey tied around the neck as was Doggie, but when the child tells Wang of beatings by former masters, the King of Masks states, "I wouldn't hit a monkey like that." More importantly, multiple close-ups on the monkey's face capture its emotional responses to events, as though it were once human.

The monkey, in fact, registers the first enlightenment of the film. When Doggie sneaks out of bed to urinate off the side of Wang's raft, we see the child pull down his pants like a girl. A close-up on the monkey's open-mouthed shock confirms Doggie's secret: she is a girl passing as a boy. Like the Living Bodhisattva, who is a male masked as female, Doggie is a female masked as a male. Indeed, the parallel is foreshadowed by the medium: a shot of Wang nestling his newly purchased "grandson" in his arms begins to dissolve so that the child's round face is superimposed on a round insignia on a stage curtain. The Living Bodhisattva then enters the stage so that his head covers the insignia, creating a graphic match between the little female playing a male with the male playing a female.

Wang's enlightenment about Doggie comes through the feet, reminding us of the shot when Doggie crawls on the Buddha's feet. When Wang's foot is severely injured, the distraught Doggie tearfully races to get her beloved "grandpa" some wine, with which he sets a rag on fire. Then he tells her, "Doggie, piss on it. Boy's piss mixed with cloth ashes will stop the bleeding." At this moment, no longer able to maintain her mask, Doggie cries out "I'm a girl," and Wang literally turns his back on her in contempt.

Significantly, Wang gets injured while competing in a contest to split a sugar cane, the shape and size of which matches the pole he uses to guide his raft. Hence, when we see him split a pole immediately before discovering Doggie's secret, we have been given a visual metaphor for the split he makes with a child he had earlier welcomed into his (c)raft. Denouncing her, Wang rushes back to his boat, Doggie chasing after him. As he grabs his pole to push the raft from shore, Doggie grabs it, wrapping her arms around it in despair, as though to unite a split sugar cane. After Wang pulls the pole from her desperate embrace, Doggie runs along the shore, dropping the money Wang has thrown her as she jumps in the water to follow him, forcing Wang to rescue her from drowning.

In the next shot we see Doggie dressed in a flowery red girl's jacket, sitting in the prow while Wang poles the boat at the stern muttering "stupid girl," their genders separated by color and space. Several shots effectively communicate the distance between them. A POV (point-of-view) shot from Wang's perspective isolates Doggie at the front of the boat, Wang out of the frame altogether. Then a long shot captures the raft sliding down the river from the side, making the boat look surprisingly long in comparison to all the foreshortened perspectives and tight shots from earlier, when Wang affectionately shared his raft with Doggie. As it glides down the river, the boat passes the huge mountainside Buddha without stopping, Doggie no longer given the "grace, compassion, and mutuality" aligned with what is often called "Big Raft" (Mahayana) Buddhism.[13] Instead, Doggie has been reduced to a servant, forced to call Wang "Boss" rather than "grandpa."

Begrudgingly training Doggie to do acrobatic tricks for his shows, Wang takes Doggie to a town where the Living Bodhisattva happens to be performing "his famous role in attaining Nirvana." In the performance, Liang impersonates the daughter of a king who has been sent to "the Buddhist hell." Though a voice on stage states that "the Princess arrives on the Boat of Kindness," we see her hanging on a rope above the stage, pleading for the life of her father, the king: "If you show no compassion, I shall cut this rope and fall into pit of death so that I may share my father's suffering." She does so, jumping in front of the stage, immediately rising again with the king. As a chorus chants "Buddha of Infinite Qualities," we are given an image of Mahayana Buddhism, which not only celebrates a bodhisattva who refuses to enter Nirvana until others attain it, but also sustains "a higher regard for the spiritual possibilities of women."[14] The medium reinforces this openness to females by cutting back and forth between the princess "turned into a god, like Bodhisattva" and Doggie in the audience watching. Significantly, after seeing the performance, Doggie starts to challenge Wang's prejudice against females, asking him "What do boys have that I don't?" When Wang answers "Just a little teapot spout," she angrily retorts "Does the [Bodhisattva] have a teapot spout?" The irony, of course, is that Liang, who plays the female Bodhisattva, *does* have a teapot spout. Doggie, undaunted, grabs a "Goddess of Mercy" statue that Wang purchased and yells, "Look, she's got bosoms! Why do you worship her?"

Wang leaves the raft without answering, and the next scene seems to endorse Wang's sexist assumptions. Doggie, now alone, takes Wang's masks from their box—forbidden to her as a female—holding one too close to a candle as she puts it against her face. Starting a fire that spreads to the boat, Doggie throws the box overboard to save Wang's art from total destruction. When Wang returns to his burned boat, the medium once again draws attention to his feet. Slowly panning left from the charred remains, the camera stops when it reaches Wang's feet, tilting up to capture his whole body, the low-angle shot emphasizing his towering power over Doggie. Rather than relying on words, the medium next communicates Wang's repudiation of the girl. A long shot from above shows her riding alone down the river on a different raft before cutting to Wang walking down an empty village street: they have gone their separate ways.

Attempting to fend for herself on land, the dirty and starving Doggie is captured by human traffickers and locked into a room with another kidnapped child. But rather than despairing, she helps the male four-year-old escape, taking him back upriver via another raft in order to leave him on Wang's boat—thus selflessly giving Wang the desire of his heart without gaining any benefit to herself. Though blessing two people at once—the boy with a loving caretaker and Wang with a grandson—Doggie watches her plan backfire from afar. Arrested for kidnapping, Wang is led away by a rope around his neck, reversing the roles from earlier, when Doggie had the rope around her neck. We see Wang placed within a cell that is entirely framed by another cell, perhaps alluding to Wang's imprisonment by *tanha*: "those inclinations which tend to continue or increase separateness, the separate existence of the subject of desire."[15] Wang has repeatedly separated himself from others, not in order to reach *bodhi*, but to selfishly preserve his art. The medium wordlessly reinforces this message through the monkey, who opens a box in the charred boat to retrieve a photograph taken of Doggie and Wang *together*: a photo that Wang angrily rips up after the monkey hands it to him.

Not coincidentally, Wang is taken to prison soon after he tears up the photograph. Wang must be handed something else, implied when Doggie brings to the jail Wang's hand-painted silk masks. As she hands the masks to the King of Masks, a surly guard snarls to Wang, "Take them with you to hell to scare off the demons," reminding us of the king sent to hell at the Sichuan opera. Doggie, then, must act the role of princess daughter, sacrificing herself to redeem her king from hell. She does so during another performance when Liang is painted as a female. At the end of the show, while actors and audience socialize on stage, Doggie lowers herself from the roof on a rope, so that she is dangling upside down over them. She then yells to a state official, "General, the King of Masks is no kidnapper. I rescued the boy and took him to the King. … If you won't help, I'll cut the rope and die." The General, who doesn't want to get involved in local politics, disbelieves Doggie's plea, and she cuts the rope. Liang lunges to catch the falling Doggie, rolling with her down a flight of stairs. The amazed General, witnessing Liang with the limp body of Doggie in his arms, states, "You live up to your nickname of the Living Bodhisattva. Though merely an actor, you have courage and character … I'll take care of this matter."

Doggie's risky act—in both senses of "act"—thus saves Wang. Inspired by Liang's art—an act portraying the Bodhisattva—Doggie does an act consonant with an authentic Bodhisattva: sacrificing her own life to save another. After Wang is released, Liang tells Wang that "Doggie is your true savior." The chastened Wang therefore returns to his boat where he teaches the artful Doggie his art, and in the last shot of the film we see both Kings of Masks—young girl and old man—holding the pole as they steer their raft *together*.

Wu Tianming has shown that art, especially performance art, can inspire merciful performances. And such can be said of Wu's cinematic art as well. In an amazing example of the interface between art and life, the stunning Zhou Ren-ying, who plays Doggie, was herself abandoned at age three, saved from starvation by joining the Xian Acrobatic Troupe. Her parents, imprisoned on drug charges, reunited with their daughter only after *The King of Masks* made Zhou's face famous. Exemplifying salvation from cinema, Wu created a raft of redemption both on and through a river of film.[16]

The (C)raft in *Beasts of the Southern Wild*

Salvation from a child similarly informs *Beasts of the Southern Wild* (Benh Zeitlin, 2012), a low-budget American film that earned numerous awards, including a Caméra d'Or at Cannes, a Grand Jury Prize at the 2012 Sundance Film Festival, and four Academy Award nominations. Offering no scenic landscapes or gorgeous bodies, the film focuses on people in the Louisiana bayou who build their shelters out of garbage heap debris, making literal the descriptor "trailer trash." The ugly images of junkyard shacks surrounded by abandoned tires, oil refinery smokestacks, dying vegetation, and sullied clothing might overwhelm some viewers with despair for the people who live in the midst of such chaos. But the film makes clear that these people consciously choose to live this way, celebrating their freedom from job expectations and civilizing influences, making do with whatever they can scavenge.

The film's protagonist is the six-year-old Hushpuppy, whose alcoholic father, Wink, provides food and shelter but shows no affection. He requires her, in fact, to live in a broken-down trailer fifty feet from his own cobbled-together shack. When a flood destroys Hushpuppy's trailer, Wink lets her sleep in his shelter, but only after he tapes to the floor a line that divides his side from her "girly" side of toys and tears. The film, then, is about the emotional divide between father and daughter, its denouement at the moment Hushpuppy finally crosses it. And, like any good film, *Beasts of the Southern Wild* offers constellations of meaning through visual motifs.

Obvious to any viewer are the repeated interpolations of "aurochs," a prehistoric elephant-sized boar with huge mammoth tusks. At least that is how Hushpuppy imagines an aurochs after her teacher mentions the extinct creatures frozen in ice: "Any day now the fabric of the universe is going to unravel. Ice caps gonna melt … You'all better learn how to survive now." The teacher thus presents an issue embedded in many religions: the end of known existence, from the floods of Gilgamesh and Noah, to the Apocalypse of St. John. This, then, becomes Hushpuppy's worry: that she will not survive if something happens to Wink, the only savior she has ever known. If the floods come, the fabric of her universe will unravel, salvation impossible.

Not much later, after watching Wink fall to the ground after a clap of thunder, Hushpuppy looks up into the sky with fear. When the shot next cuts to another image, we are trained by the medium to expect a POV shot, in this case Hushpuppy's view of lightning and/or rain. However, the medium inserts, instead, a shot of huge polar ice cliffs breaking off into the sea, sounding like thunder. Because the film has acclimated us to Hushpuppy's point of view via her multiple voice-overs, we realize that this inserted shot is her *psychological* POV, a visualization of her fears that the universe is falling apart. Indeed, as floodwaters advance, we watch Wink and Hushpuppy float in a re-purposed truck-bed—their raft of redemption—while listening to Hushpuppy's voice-over: "For the animals that didn't have a dad to put them in a boat, the end of the world already happened."

Hence, each time that Hushpuppy realizes something may be wrong with *her* dad, we see another POV insert of aurochs on the move. The motif reaches its culmination as Wink lies dying in his squalid shack. Hushpuppy runs toward the shack with a herd of aurochs chasing behind her. Significantly, this is the first time that the girl and the beasts have appeared together in the same shot, implying that her fears are overtaking her. But then we see something amazing: Hushpuppy turns and faces her fears, telling the first aurochs towering above her, "You're my friend, kind of ... I gotta take care of mine." In other words, she has to acknowledge her fears in order to take care of Wink; and, because facing her fears makes her stronger, those fears become her friends, enabling her to survive Wink's demise. Indeed, after Hushpuppy greets the aurochs as friends, the beasts turn and walk away. The medium is thus key to the message: just as the technical divide between shots of aurochs and shots of Hushpuppy has been crossed by placing beasts and girl into the same mise-en-scène, so Hushpuppy crosses a psychological divide when she faces her mammoth fears. And she literally crosses the divide taped in Wink's shack to feed the dying man.

This constellation of meaning is enhanced by another motif: repeated alligator images. Like the aurochs, alligators are fearsome creatures with prehistoric roots. But rather than frozen in ice, they continue to roam Eastern Gulf states seeking whom they may devour. The first time we see an alligator is during an interpolated flashback of the moment Hushpuppy was biologically conceived. When Wink begins to tell the tale of "Hushpuppy's conception" to a room filled with children, viewers should feel uncomfortable with Wink's inebriated decision to recount a moment of coitus. However, what we see, instead, is Hushpuppy's POV "conception" of her moment of conception, via flashback.

At the start of the POV flashback, we hear that Wink and Hushpuppy's mother were divided by their shyness. What we see is an image of Wink lying on a plastic lounge chair, oblivious to an alligator advancing upon him. The back of a woman half enters the frame, her body covering Wink's, and she shoots the alligator with a rifle. That's all we see of Hushpuppy's biological "conception," perhaps because this is the only way a six-year-old can *conceive* it—especially since she does not know her mother's identity. Nevertheless, in combination with the aurochs constellation, the image implies that the shyness barrier, like the alligator, had to be destroyed for life to go on. With the alligator dead, Wink can break sexual barriers in order for Hushpuppy to come into existence. Of course, we do not recognize this symbolism until the alligator motif is complete, just as we cannot recognize a constellation by seeing only one star.

The second star in the alligator motif is very important in this regard. After the flood has inundated their entire shanty town, Wink and two friends decide to drain their land by blowing a hole in the levee that protects established neighborhoods from the waters that flood their own makeshift shanty-town. They do so by placing dynamite in the belly of an alligator carcass. Significantly, it is Hushpuppy who pushes the button to ignite the alligator bomb. She and Wink together thus enable life to return to their land by breaking a literal barrier: the levee.

The next star in the constellation appears during another emotional breakthrough. Having run away from a shelter where her shanty-town people have been taken after the flood, Hushpuppy and several girls wade into the ocean until a boat picks them up and takes them to a floating saloon. There Hushpuppy encounters a female cook whom she imagines to be her mother. The woman, who shows Hushpuppy how to cook alligator meat, picks the girl up for an extended hug, and we hear Hushpuppy say, "This is my favorite thing," followed immediately by her voiceover: "I can count all the times I've been lifted on two fingers." Once again, a destroyed alligator—this one cooked—is aligned with the breaking of a divide.

The final star in the constellation shines at the very end of the film. Immediately after Hushpuppy stares down the aurochs, she enters Wink's shack carrying a paper sack. She kneels on the floor and starts feeding her dying father food from the sack: the cooked alligator meat from the floating saloon. As Hushpuppy breaks off a piece of alligator, dipping it in red sauce, it looks like communion via intinction enacted at many Christian churches. As Wink opens his mouth to receive the alligator, he starts to cry, despite his repeated demands, throughout the film, that Hushpuppy not cry. Using shot/reverse-shot, the camera cutting back-and-forth between father and daughter, the medium shows Hushpuppy crying as well. Like the levee, the emotional divide has been breached, allowing tears to escape like the floodwaters that escaped through the levee hole: both mediated through an alligator. The camera then cuts to Hushpuppy lying on Wink's chest, and we are given a close-up on Hushpuppy's dark face and one brown eye. Shot at a strange angle, the medium calls attention to the low-angle, thus reminding us of a similar close-up on an aurochs's one brown eye surrounded by its black skin. The graphic match implies that Hushpuppy's fears have been fulfilled—Wink has died—but that her communion with him during his last moments of life has been her salvation.

Indeed, at the very end of the film, we see Hushpuppy with head held unusually high as she watches Wink's body float in his car-raft downstream. According to his request, she has set Wink's body on fire, honoring him as in Hindu cremations. As we watch the sparks fly up, we hear a voiceover in which Hushpuppy states, "When it all goes quiet behind my eyes, I see everything that made me flying around in invisible pieces ... When it all goes quiet, I see they're right here. I see I'm a little piece of a big big universe. And that makes things right ..."

Hushpuppy's closing statement thus connects to another visual motif in *Beasts of the Southern Wild*: repeated images of sparks floating up into the air, looking like stars. Though these graphic "pieces" are right there in the film, they remain "invisible" to spectators who fail to cross the divide between medium and message. For those with eyes to see, however, the visual motif "declares knowledge" despite having "no speech," proclaiming the power of the medium itself.

Ending with the Light

When the Psalmist looks at the heavens, he aligns stars with beasts of the field, if not of the southern wild:

> When I look at your heavens, the work of your fingers,
> > the moon and the stars that you have established;
> what are human beings that you are mindful of them,
> > mortals that you care for them?
> Yet you have made them a little lower than God.
> > and crowned them with glory and honor.
> You have given them dominion over the works of your hands;
> > you have put all things under their feet,
> all sheep and oxen,
> > and also the beasts of the field,
> the birds of the air, and the fish of the sea,
> > whatever passes along the paths of the sea.
>
> (Psalm 8:3–8)

Many have interpreted these lines to mean that humans are encouraged to extract whatever they need from earth—fish, coal, oil, timber—in order to enhance their own lives. Like Jake LaMotta extracting gems out of his championship belt in *Raging Bull*, such interpreters are blind to the greater value of the whole, to the environmental context that gives meaning and sustainable value to their extractions, whether sheep or oxen, alligators or aurochs.

This, of course, also happens in the field of religion and film, many authors extracting profundities without considering the entire visual environment in which gems of insight are embedded like stars in constellations. *Salvation from Cinema* therefore encourages those in the field to consider the word *consider*. Meaning "to examine carefully," *consider* derives from a Latin term meaning "with the stars."[17] Constellations on the screen proclaim glory within the medium itself—but only for those with eyes to see.

Notes

1 Rudolf Arnheim in *Film as Art* (1957), quoted in James Monaco, *How to Read a Film: The Art, Technology, Language, History, and Theory of Film and Media*, rev. ed. (New York: Oxford University Press, 1981), 318; Marshall McLuhan, *Understanding Media: The Extensions of Man* (New York: McGraw-Hill, 1964), 287.
2 Johannes Ehrat, *Cinema and Semiotic: Peirce and Film Aesthetics, Narration, and Representation* (Toronto: University of Toronto Press, 2005), 436.
3 Clive Marsh has a similar response to *Koyaanisqatsi*: "It confronts us, by beautiful means, with the world's beauty." See *Theology Goes to the Movies: An Introduction to Critical Christian Thinking* (London: Routledge, 2007), 67.
4 John C. Lyden, *Film as Religion: Myths, Morals, and Rituals* (New York: New York University Press, 2003), 24. For similar cautions against the "discovery" of Christ-figures in film, see Christopher Deacy, "Theology and Film" in *Theology and Film: Challenging the Sacred/Secular Divide*, ed. Christopher Deacy and Gaye Williams Ortiz (Malden: Blackwell, 2008), 5–6, 27–8.
5 Christian Metz, *Film Language: A Semiotics of the Cinema*, trans. Michael Taylor (Chicago: University of Chicago Press, 1974), 119. Problems with Metz's film theory are addressed in Chapter 5.

6 David Bordwell and Kristin Thompson, *Film Art: An Introduction*, 2nd edn (New York: Knopf, 1986), 119. As the authors make clear, "Mise-en-scène is at bottom a theatrical notion: the filmmaker stages an event to be filmed" (151).
7 Metz discusses the different connotations between a dissolve and a fade to black. The latter implies "a straightforward spatiotemporal break" between shots, while a dissolve connotes a "transitive" connection between scenes (*Film Language*, 99).
8 The film was adapted from an internationally best-selling 2002 novel by Turkish writer Zülfü Livaneli.
9 The novel explains that the village "imam" had "forbidden all 'non-Muslim inventions,' including radio and television." O. Z. Livaneli, *Bliss*, trans. C. A. Fromm (New York: St. Martin's, 2006), 49, 13–14. "In Turkey," Livaneli states in a printed interview at the end of the novel, "honor killings are most frequently seen in regions where tribal/feudal ties and relations continue to exist. In certain parts of eastern Anatolia, patriarchal norms and hierarchies can still be found in their harshest and most anachronistic forms and women are denied all of their rights" (279–80).
10 Huston Smith, *The Religions of Man* (New York: Harper & Row, 1965), 115.
11 Ibid., 153. As with any religion, Buddhism is much more complicated than my brief overview allows. For example, Hinayana has been renamed Theravada, and some scholars insist that the Enlightened in Theravada Buddhism are called *Arhat*, not *Bodhisattva*. Furthermore, Mahayana continues to divide into multiple schools, like the multiple denominations of Protestant Christianity.
12 Ibid., 210.
13 Ibid., 139.
14 Ibid., 138.
15 Christmas Humphreys, *Buddhism* (Harmondsworth: Pelican, 1951), 91.
16 For this discussion of *King of Masks*, I borrow extensively from my essay "(C)rafting Redemption," *Cresset* 69.3 (February 2006): 36–9. However, the thesis of the earlier essay is radically different from the discussion here.
17 Eric Partridge, *Origins: A Short Etymological Dictionary of Modern English* (New York: Greenwich House, 1983), 116.

3 Gazing at the Stars
Nudity on the Screen

The preceding chapter defined cinematic beauty in terms of star-like constellations. This chapter considers cinematic stars in the more conventional sense, presenting theorists who interrogate human beauty on screen. It does so in order to grapple with an issue that has concerned devout people since the earliest days of Hollywood: the sexualized body and cinematic nudity.

Just as some people never look in awe at the constellations, others never thoughtfully reflect about the way they look at bodies on a movie screen, preferring to focus on the preposterous movie scenarios that carry cinematic stars to artificially happy endings. As famed film theorist Laura Mulvey has lamented, "cinema has distinguished itself in the production of ego ideals as expressed in particular in the star system, the stars centering both screen presence and screen story as they act out a complex process of likeness and difference."[1] By "difference," Mulvey implies that beautiful stars move beyond our reach, like the stars in the night sky. But, at the same time, spectators project themselves into stories on screen, establishing "likeness" with the characters that stars perform. Nevertheless, such spectators usually do not think about *how they view* beauty, whether cinematic or human, on the screen.

A Room with a View of Beauty: The Male Gaze

For the last decades of the twentieth century, a "beautiful film" was often associated with Merchant Ivory Productions: a collaboration between producer Ismail Merchant and director James Ivory, with scripts usually written by Ruth Prawer Jhabvala. Their style, using elaborate sets and costuming to capture the feel of late nineteenth- and early twentieth-century British culture, became so famous that people began using the phrase "like a Merchant Ivory film" to describe any period piece containing superb actors set in one gorgeous mise-en-scène after another. For several decades, then, "Merchant Ivory film" meant, to many, "beautiful film."[2]

With Academy Awards for Art Direction and Costume Design, one of the most stunning Merchant Ivory films is *A Room with a View* (1985), based on E. M. Forster's 1908 novel. And while each mise-en-scène is breathtaking, the medium also appeals to beautiful minds, encouraging viewers to think about *how they see* beauty in any room that contains a viewing screen. Beginning in Italy, *A Room with a View* offers gorgeous shots of Florence and the sun-drenched fields of Fiesole, a scenic village to its north. The story then moves to the more subdued England, where the Edwardian protagonist, Lucy (Helena Bonham Carter) becomes engaged to the effete Cecil (a wonderfully funny Daniel Day-Lewis). What some people remember more than anything else, however, is an incident when Cecil, Lucy and her mother take a walk to a secluded pond where they happen upon three men, including their rotund rector, skinny-dipping with joyous abandon. As the bathers shamelessly jump in and out of the water in a jubilant game of tag, we see their genitalia.

Though the scene is not at all erotic, is in fact quite humorous, I occasionally hear gasps from students during screenings, primarily because they are not used to *seeing* fully nude males on screen. In contrast, they have gotten so used to female nudity in movies that they think nothing of it. But that is just the problem: not thinking.

Wanting viewers to *think about* how they look at human beauty in cinema, Laura Mulvey incited a revolution with her 1975 publication of "Visual Pleasure and Narrative Cinema." Appearing in almost every anthology of film theory ever published, Mulvey's essay energized feminist film studies, often through critiques of her assumptions by other feminists.[3] In 2004, Mulvey acknowledged that her watershed essay depended upon cinematic technology of the 1970s, wherein the exhibition of film required "darkness, the projector beam lighting up on the screen, the procession of images that imposed their own rhythm on the spectator's attention." Reminding us of Plato's allegory of the cave, Mulvey here implies that spectators in the 1970s were chained to the cinematic apparatus, whereas in the twenty-first century viewers can take charge of their gaze by watching movies on apparatuses they control: computer, television, and phone screens.[4] Though critiqued as reductive—like Marx, Freud, and McLuhan—Mulvey can nevertheless help theologians and religion scholars assess how to regard human beauty on the cinematic screen.[5]

Mulvey begins her famous essay by distinguishing two kinds of "pleasurable structures of looking": narcissistic versus scopophilic. She defines narcissistic viewing as a projection of oneself into the movie through identification with the screen protagonist. Far more problematic is scopophilia: a term Mulvey borrows from Freud to describe "using another person as an object of sexual stimulation through sight."[6] Not surprisingly, narrative cinema, from its very start, has tended to code females, and not males, as objects of scopophilia.

Mulvey thus suggests that Hollywood cinema genders viewers as male. In other words, the camera identifies with the "male gaze," such that females function as either rewards for or seductive impediments to male protagonists. Hence, even female viewers of a film identify with the "male gaze," angry at any *femme fatale* who impedes the male protagonist, while rooting for the good woman who functions as a beautiful reward for his endeavors. As Mulvey puts it:

> The determining male gaze projects its fantasy onto the female figure, which is styled accordingly. In their traditional exhibitionist role women are simultaneously looked at and displayed, with their appearance coded for strong visual and erotic impact so that they can be said to connote *to-be-looked-at-ness.*[7]

Significantly, in *A Room with a View*, both the novel and the film, the prim and proper Cecil repeatedly compares his fiancée, Lucy, to "a Leonardo": a painting (by Leonardo da Vinci) to be looked at. Hence, when he first tries to kiss Lucy, "his gold pince-nez became dislodged and was flattened between them," rendering the kiss ineffectual.[8] In other words, when Cecil tries to connect with a real flesh-and-blood woman, his reliance on "the gaze" through his spectacles undermines their connection. Not coincidentally, Merchant and Ivory, like Forster, place this moment at the side of the same lake where skinny-dipping men will later undermine our own complacency about "the male gaze."

Perpetuating the Male Gaze in the Twenty-First Century: Chick Flicks

Though much has changed since Mulvey coined the term *to-be-looked-at-ness*, thanks in part to the very fact that she coined it, I would argue that twenty-first-century culture still celebrates the male gaze. Consider, for example, the review of a 2012 book about the James Bond franchise: "Page after page of photos display the villains, the gadgets and the girls, making 'Bond on Bond' a kind of 007 family album for those who grew up with the British secret agent."[9] Notice how the term "girls" follows a reference to the "display" of Bond's impediments and aids: "villains" and "gadgets." Indeed, most females in James Bond movies are coded as either sexy villains to be overcome or sexy gadgets to be used, whether for information or gratification. Even as late as 2012's *Skyfall*, Bond (Daniel Craig) responds to a gunfire attack by regretting the shattering of a good bottle of Scotch more than the death of a female he had bedded. The woman's sexy body is a container of stimulation less valuable than a container of alcoholic stimulants.[10]

Though male chauvinism in James Bond movies is self-consciously campy, Hollywood continues to code women as "sexy," not only through provocative dress and gestures, but through manipulation of the medium. As Mulvey notes, *close-ups*—on legs, lips, arms, eyes, breasts—draw attention to body parts as objects of the gaze.[11] The woman is thus dehumanized as the camera fragments her body into parts. In contrast, notice how often, when a naked male appears on screen, we see a man's entire body: our gaze regards him as a whole person (as in the skinny-dipping scene in *Room with a View*).

Of course, numerous films avoid such fragmentation of the female form, communicating value for the whole woman in what are often called "chick flicks." But this designation should give us pause. When people describe films as "chick flicks," they imply a dichotomy between regular/real/authentic movies and those for "chicks." Why the distinction? Perhaps because the so-called "chick flick" identifies with a female perspective. And since most viewers—including females—are programmed to look with the "male gaze," they distinguish films that stand out *against the norm* with a special term: chick flick.

Without renouncing the idea of the "male gaze," Mulvey later admitted that her watershed essay was caught in an "either/or" binary: "masculine/feminine, voyeuristic/exhibitionist, active/passive."[12] The idea of a "chick flick" can get caught in binary thinking as well, and can be illustrated as follows, where the term on top is considered "authentic" or "standard" and the term underneath sub-par:

Male perspective	=	Normal film	=	Woman as object
Female perspective	=	Chick flick	=	Woman as subject

Unfortunately, some feminists react by inverting the binary, making a female perspective primary while disdaining any kind of male viewpoint. Arguing against such an inversion, E. Ann Kaplan responds to Mulvey by asserting, "What rather has to happen is that we move beyond long-held cultural and linguistic patterns of oppositions … we need to think about ways of transcending a polarity that has only brought us all pain."[13] While Kaplan talks about "transcending" oppositions such as "dominant/submissive" or "matriarchal/patriarchal," other feminists talk about deconstructing them, encouraging "both/and" thinking rather than "either/or" thinking.[14] Deconstruction—which will be discussed more thoroughly in Part II—occurs as viewers think about *both* male *and* female "seeing," in *both* senses of the word: being seen *and* the act of seeing. This, of course, is what Merchant and Ivory did in *A Room with a View*: they encouraged viewers to think about *the seeing of* skinny-dipping males, not only by characters walking through the woods, but also by audience members sitting in a theater.

A Room with a View of Art

Merchant and Ivory signal their interest in spectatorship by including moments in *A Room with a View* when characters appear next to famous works of art. Early in the film, a group of people tour a church in Florence, a British rector directing their gaze toward specific paintings. A crane shot captures them from above, such that we see the tops of their heads simultaneously swivel as they briefly look toward each painting the rector describes. This captures one of the novel's themes: how people see what they have been trained to see, without looking in depth at the art itself. But it also might comment on scholarship about religion and film: like the rector in *A Room with a View*, all too many scholars direct our attention to theological/religious issues films suggest, turning our heads toward brilliant insights without encouraging us to look in depth at the art on screen.

The rector's swift tour of church art in Florence contrasts with a later scene in London when Merchant and Ivory force the camera to linger on one painting hanging in the National Gallery: Paolo Uccello's *Battle of San Romano* (c. 1440).

The work fills the entire mise-en-scène as three film characters converse in front of it. Though the novel alludes to the three meeting in London, Forster does not mention any paintings, let alone Uccello. We therefore need to consider the artistic intent of the filmmakers, who frame the painting with the frame of the movie screen. Their unusually long take on the full-frame painting forces attentive viewers to think about looking at film the way they look at art: for beauty as well as content. The content of Uccello's *Battle of San Romano*, with armored horsemen facing each other, alludes to the battle for Lucy's love developing between the two young men who face each other in front of the Uccello: one who sees her as "a Leonardo," the other who embraces her as a woman. More importantly, by filling the mise-en-scène with a work by Uccello, a Quattrocento (fifteenth-century Italian) painter famous for pioneering perspectivalism in art, the filmmakers seem to endorse an assumption held by many film theorists: that the monocular perspective developed in Quattrocento art "defined to a significant degree" the "visual field" of cinema.[15] The inclusion of paintings in a film's mise-en-scène—what what Sylvain De Bleeckere calls "image grafts"—encourages viewers to consider *how* they view beauty—both artistic and human.[16]

Artistic Beauty: *Girl with a Pearl Earring*

The parallel between gazing at art and the gaze elicited by cinematic bodies is intensified by *Girl with a Pearl Earring* (Peter Webber, 2003). Based upon the *New York Times* bestseller by Tracy Chevalier (1999), *Girl with a Pearl Earring* focuses on work by the painter Johannes Vermeer (1632–75). While the novel shows us only one Vermeer painting—on its cover—the film captures interiors reminiscent of seventeenth-century Dutch realist paintings by Jan Steen, Pieter de Hooch, and Nicolaes Maes, as well as by Vermeer himself. In addition, warm yellows and reddish browns often bathe the film's mise-en-scène, generating the aura of Rembrandt van Rijn. This stunning film earned accolades for its relatively unknown director, Peter Webber, and well-earned Oscar nominations for art direction, set decoration, cinematography, and costume design.

Since not much is known about Vermeer, Chevalier had the artistic license to create a story about one of the Dutch realist's actual portraits called *The Girl with a Pearl Earring* (c. 1665). Unlike most of Vermeer's paintings, which place individuals into highly detailed interior spaces, with hangings in the background and meticulously rendered domestic objects in the foreground, *The Girl with a Pearl Earring* surrounds its subject in black: a background as dark as our knowledge of the pearl-wearer's life. Chevalier therefore paints a background in words, inventing a 16-year-old named Griet who narrates how she became a servant in Vermeer's household. Hired to wash clothes and clean the painter's studio, Griet is secretly recruited by Vermeer to help him grind colors for paint and eventually sit for the portrait. When the artist's wife, Catharina, discovers her own pearl earrings were worn by a servant girl in a secret painting, she evicts Griet from the house.

The novel focuses primarily upon *the seeing of* Griet—in both senses of the italicized phrase. Narrated by her, it communicates not only the beauty she sees in Vermeer's studio, but also her concerns about the various ways people see and respond to her body. In its cinematic form, then, *Girl with a Pearl Earring* must somehow get inside Griet's head in order to transmit both kinds of seeing: female as both subject and object of "the gaze." Assessing how the film does so provides an education in cinematic artistry and the subversion of *to-be-looked-at-ness*: a necessary step before we consider how to view, both literally and figuratively, nudity on screen.

Externalizing the Internal in *Girl with a Pearl Earring*

Filmmakers employ several film techniques to externalize thought. The most obvious is the use of *voice-over*, in which either an omniscient narrator tells us what is going on or we hear a character voice her/his thoughts. Many filmmakers consider voice-overs as cinematic cheating.[17] For them, a truly artistic film externalizes the internal rather plastering a sonic band-aid over the mise-en-scène.

Rather than voice-overs, *Girl with a Pearl Earring* relies on eyeline match cuts. Several times we see Griet (Scarlett Johansson) gazing at paintings or still-life arrangements in Vermeer's house, tilting her head or narrowing her eyes as she assesses their beauty, establishing her as subject of the gaze, in control of how she looks at beauty. She shows less control, however, when she looks at the smouldering Vermeer (Colin Firth).

Movies can easily make sexual attraction explicit by putting two people in a shot (a two shot) and using a long take to linger over their desire, their heads slowly moving closer as they stare into each other's eyes while glancing at lips waiting to be kissed. But *Pearl Earring* hesitates to follow this generic scenario, for it would dishonestly represent a seventeenth-century class system in which attraction between an employer and servant was unthinkable. (Of course, that didn't prevent seventeenth-century employers from having their way with beautiful servants, but such behavior usually reflected lust-bred power-plays, not the mutual attraction which many so-called "historical" films artificially inculcate in order to titillate viewers.)

While the novel could make explicit Griet's hidden attraction to Vermeer through the way she writes about him, the film had the more difficult task of suggesting *unspoken, undemonstrated* sexual desire. One way it does so is through the classical Hollywood convention of shot/reverse shot, by which a close-up on one person's face, looking in one direction, is followed by a close-up on another person's face, looking in the opposite direction—signaling that the two are looking at each other. Because Vermeer's stare lingers, while Griet furtively turns her eyes away, we get a sense that looking reflects one's station in life. People have been trained to look a certain way—in both senses of the phrase. And gender, of course, contributes to the way one looks—in both senses of the phrase. As Kaja Silverman notes in her assessment of Laura Mulvey, "Classic cinema abounds in shot/reverse shot formations in which men look at women."[18]

Girl with a Pearl Earring also draws attention to the concept of "looking" through a significant motif *not in the novel*. Several times characters appear behind door jambs as they watch activity in a room, half their face hidden behind the frame. Because a close-up on a whole face conventionally represents the entire person, these shots with only one eye facing the camera force attentive viewers to think about the organ of seeing. At one point Vermeer, half his face hidden, surreptitiously watches the beautiful Griet expose her luxurious tresses, and he leaves only when she looks up and sees him watching.

Significantly, the different ways characters in the movie look at Griet fulfills a distinction made by Laura Mulvey: voyeurist versus fetishistic scopophilia. As Mulvey explains, "fetishistic scopophilia builds up the physical beauty of the object, transforming it into something satisfying in itself. ... [V]oyeurism, on the contrary, has associations with sadism: pleasure lies in ascertaining guilt ..., asserting control and subjugating the guilty person through punishment or forgiveness."[19] The way people inside the film look at the seventeenth-century Griet, in other words, comments upon the way viewers outside the film look at Scarlett Johansson's twenty-first-century embodiment of Griet.

Indeed, Vermeer is not the only character whose one eye watches behind a door jamb. We also see the one eye of his daughter Cornelia (Alakina Mann), who spies on Griet around door frames, as though to catch her in some illicit activity. Quite clearly her "pleasure lies in ascertaining guilt," explaining why she subjugates Griet to "punishment." Not only does Cornelia wipe her dirty hands on freshly clean sheets that Griet has hung to dry, she also dirties Griet's clean reputation by implicating her in the disappearance of an expensive comb.

The image of clean laundry connects Cornelia's voyeurism with that of another character. As Griet hangs out the wash, van Ruijven, Vermeer's patron, squeezes her breast. Punishing Griet by groping her every chance he gets, van Ruijven has a similar attitude toward artistic beauty: it is the object of his desire, something that he wants to possess, to control. Owning paintings, like groping Griet, adds to van Ruijven's sense of power. When Griet repeatedly rebuffs his advances, van Ruijven asserts his control by commissioning a painting of her: the portrait that becomes *The Girl with a Pearl Earring*. If he can't have her as a sexual object, he'll own her as an art object. His seeing, like that of many film viewers, serves merely to arouse self-serving pleasure.

However, as Mulvey notes, not all voyeurism seeks to punish the object of the gaze. Control can also be asserted through "forgiveness" of presumed guilt. Such is the tactic of Maria Thins, Vermeer's mother-in-law, who, true to historical accounts, owns and runs the house where the painter lives with Maria's daughter, Catharina. In contrast to the flamboyantly dressed van Ruijven, who wants to possess beauty for his own stimulation, the angular Maria, always dressed in Puritan black, primarily wants to make money. Deciding that Griet is "useful" because she helps Vermeer paint faster and hence earn money more quickly, Maria forgives Griet for her enticing beauty. She goes behind Catharina's back, not only by allowing Griet to help Vermeer prepare paint, but also by absconding with Catharina's earrings so that Vermeer can add them to Griet's portrait. Maria thus voyeuristically exercises control over Griet's *to-be-looked-at-ness* in order to serve her own financial interests—like filmmakers who insert gratuitous female nudity only to sell tickets. (More of that later.)

Unlike her mother, Catharina regards Vermeer's paintings as objects of the gaze that take attention away from her own needs. Currying the gaze of Vermeer the man, Catharina seems to fear Vermeer the artist. Indeed, he will not allow her to enter his studio because her carelessness—in both senses of the word—interferes with his art. Nevertheless, due to whisperings of guilt by the voyeuristic Cornelia, Catharina storms the studio expecting to see evidence of sexual dalliance between Griet and her husband. But all she sees is a painting called *The Concert* (c. 1665-6). When the annoyed Vermeer pulls *The Concert* off its easel, we see Griet standing behind it, framed by the easel's empty limbs. The medium thus makes the point clear: rather than hiding adultery, Vermeer is hiding the subject matter of his next painting. Indeed, Griet's face will soon appear on a canvas held by the same easel. Significantly, easels were invented in Vermeer's lifetime, emphasizing, according to film theorist Stephen Heath, spectatorship: "the painter is definitely upright, an eye on the world, an eye that stations itself," much like a moviegoer stationed in front of a screen. Vermeer, then, like many moviegoers, enjoys "fetishistic scopophilia" as Mulvey defines it: "the erotic instinct is focused on the look alone."[20]

An erotic connection is established between Vermeer and Griet, then, not through sexual love but through scopophilia, the love of looking. First recognizing her sensitivity to beauty by the way she arranges vegetables on a tray, Vermeer eventually arranges for Griet to sleep in an attic connected to his studio—not so he can bed her, but so she can help create beauty. In this way, *Girl with a Pearl Earring* subverts a common Hollywood cliché in which two people, having become strongly attracted to each other despite radical differences in class, vocation, or personality, finally consummate their attraction sexually. In *Girl*, consummation occurs not in the flesh but through art, seen when Griet becomes Vermeer's art: his *Girl with the Pearl Earring*.

In order to wear the earring, however, Griet must have her ears pierced. While in the novel she does the task herself, the film shows Vermeer piercing her ears with a hot needle, implying that he penetrates her for his art rather than with his flesh. He therefore seems to use Griet as does his lustful patron: both regard her as the object of the gaze, one voyeuristically, the other fetishistically. For example, in one scene, Vermeer strokes Griet's face with his finger as she sits for his painting, but when she moves toward him with longing, he pulls back and swiftly paints her look of arousal on his canvas. Rather than kiss her, he fetishistically paints, and thus preserves, her beauty. He is like a film director eliciting enticing poses from a female star that others will pay to view. What saves Vermeer from our Mulvey-bred disdain is the agency he allows Griet as she takes control of the gaze. In one early scene, Vermeer sees Griet gazing out a window. But rather than scolding her for ignoring her cleaning duties he joins her to discuss what *she sees*, helping her to distinguish subtle variations in cloud color.

Vermeer's respect for Griet's seeing—making her the subject rather than merely the object of the gaze—may explain a bold move she later makes. While cleaning the studio, Griet becomes disturbed by a subtle lack of balance in the background of a current Vermeer project, *Young Woman with a Water Jug* (1665-6). After intently surveying the still-unfinished painting, Griet finally drags a chair out of the painting's mise-en-scène. Vermeer changes his painting to incorporate Griet's aesthetically astute alteration, thus *submitting his seeing to hers*.[21]

This focus on Griet's seeing, as opposed to people merely seeing her, is reinforced by another scene changed from the novel. Chevalier, who researched seventeenth-century Holland as well as Vermeer's painting practices, discovered that Vermeer employed a camera obscura to help him conceptualize how arrangements of subject matter might look when rendered on canvas.[22] Key to the development of photography, the camera obscura was originally a dark room with a hole in one wall, such that light entering from the outside would cast an inverted image of objects outside onto the opposite wall of the room. By Vermeer's day, the camera was a portable box with a viewing porthole and lenses: one lens was attached to the hole and another inside the box turned the image right side up. In both the novel and the film, then, Vermeer invites Griet to look into a camera obscura set up in his studio. The film, however, proceeds to externalize Griet's internalized wonder by cutting to a close-up of Griet's single eye looking in, as though taken from within the camera obscura itself. By focusing on Griet's eye—like those single eyes behind door frames gazing at her—the cinematic camera draws attention to *her* gaze, *her* seeing.

Reinforcing how the cinematic medium tells stories differently than their written source texts do (a distinction under-theorized by scholars in religion and film), *Girl with a Pearl Earring* next makes a profound change. In the novel, Griet notes how the camera obscura intensifies the scene that Vermeer has arranged to paint, calling it "a painting that was not a painting." Griet's phrase seems a perfect description of multiple scenes within the film: arranged by a set designer and then captured by a movie camera, they are paintings that are not paintings, viewed through an intensifying camera lens. The film, however, has a different point to make. Instead of "a painting that was not a painting," Vermeer tells Griet that what they see through the camera obscura is "a picture made of light": a phrase traditionally used to describe cinema. It is as though the filmmakers want to capture the insight of Stephen Heath, who famously argued that easel painting, in combination with the camera obscura, "is a step in the direction of the camera, a camera that will provide screen and frame and the image reflected, fixed, painted with light."[23] *Girl with a Pearl Earring* thus calls attention to its own status as art, a beautiful "picture made of light" captured by a *camera* lens. But that is not all. By showing us what Griet sees through the camera obscura, the film forces us to look *with* Griet's eyes rather than merely look *at* her body.

The medium, in other words, is the message, encouraging us to consider how we see the pictures made of light projected onto our movie screens. Many people watch movies with the motivation of a van Ruijven, seeking voyeuristic titillation. Others look with the eye of Maria Thins, valuing movies in terms of how much money they make. Some devout people view films like Cornelia, ready to report on the number of vulgar words and activities they witness.[24] Others primarily focus on the celebrities who make movies, paralleling Catharina, who obsesses over Vermeer while oblivious to his art. *Girl with a Pearl Earring* implies that we should instead watch films with the eye of Griet: seriously contemplating how—and why—painters of light have arranged every element on the canvas of our screens.

Seeing Nudity: Gratuitous or Justified?

These different approaches to seeing beauty relate, of course, to viewing the naked body on screen. Is the nudity artistically justifiable, or does it pander to problematic scopophilia? Unfortunately, even good filmmakers often indulge van Ruijven viewers by inserting unnecessary nudity and/or sex. Just as Vermeer needed a patron like van Ruijven to buy his art in order to support his family, so filmmakers, overseen by producers reminiscent of Maria Thins, need the van Ruijvens of the world to patronize their films.

Interestingly, filmmakers often put a nude sex scene in the opening minutes of a film—with little to no sex and/or nudity to follow. One famous example is the graphic sex shared by Julie Christie and Donald Sutherland that begins *Don't Look Now* (1973), a scene considered a watershed moment in non-pornographic film history.[25] Such titillating beginnings seem gratuitous: inserted to keep voyeuristic viewers attentive. But maybe that is the point: directors serious about cinema as an artistic medium give their Maria Thins producers just what they want, putting nude sex scenes up front as though to say, "You want gratuitous? Well, I'll give you gratuitous, you studio rascals! I'll satisfy your van Ruijven viewers by slapping some steamy sex into the first scene to get it out of the way. Then I'll proceed to make a good film." Doing so, they emphasize the gratuitous scene's insignificance, viewers often forgetting how the movie started since the sex scene had so little to do with the film's actual narrative trajectory. Of course, this is mere speculation—much as Tracy Chevalier speculated about the girl Vermeer painted in *The Girl with the Pearl Earring*.

The question still remains: how do we know when nudity in cinema is justified? We certainly don't want to go to the opposite extreme, mimicking viewers like Catherina and Cornelia who, indifferent to art, establish the "guilt" of a movie by counting up the number of nude shots it contains. That's simply a different kind of voyeurism. In contrast, I would suggest that justifiable nudity in a film functions like the nudity we see in art museums. When we look at a nude painting, in either a museum or an art history book, we are aware of our process of seeing. After all, we entered the museum or opened the book intending to *thoughtfully view* the art rather than to seek mindless stimulation. I would argue, then, that nudity is not gratuitous in cinema when the medium of film encourages attentive viewers to become conscious about their process of seeing, making them aware of the gaze.

For examples, I will end this chapter discussing two beautiful films: one in which the protagonist is female, the other in which the protagonist is male. Both are directed by females, illustrating a point made by Ally Acker in *Reel Women*: "Distinct uses of the camera: a focused eye and heart toward aspects of women's lives previously ignored or pooh-poohed by male cinema, because of a lack of shared experience—all this is what distinguishes a female gaze."[26]

Take the Marriage in *Take This Waltz*

Take This Waltz, directed by Sarah Polley (2011), focuses on the eye and heart of Margot (Michelle Williams), who has been married to Lou (Seth Rogen) for five years. It is a best-buddy kind of marriage: lots of cuddling, baby talk, and laughter. We get a clue that Margot is dissatisfied with something, however, when she pushes Lou away after he kisses her during one of their "bad little baby" games, suggesting that she doesn't want to associate sex with baby behavior: "Not both together," she winces. Indeed, when Margot later makes overtures toward Lou, she seems to desire the steamy passion usually portrayed in cinema: more sensual than playful. However, as Margot hugs him from behind several different times, Lou gently rebuffs her, always because he is in the middle of cooking chicken, seeking to generate recipes for a cookbook he is writing.

The medium symbolizes Margot's sexual frustration with a glass motif. The film begins and ends with Margot leaning against the glass of an oven door, mournfully looking at the warmth within, as though longing for hotter sex. And twice we see Lou and Margot on opposite sides of a window in their house, he sitting on the back porch while she sits in the kitchen. When they try to talk through the window they cannot hear each other, and when they hold their hands up on the window and then their lips, the glass impedes the warmth of their touch. The symbolism is clear: Margot experiences a failure of communication about her inability to arouse the warmth of passionate sex. Hence, the second time we see them on either side of the window, Margot has just told Lou she is leaving him. And rather than touch the window, she turns her back and walks out of the room.

Inspiring Margot to leave Lou is the handsome neighbor across the street: Daniel (Luke Kirby). Attracted to the quirky but cute Margot, Daniel arranges ways to spend time with her, at one point sitting in the bleachers at the side of a community pool while Margot joins a dozen women in the water for an exercise class. A generic film would reinforce Margot as the object of Daniel's gaze—and our own—by putting her in a revealing swimsuit. However, while in *My Week with Marilyn* (Simon Curtis, 2011), released the same year, Michelle Williams turned in an award-winning performance playing Marilyn Monroe, a woman famous for soliciting "the male gaze," *Take This Waltz* radically subverts the gaze. When she laughs at the silly exercise routine that Daniel is watching, Margot accidentally pees in the pool, causing a blue stain to swirl up around her middle: not at all a sexy moment.

And then comes the nudity. The camera takes us inside a locker room, showing us the women from the pool showering together. However, rather than focusing on body parts, the view comes through a long shot, such that we see multiple women's entire bodies, most of them middle-aged and overweight, some excessively so. Since female nudity in generic Hollywood cinema is almost always beautifully sleek (and slick), we feel uncomfortable as we watch everyday normal female bodies, making us aware of two things: (1) our own voyeuristic status as Peeping Toms, watching women doing something private; and (2) the artifice of the gorgeous bodies that cinema usually offers as objects of the gaze. In other words, nudity in *Take This Waltz* forces us to think about Hollywood scopophilia: how we have been conditioned to look at the naked female form.

Furthermore, the long shots cut back and forth between a shower stall containing three middle-aged overweight women to a stall containing Margot and two other twenty-somethings: one skinnier than she, the other fatter. Hence, rather than viewing something erotic, we simply see difference, not only the difference among their shapes, but also the more pronounced difference between younger lithe limbs and the sagging bodies of older women. In the midst of this contrast occurs a significant conversation. As one naked young woman wonders why she shaves her legs since her husband never notices them any more, another states, "Sometimes I just want something new ... New things are shiny." The shot then cuts to the shower stall with the older women, one commenting, "New things get old." To make sure we hear it, the filmmakers cut back to the young naked women in order to have the leg-shaving woman concur: "That's right; new things get old." We cannot help thinking, then, that the bodies of the twenty-somethings will someday lose their youthful contours, looking more like those of the portly older women: new things get old. But the comment, embedded in a "nude scene," has even more profound implications, unlocking the entire film.

Refreshingly, Daniel finds Margot attractive for her personality rather than for her body. But he seduces her by appealing to her fear that she has missed out on movie-like hot sex and therefore authentic love-making. The film shows Margot repeatedly seeking out the romantic Daniel, but then resisting Daniel's sexual overtures, not wanting to betray her husband. And here the film does something else unusual. Unlike conventional (and highly lucrative) films that make annoyingly clear which man we are to root for and which one to despise, *Take This Waltz* shows us the weakness and strength of both men: Lou lacks erotic passion but is affectionate and playful, Daniel unremittingly pursues Margot, a married woman, but doesn't pressure her into anything. Viewers thus feel something of the ambivalence Margot experiences, which is important to our understanding of the film. For, after assiduously fighting her adulterous urges, Margot finally gives in to the desire for shiny eroticism once Daniel moves to another part of town. Evidently fearing the loss of the one opportunity she may have to experience movie-like passion, Margot tracks Daniel down and offers her body to him.

The film presents the sex the way many movies do: starting with a chaste kiss and then moving to greater eroticism. Here, however, the shiny, sleek nudity is intensified by its radical contrast with the nudity of the shower scene. People conditioned by Hollywood convention will view Margot's experience of sex as the denouement: happiness at last! The medium, however, delivers a different kind of message. Using long shots, the camera circles the lovers in the middle of Daniel's empty loft. With each circle the mise-en-scène changes. After an image of the fully clothed Daniel and Margot sharing their first kiss, the camera circles them, going behind a ladder and coming out the other side to reveal them lying on the floor embracing. When the camera next circles behind a plant stand, we see their naked bodies in a more kinky pose on a mattress. With each circle, the camera shows more and more furniture around the mattress, and more and more kinky sex on the mattress: first another naked woman joins Daniel and Margot, and then, after the next circle, a male joins the two. Though it sounds semi-pornographic, the camera moves fast enough and is far enough away that we only see enough to understand what is going on. And I would argue the nudity and sex are not gratuitous; for the circling shots comment on the inadequacy of erotic sex to provide satisfaction. Though clearly experiencing hot sex, the lovers become dissatisfied, accumulating sexual techniques and lovers the way they accumulate new furniture to satisfy a lack: new things get old.

Indeed, we soon see Margot and Daniel in shots very similar to shots of Margot and Lou earlier in the film. The last time the camera circles Margot and Daniel, they are sitting on a couch watching television, she wearing the exact same glasses that she wore to watch television with Lou. When she turns to Daniel to say "I love you," she has as much trouble getting a response from him as she did when she tried to seduce Lou. More dramatically, we next see Margot sit on a toilet urinating while Daniel flosses his teeth at the sink, establishing a graphic match with an earlier scene when Margot sits on a toilet urinating while Lou brushes his teeth at the sink. The medium, through graphic matches and circling shots, makes clear that Margot's life has come full circle.

The film, in fact, literally comes full circle when, at the end, it repeats its opening shot. As Margot mournfully leans her head against a warm oven door, she watches someone enter the kitchen. The low-angle shot (the camera on the floor with Margot) shows only the legs of a man who walks by the sullen woman. When the film starts this way, we assume the scene encapsulates the marriage between Lou and Margot. However, when the shot is repeated at the end of the film, we realize it is actually about the affair between Daniel and Margot. *Take This Waltz* thus exposes the artifice offered by much Hollywood cinema, in which finding the perfect sexual partner ameliorates life's frustrations and boredom. The nudity and sex thus contribute to a message far more consonant with religious values about the importance of the whole person than a PG-rated film that implies sexual love conquers all. And it is the medium that delivers the message.

We could chart the film's narrative symmetry as follows:

Leaning against the oven door
Nudity in shower → Toilet scene with Lou
Margot and Lou on opposite sides of a window

CENTER

Margot and Lou on opposite sides of a window
Nudity of hot sex → Toilet scene with Daniel
Leaning against the oven door

What the filmmakers place at the CENTER, then, is extremely significant, especially since it has its own narrative symmetry: Daniel offers to give the married couple a ride on his rickshaw for their wedding anniversary. As he pulls the conveyance, Daniel becomes the object of Margot's gaze, the camera cutting back and forth between her face and Daniel's muscular body parts with eyeline match cuts. We next see Margot and Lou eating at a fancy restaurant, where Margot expresses dissatisfaction that Lou does not make conversation over the meal. Margot therefore spends the next day with Daniel: first they eat together at a picnic table, then they sit together in one of those amusement park rides that has seats spinning at the end of metal arms which circle the ride's center.

The day with Daniel seems much more exciting than the anniversary with Lou—until we notice the parallels. During the picnic lunch Daniel and Margot have no conversation, and though the amusement park ride is exhilarating—music blaring, lights popping, people screaming—it eventually stops. In fact, when Margot and Daniel step off the exciting ride, the mise-en-scène is entirely gray, the sound entirely silent, and the seat Margot shared with Daniel is similar in size and shape to the one Margot shared with Lou on the rickshaw. We could therefore schematize the symmetry at the CENTER of the chart above as follows:

> Rickshaw ride with Lou
> Meal with Lou without conversation
> Meal with Daniel without conversation
> Amusement ride with Daniel

Like the hub around which the amusement park ride circles, this symmetrical center is the hub around which the symmetry of the entire film circles. The medium itself, then, draws attention to its own circular structure, communicating that, like the amusement park ride going around in circles, sex between Daniel and Margot is exciting while the camera goes around in circles. But once the titillation of the ride/sex stops, Margot again encounters the gray of real life, like urinating as a partner attends to his teeth: new things get old.

The artistically structured medium, as carefully crafted as a medieval triptych, demonstrates that hot sex with a gorgeous body is not the answer to life's dissatisfactions. We see this confirmed toward the end of the film when Margot returns to her former house in order to help with a family crisis: Lou's sister Geraldine, whom Margot loves dearly, has been arrested for leaving her four-year-old alone to go on an alcoholic bender. When Margot asks Geraldine what happened, the still inebriated woman tells Margot that their actions are not that different: "I think you're a bigger idiot than I am ... In the big picture, life has a gap in it; it just does. You don't go crazy trying to fill it like some lunatic!" In other words, while Geraldine insanely tried to fill the gap with alcohol, and hurt other people in the process, so Margot tried to fill the gap with hot sex.

The medium confirms the connection between the two women by having the drunk Geraldine hand her husband, James, a box of live chicks, reminding us of Margot's husband who is obsessed with cooking chicken. Significantly, Geraldine was the naked woman in the shower scene talking about shaving her legs. But she concluded her remarks with these words: "I still like James. Is it worth trading all that in for someone exciting that I may not like in ten years?" This explains why she repeats the words of the naked older woman—"New things get old"—like chicks that turn into chickens.

The truth of the film, then, comes from a conversation embedded in real-life nudity, which comments upon the camera-swirling Hollywood-slick nudity in Daniel's loft. Significantly, after the police take his sister away, Lou yells to Margot, who stands across the street, one of their baby-game phrases. With tears of regret on her face, Margot speaks back "Me too": a common rejoinder to expressions of love. What Margot had with her husband was real love, like the real nudity in the shower scene: not artificially exciting but authentically companionable. What follows is the bookend device of Margot leaning against the oven door as Daniel walks past her. The film ends with a different shot, however, the powerful significance of which I will allow viewers to discover on their own. For now, suffice it to say that the sex and nudity in *Take This Waltz* offer a more profound endorsement of marital fidelity than many "family-friendly" movies endorsed by Christian websites—at least for those with eyes to see the medium itself.

An Elegy for Nudity

While *Take This Waltz* contrasts realistically naked bodies with slick Hollywood nudity, *Elegy* (Isabel Coixet, 2008) offers to the male gaze more conventional nude shots. I end with this film because it ties together various threads woven throughout this chapter: from Mulvey's scopophilia to the cinematic power of paintings in a film's mise-en-scène.

Based on Philip Roth's novel *The Dying Animal* (2001), *Elegy* is about David (Ben Kingsley), a college professor who is something of a "celebrity" (as one character puts it) due to his weekly radio show and numerous television interviews. He takes advantage of his star status by seducing his beautiful female students, albeit waiting until after he has turned in their grades. He restrains himself, however, not due to any ethical code but in fear of sexual harassment charges. In other words, David is committed primarily to his own best interests.

Though the movie shows David engaged in steamy sex several times, it does not glorify promiscuity the way many romantic comedies that *avoid* nudity often do. Instead, *Elegy* makes clear the emptiness of David's life. His son, now a physician, resents David for abandoning him and his mother in order to pursue "emancipated manhood." And after David makes his most recent conquest, a gorgeous student named Consuela (Penélope Cruz), he experiences as much agony as pleasure. Though obsessed with her to the point of jealousy, he still cannot bear to make a commitment after a year of dating, never telling her that he still beds another former student on the side. When, fearing to meet her parents, he fails to show up at an event Consuela told him was extremely important to her—and then lies about it—Consuela ends the relationship. Thinking only of himself, David responds with disgust.

What David seems to miss most after the break-up, then, is Consuela's beauty. During their first sexual encounter he expresses awe over her perfect breasts, the camera lingering on them in order to give viewers David's male gaze. Unlike the myriad other movies that inculcate fetishistic voyeurism, however, *Elegy* forces us to question how we look at the breasts. The questioning begins when a friend tells David, "Beautiful women are invisible." Like us, David is baffled by this statement until the friend explains what he means: people are usually so stunned by a gorgeous woman that they look only at her surface, never seeing beyond her beautiful body to the person underneath. Her real self is therefore "invisible." Or, to use the language of Laura Mulvey, beautiful women are defined solely by their *to-be-looked-at-ness*.

The issue of *to-be-looked-at-ness* is reinforced as David and Consuela look through art history books. Famous paintings become the "object of the gaze" both to them and to us, eyeline match cuts showing us the reproductions they view. David, in fact, proclaims that Consuela looks like the woman they/we see in a painting by Goya (1746–1828)—reminding us of Cecil comparing Lucy to "a Leonardo" in *A Room with a View*. Later, they/we look at the famous Velázquez painting *Las Meninas* (1656), in which the object of the gaze seems to be the young princess in the foreground of the painting. However, as David points out, barely visible at the center of the painting appear images of the girl's parents, the king and queen, reflected in a tiny mirror. To the left of the princess is a painter who looks out of *Las Meninas* toward viewers. We therefore assume that what he sees, and paints, are the king and queen reflected in the mirror behind the princess. The painting, in other words, places spectators into its own mise-en-scène.

Significantly, several film theorists discussed *Las Meninas* decades before the making of *Elegy*. They did so in order to analyze the role of cinematic spectatorship. In *Cahiers du cinéma*, Jean-Pierre Oudart argues that "the text of [Velázquez's] painting must not be reduced to its visible part; it does not stop where the canvas stops."[27] In other words, Velázquez creates spectators outside the frame of the painting, controlling their gaze. Like the painter of *Las Meninas*, then, filmmakers control the gaze of their viewers, who, like the king and queen painted into the background, become "sutured" into the mise-en-scène, oblivious to the apparatus that manipulates their perception. As Steve Nolan notes in his discussion of Oudart, "the spectator reduces his *knowledge about* the object to his *vision of* it"—much as David reduces his knowledge about Consuela to *visions of* her beautiful body.[28]

By drawing attention to *Las Meninas*, *Elegy* encourages viewers to consider what has become "invisible" to them, what Oudart calls "the absent-one (l'absent)" outside the frame: the unseen apparatus of camera and editing.[29] Coixet, the director, thus seems to query viewers about her own camera work and cinematic technique: are they invisible the way beautiful women are invisible, valued only for their projection of *to-be-looked-at* surfaces? Indeed, David seems unaware of the superficiality of his own viewing, unable to focus on what is beyond the frame of Consuela's body: the soul that is her real self. The *Las Meninas* painting thus foreshadows that which breaks up their relationship: David's refusal to meet the shadowy parents at the unseen center of Consuela's existence.

After nearly two years, however, Consuela reconnects with David. Viewers therefore anticipate a typical Hollywood ending, the protagonists recognizing that they cannot live without each other, David finally willing to commit. But *Elegy* subverts such superficial generic closure. Consuela reconnects with David in order to tell him that she has cancer, asking him to photograph her breasts before she has one removed. As she poses topless on the couch, both voyeuristic and fetishistic scopophilia are challenged when the film draws attention to the mechanics of filming as David looks through his camera at Consuela on the couch.[30] Hence, just as Velázquez's *Las Meninas* shows a painter with mechanisms of reproduction—canvas and brush—so *Elegy* shows David with the mechanism of reproduction: his camera.

Significantly, Coixet shoots the scene using shot/reverse shot, cutting back and forth between the partially naked Consuela and close-ups on David's camera, which stares straight at viewers in the audience. This aligns spectators not only with the camera gazing at a female body but also with the woman looking back at the camera. Hence, rather than mindlessly identifying with an unseen movie camera that generates a salacious male gaze, attentive viewers become aware of what is usually "the absent one" in cinema—the camera—and their own viewing bodies in relation to it.[31] Furthermore, during the shot/reverse shot sequence, even casual spectators can't help thinking that one of Consuela's beautiful breasts, photographed by David, will soon be an absent one. Coixet seems to suggest that once Consuela's breast is made invisible, quite literally through mastectomy, her unseen spiritual beauty may finally become visible: the absent made present. In *Elegy*, then, as in other films that employ "image grafts" from famous paintings, spectators are "exposed to the possibility of looking at the naked human body in a religious way that stands in stark contrast to the countless films in which the human body is visually reduced to the level of a sex object."[32]

Elegy ends with David once again in bed with Consuela, only this time it is Consuela's hospital bed, onto which David has crawled to chastely comfort her. As he whispers "I am here" to the sallow patient, we sense that David finally embraces true beauty. And so might we, while sitting in movie theaters, whisper "I am here" to the medium itself, opening ourselves to beauty that lies beyond the surfaces of gorgeous stars.

Notes

1. Laura Mulvey, *Visual and Other Pleasures* (Bloomington: Indiana University Press, 1989), 18.
2. When Merchant died in 2005 the term "Merchant Ivory film" lost cachet. In addition to *A Room with a View*, the most famous Merchant Ivory films are *Howards End* (1992) and *The Remains of the Day* (1993).
3. For an excellent overview of feminist film theory, see Gaye Williams Ortiz, "Feminism," in *The Routledge Companion to Religion and Film*, ed. John Lyden (London: Routledge, 2009), 237–54.
4. Laura Mulvey, "Looking at the Past from the Present: Rethinking Feminist Film Theory of the 1970s," *Signs: Journal of Women in Culture and Society* 30.1 (2004): 1288–9.

5 For summaries of feminist theorists who have challenged Mulvey, see Robert Stam, *Film Theory: An Introduction* (Malden: Blackwell, 2000), 174–7; and Julie Kelso, "Gazing at Impotence in Henry King's *David and Bathsheba*," in *Screening Scripture: Intertextual Connections between Scripture and Film*, ed. George Aichele and Richard Walsh (Harrisburg: Trinity International, 2002), 165.
6 Mulvey, *Visual and Other Pleasures*, 18.
7 Ibid., 19.
8 E. M. Forster, *A Room with a View* (New York: Dover, 1995), 88.
9 Douglass K. Daniel, "'The Name's Bond, James Bond': Roger Moore Reflects on 50 Years of 007 in New Book," *The Patriot-News* (Harrisburg, PA), October 25, 2012, B-4.
10 Even though the Bond franchise made the leader of Britain's spy agency a woman (beginning with 1995's *GoldenEye*), the female "M" (Dame Judi Dench) still submits to Bond's directives in *Skyfall*.
11 "The beauty of the woman as object and the screen space coalesce; she is ... a perfect product, whose body, stylised and fragmented by close-ups, is the content of the film, and the direct recipient of the spectator's look" (Mulvey, *Visual and Other Pleasures*, 22).
12 Ibid., 162. Mulvey admits that "'Visual Pleasure and Narrative Cinema' was written in the polemical spirit that belongs properly to the early confrontational moments of a movement" (161).
13 E. Ann Kaplan, "Is the Gaze Male?" *The Film Theory Reader: Debates and Arguments*, ed. Marc Furstenau (New York: Routledge, 2010), 210. This essay, first published in 1983, influenced Mulvey's change in emphasis. Arguing similarly about binary oppositions, Mary Ann Doane notes that "the reversal itself remains locked within the same logic." See *Femmes Fatales* (New York: Routledge, 1991), 21. Mulvey's "male gaze" is also problematic for many scholars because it does not consider "the gaze" of gay and lesbian viewers. See Kenneth MacKinnon, "After Mulvey: Male Erotic Objectification," in Michelle Aaron, ed., *The Body's Perilous Pleasures: Dangerous Desires and Contemporary Culture* (Edinburgh: Edinburgh University Press, 1999), 13–29.
14 Irena Makarushka illustrates deconstruction in her feminist reading of Adrian Lyne's *9½ Weeks*, discussing "an ambiguity of experience that resists the reductive dichotomies of either/or: either victim or victimizer, either good or evil, either oppressor or liberator, either fall or redemption." See "Women Spoken For: Images of Displaced Desire" in *Screening the Sacred: Religion, Myth, and Ideology in Popular American Film*, ed. Joel W. Martin and Conrad E. Ostwalt Jr. (Boulder: Westview, 1995), 143.
15 Kaja Silverman, *The Threshold of the Visible World* (New York: Routledge, 1996), 125.
16 Sylvain De Bleeckere, "The Religious Dimension of Cinematic Consciousness in Postmodern Culture," in *New Image of Religious Film*, ed. John R. May (Kansas City: Sheed and Ward, 1997), 109.
17 While voice-overs are often used in post-classical cinema, filmmakers committed to classical Hollywood style consider them unacceptable. See Eleftheria Thanouli, *Post-Classical Cinema: An International Poetics of Film Narration* (London: Wallflower, 2009), 153. A famous example is the voice-over Ridley Scott was forced to add to *Blade Runner* (1982). Reportedly angry about Scott's capitulation to studio bosses, Harrison Ford delivered his voice-over in a monotone voice.
18 Kaja Silverman, *The Subject of Semiotics* (New York: Oxford University Press, 1983), 225.
19 Mulvey, *Visual and Other Pleasures*, 21–2.
20 Stephen Heath, *Questions of Cinema* (Bloomington: Indiana University Press, 1981), 35. Heath notes that the "first recorded instance" of the word *easel* is around 1634 (34); Mulvey, *Visual and Other Pleasures*, 22.
21 The novel uses a different painting, "A Lady Writing" (c. 1665–66), having Griet rearrange a blue cloth in the still life. By having Griet, instead, move a large table, the filmmakers draw more attention to the fact that Vermeer's scene shapes the film's mise-en-scène.

22 For Vermeer's use of the camera obscura, see Philip Steadman, *Vermeer's Camera: Uncovering the Truth behind the Masterpieces* (Oxford: Oxford University Press, 2001).
23 Heath, *Questions of Cinema*, 35.
24 For a contemporary Christian website that begins movie reviews by charting the number of nude shots, see www.movieguide.org.
25 Another example is the otherwise well-crafted German movie *Circle of Deceit* (1993), which starts with an explicit sex scene. The same phenomenon also occurs in intelligently written and acted HBO and Showtime series on television, as in the first episodes of *Rome* and *Homeland*.
26 Ally Acker, *Reel Women: Pioneers of the Cinema, 1896 to the Present* (New York: Continuum, 1991), 287.
27 Inspired by Michel Foucault's famous discussion of *Las Meninas* in *The Order of Things* (1970), Jean-Pierre Oudart published several French essays in *Cahiers du cinéma* between 1969 and 1971. His work became known to English speakers through Daniel Dayan's discussion in "The Tutor-Code of Classical Cinema" (*Film Quarterly* Fall 1974). I quote from a reprint of Dayan's famous essay in *Film Theory and Criticism*, 6th edn, edited by Leo Braudy and Marshall Cohen (New York: Oxford University Press, 2004), 112.
28 Steve Nolan, *Film, Lacan and the Subject of Religion: A Psychoanalytic Approach to Religious Film Analysis* (London: Continuum, 2009), 91. Oudart and Dayan are known as "suture" theorists, having borrowed the word "suture" from Lacan, a psychoanalytic theorist who will be discussed in Part II. Also famous for suture film theory is Stephen Heath, author of "Notes on Suture," *Screen* 18.4 (1977/8): 48–76.
29 Dayan, *Film Theory and Criticism*, 115.
30 Because Consuela's pose is reminiscent of Goya's *Nude Maja* (c. 1800), attentive viewers are reminded of the photographed paintings from earlier in the film: images that David compared to Consuela.
31 Exploring the relationship between cinema viewing and viewers' bodies, Vivian Sobchack notes that the spectator "feels his or her literal body as only one side of *an irreducible and dynamic relational structure of reversibility and reciprocity* that has as its other side the figural objects of bodily provocation on the screen." See *Carnal Thoughts: Embodiment and Moving Image Culture* (Berkeley: University of California Press, 2004), 79, emphasis hers.
32 De Bleeckere, "The Religious Dimension of Cinematic Consciousness," 109.

4   Breaking the Fourth Wall
Salvation from the Screen

Salvation from Cinema began with a discussion of Marshall McLuhan's famous aphorism, "the medium is the message." This chapter begins with the living body of McLuhan in order to explore theology generated by the cinematic medium. Rather than extracting salvation messages from film stories, it demonstrates how a cinematic technique—related to "the absent one" that closed the preceding chapter—can have profound religious implications.

Marshall McLuhan and "Cool Media"

Ironically, McLuhan considered the benefits of cinema to be minimal. In *Understanding Media*, he places visual media on a continuum between "cool media," which elicit user participation, and "hot media," which generate user passivity.[1] He illustrates the difference between "cool" and "hot" with the communication systems inside college classrooms. Professors who lecture at their students use a "hot media" format, such that students become passive thinkers, internalizing and regurgitating someone else's thoughts. In contrast, professors who encourage students to participate in class discussion while grappling with complex theoretical issues employ a "cool medium."

McLuhan identifies television as a "cool" medium, since viewers, in the privacy of their homes, can exercise agency by yelling at the screen, changing the channel, muting or enhancing the sound, and talking with those who watch with them. Cinema, in contrast, is a "hot" medium: viewers passively sit in a darkened space, all facing one direction while they silently absorb the action on a huge screen, losing themselves in an alternate reality.

Published in 1964, McLuhan's distinction between cool and hot media dissolved once VCRs enabled people to watch theatrical releases on their television screens. Furthermore, a 2010 study by a psychologist at York University in Canada established that children who watched movies had a "keener ... theory of mind" than children who only watched television.[2] And I suspect that even in McLuhan's day many people watched television with passivity—even as many moviegoers were actively exercising their brains in darkened theaters. The term "couch-potato," after all, was coined to describe semi-comatose viewers in front of their living-room TVs.

This qualification of McLuhan helps explain why my approach to the "medium" of film differs from his. Whereas McLuhan focuses on effects of the technology itself—the presence of a viewing-box in the living room versus a viewer boxed in a theater—I focus on what people see (or don't see) on screen, arguing that whether media is "hot" or "cool" depends, to a significant extent, upon viewers themselves. Too many people fail to consider *how* transmitted images, on both kinds of screens, communicate their message. Slipping into escapist reveries— what McLuhan calls a Narcissus trance—they gladly turn off their brains while reveling in the hot bombs and hotter bombshells of projected fantasies.

Of course, many Hollywood filmmakers count on viewers not thinking too much about the implausibility of their screen scenarios. This should make us appreciate all the more those filmmakers who attempt to cool down McLuhan's so-called hot medium. By drawing attention to the medium of cinema artistry, they encourage us to actively think, not only about how we view movies, but also about how we view the meaning of life. In fact, if we were to extrapolate from numerous neurological studies, we might say that one effect of well-wrought cinema is a "roused sensory cortex." For, as an Emory University study reveals, conventional clichés generate much less brain activity than new ways of seeing.[3] This chapter therefore explores a manipulation of the cinematic medium that challenges hot Hollywood clichés, so much so that Marshall McLuhan agreed to be part of the medium itself.

A Very Cool *Annie Hall*

Considering his animus against the Narcissus trance generated by "hot media," it may come as a surprise that McLuhan agreed to appear in a major cinematic release: Woody Allen's *Annie Hall* (1977), which received Oscars for Best Picture, Best Director, and Best Screenplay. The scene containing McLuhan takes place, significantly enough, in the lobby of a movie theater, where Alvy Singer (Allen) and Annie Hall (Diane Keaton, winning an Oscar) argue about their "sexual problems." The couple are distracted by a man in line behind them, who loudly pontificates about Italian film director Federico Fellini, Irish playwright Samuel Beckett, and, finally, about communication theorist Marshall McLuhan.

Alvy therefore steps out of the movie line and looks straight into the camera in order to speak to us, the viewing audience, about the deficient perceptions of the arrogant pontificator. The latter then does the same, speaking directly to us in order to establish his credentials as a media specialist at Columbia University. In exasperation, Alvy walks over to a huge free-standing movie advertisement at the edge of the lobby, pulling from behind it a real live Marshall McLuhan. The world-famous media specialist proceeds to inform the pompous academic, "You know nothing of my work … How you ever got to teach a course in anything is totally amazing." Alvy then looks into the camera to speak to us once again, exulting "Boy, if life were only like this!"

Annie Hall thus draws attention to the medium of film and the fantasies it creates. In this case, the fantasy is one imagined by many people who have withstood the denunciations of arrogant pontificators. Indeed, those who have been victim to condescending dismissals of their faith often wish they could miraculously produce, just at the right moment, a higher power that might prove pompous skeptics to be wrong. Tellingly, *Annie Hall*'s Alvy moves to the edge of the movie screen in order to retrieve his higher power. Because we viewers just barely see a sliver of the A-frame poster-board at the screen edge, it looks like Alvy pulls his authority from beyond the frame of his environment, just as reviled Christians sometimes wish they could produce supernatural proof—or at least a renowned theologian—from beyond the frame of everyday reality to verify the Gospel message. In the case of Christian desire for supernatural intervention, the medium of that intervention quite literally becomes the message.

The proof Alvy produces, of course, is Marshall McLuhan, who coined "the medium is the message." Allen thus signals that the entire scene, set in a movie theater foyer, has been about the medium of film. In the process, Allen challenges both the fictional academic inside the film and the non-fictional McLuhan from beyond it. For he has the arrogant academic erroneously say that McLuhan regards television as a "hot medium." This is why McLuhan rebukes him, having suggested just the opposite: that television is a "cool medium." Ironically, however, by setting up the scene this way, Woody Allen challenges McLuhan's relegation of film to "hot medium." For by having Alvy address movie viewers outside the frame of the film, Allen gets us to think about the medium itself, about the artifice of what any movie screen frames. Allen thus nudges attentive viewers out of their passivity, encouraging them to think of theoretical issues beyond the "frame" of most movies.

Breaking the Fourth Wall: Theatrical Precedent and Comic Employment

In theater, this technique of speaking to the audience is called "breaking the fourth wall," referring to the imaginary wall between actors and seated viewers. The back of a stage and its two sides, usually covered with scenery, scrims, or curtains, create the illusion of a separate realm in which the actors live: it is their world as opposed to that of the audience. We viewers therefore imagine, if even subconsciously, that the space between actors and audience is a transparent fourth wall, like the one-way windows in police interrogation rooms. Though we can see the actors, they can't see us from the imaginary divider that separates their realm from ours. As a result, when actors "break the fourth wall," they call attention to the fiction of theater, reminding us that we are complicit with their illusion, that we choose to believe in their separate world. Film critics have therefore borrowed the phrase "breaking the fourth wall" to talk about similar moments in cinema, when a character stares directly into the camera, thus seeming to look at the viewing audience.

Some readers may not remember ever seeing a film actor break the fourth wall. Indeed, it is not a common device, perhaps because it is hard to do without seeming gimmicky. Movies that break the fourth wall often do so merely for laughs, as in *Horse Feathers* (Norman McLeod 1932), starring the Marx Brothers. When Baravelli (Chico) sits down to play the piano, Professor Quincy Adams Wagstaff (Groucho) looks into the camera and says to the movie audience, "I've got to stay here, but there's no reason why you folks shouldn't go out into the lobby until this thing blows over."

While *Horse Feathers* appears in some film history books due to the anti-establishment creativity of Marx Brothers craziness, other comedies reduce the fourth wall to a silly sight-gag. Take, for example, the plot-thin "*Road to …* " movies of the 1940s and 1950s starring Bob Hope, Bing Crosby, and Dorothy Lamour. Bob Hope would frequently break the fourth wall in order to deliver some snide remark about other characters in the movie. In *The Road to Bali* (1952), he echoes Groucho Marx in *Horse Feathers* when he looks into the camera and comments, "[Crosby's] gonna sing, folks. Now's the time to go out and get the popcorn." He had me at "go out."

In contrast, avant-garde filmmakers break the fourth wall to call attention to their films as constructed artifacts, signaling a commitment to art more than to commercial entertainment. In *Breathless* (1960), one of the defining films of the French New Wave, director Jean-Luc Godard has his insouciant protagonist break the fourth wall early in the film. While driving a stolen car, Michel (Jean-Paul Belmondo) turns toward the empty passenger seat and looks straight into the camera to explain the attractions of France. We viewers thus become his passengers while transported by the film that contains him. This implication is reinforced after Michel arrives in Paris. Walking down the street, he stops to look at a movie poster of Humphrey Bogart, the image filling the mise-en-scène in such a way that the piercing eyes of Bogart seem to look straight into our eyes. Permeated with other allusions to cinema, *Breathless* thus signals its own status as cinematic medium, thus distinguishing it from the classical Hollywood style, which seeks to disguise its artifice.[4]

Synthesizing Godard-like self-reference with Marx-brothers zaniness, Woody Allen breaks the fourth wall not simply for humor but also for art. As he remarked to one interviewer, in *Annie Hall* he wanted to "make some deeper film and not be as funny" as in his earlier films: "maybe there will be other values that will emerge, that will be interesting or nourishing for the audience."[5] Indeed, while challenging McLuhan's relegation of cinema to "hot medium," Allen's choice to break the fourth wall also questions one of the fundamental genres of cinema itself: the romantic comedy.

The Hot Fantasies of Romantic Comedies

Immediately before Allen's Alvy turns in disgust to look at the pontificating professor in *Annie Hall*, the man standing in front of Alvy turns to look at him and Annie, whose argument about "sexual problems" has gotten a little too loud. The attentive viewer will notice that, unlike the arguing couple, the two men on either side of them wear coats and ties, establishing a visual parallel. Hence, when one man in suit and tie turns to look at Alvy behind him, followed by Alvy turning to look at another man in suit and tie behind him, a connection is made between the two annoying conversations. We should take note, then, when the pompous professor proceeds to talk about writers famous for the lack of realism in their scripts: Samuel Beckett (1906–89) who wrote absurdist plays for the stage and Federico Fellini (1920–93) who wrote screenplays filled with surreal imagery. The medium thus implies that we are to regard the romantic relationships we see in movies (remember that Alvy and Annie are standing in a cinema lobby) as absurd and/or surreal as well: love-at-first-sight happily-ever-after fantasies that rarely reflect real life. Indeed, while most romantic comedies deliver a generic happy ending wherein a couple, after facing seemingly insurmountable odds, end up expressing their undying love (the fantasy), *Annie Hall* explores not just the development of a romantic relationship but also its demise.

In fact, Allen begins the entire film by breaking the fourth wall, Alvy talking to viewers as though he were a newscaster reporting on the disintegration of a relationship. The remainder of the film therefore delivers non-consecutive flashbacks about falling in and out of love. The first flashback shows Alvy waiting for Annie in front of a movie theater, where we see a poster for Ingmar Bergman's 1976 film *Face to Face*. Allen thus subtly alludes to his tactics: not only to speak "face to face" with viewers of *Annie Hall*, but also to create a more artistic film— like those by Bergman. Indeed, people familiar with the Swedish director's work will recognize that *Annie Hall* echoes, though with considerably more humor, *The Passion of Anna*, a 1969 film about problems in a love relationship: a film that breaks the illusion of cinema when Bergman inserts shots of actors commenting on characters they play.

Like Bergman, Allen breaks the illusion that the cinema screen provides a window on reality. Furthermore, when his character Alvy turns to address viewers, he echoes how the man in front of him in line turned to view him, followed by his turning to view the Columbia professor. By thus emphasizing the idea of multiple viewing audiences in a movie theater, Allen exposes not only the professor's inaccurate portrayal of McLuhan and McLuhan's inaccurate portrayal of film, but also cinema's inaccurate portrayal of romance. Indeed, the last time Allen breaks the fourth wall, near the end of the film, he comments on the artificiality of happy endings. We see two actors rehearsing a play written by Alvy, speaking lines that reiterate, nearly word for word, a conversation we earlier heard between Annie and Alvy that had ended the relationship. When the shot cuts to Alvy watching the actors rehearse, a mirror behind him reflects the entire scene, signaling that the play mirrors Alvy's life. The following shot, however, eliminates the mirror as the female actor speaks a new line: "Wait! I'm going with you; I love you!" Immediately after this unrealistic happy ending, Alvy breaks the fourth wall in order to comment on the artifice of romantic "perfection" he had created for the actors: "What do you want? It was my first play!"—a play that no longer reflects, as in a mirror, real life. The medium thus becomes a message about the medium itself: a self-referential gesture that, as we shall see, can have profound religious implications.

A History of Cinematic Self-Reference: *The Great Train Robbery*

Though often employed by avant-garde filmmakers, breaking the fourth wall is nothing new. In 1903 Edwin S. Porter ended his twelve-minute tour-de-force, *The Great Train Robbery*, by breaking the fourth wall. In a full-frame medium shot, the character leading the train robbers looks out of the screen and fires his gun straight at the viewing audience. Porter thus created a pun on "shot": the *shot* of the gun is the final *shot* of the film.

This moment is so famous in cinema history that other filmmakers intentionally allude to it, making it not a cliché but a quotation.[6] Admitting to a "taste for quotation," Jean-Luc Godard has the protagonist in *Breathless*, who is a thief like the shooter in *The Great Train Robbery*, fire a gun in the same direction that he just broke the fourth wall, as though taking aim toward viewers.[7] This anticipates the ending of *Breathless*: after police gun the thief down, his girlfriend breaks the fourth wall in the last "shot" of the film.

Familiar with both Porter and Godard, Martin Scorsese alludes to Porter's famous "shot" several times. His first critical success, *Taxi Driver* (1976), has the protagonist, Travis Bickle (Robert De Niro), aim a gun at the camera while practicing at a shooting range. More obvious is the ending of *GoodFellas* (1990), where a character fires directly at the camera. And Scorsese includes a clip of Porter's 1903 shot in *Hugo* (2011), his homage to film history that will be discussed in my conclusion. Another New Hollywood director, Ridley Scott, quotes the historical shot after the closing credits of *American Gangster* (2007), when Denzel Washington fires a gun into the camera.[8] Even directors outside Hollywood allude to Porter's closing shot. Romanian theater and film director Lucian Pintilie ends *Balanta* (*The Oak*, 1992) with a shot of his two protagonists breaking the fourth wall, one of whom points a gun at the camera.[9]

Perhaps these filmmakers, like Porter before them, want us to think about our complicity in film violence: a complicity that occurs whenever we unthinkingly enjoy criminal activities on the screen. As the guns break the fourth wall, we become victims of the evil deeds we witness—victims not literally, of course, but figuratively. Violence that should radically distress us penetrates our psyches like a bullet, killing our abhorrence of bloodshed. Guns shooting at the camera allude to cinematic "shots" that kill our discomfort with murder.[10]

Killing *eXistenZ*

The metaphor between film shots and gun shots becomes explicit in David Cronenberg's 1999 cult classic *eXistenZ*, which also ends with the iconic shot. This time, two people aim their guns out of the screen, although we know, via shot/reverse shot, which character they actually threaten. We might therefore question whether they legitimately break the fourth wall if it were not for the last spoken line of the film, which voices exactly what we are thinking: "Are we still in the game?"

eXistenZ is about a virtual reality video game called eXistenZ that players plug into their spines with an "umbycord." The game is therefore acted out in participants' brains, mimicking lived experience so well that players lose their ability to differentiate authentic reality from virtual reality: eXistenZ feels like their own existence. The medium of *eXistenZ* reinforces this message. As scenes morph into new scenarios the way video games do, viewers of the film become confused as to what is virtual and what is the "real" world of the characters.

We assume all is explained near the end of the film when we witness the characters, whose adventures we have been following, sitting on a stage while holding their game boxes. At this point we learn that, when the primary gaming couple Ted (Jude Law) and Allegra (Jennifer Jason Leigh), who designed eXistenZ, enter into the game at the beginning of the film, they were actually playing an encompassing game called transCendenZ. Like a nut in a shell, then, eXistenZ takes its meaning from transCendenZ: the religious significance obvious. However, near the film's ending, Ted and Allegra exit transCendenZ, leaving their game boxes on stage, and proceed to confront the game's designers, accusing them of "deforming reality." In order to free themselves from a corrupt design, Ted and Allegra gun down the controllers of transCendenZ. The implied death-of-God theology becomes explicit as Ted yells, "Death to transCendenZ." Indeed, Cronenberg comments that "The title eXistenZ is a reference to the existentialist's accepting total responsibility for his actions."[11] After all, Allegra designed the eXistenZ that she and Ted enact before they kill the transCendenZ designers.

In addition to this religious/philosophical message, *eXistenZ* explores the message of the medium: how moving images shape our understanding of existence. To that end, the last shot of film breaks the fourth wall as Ted and Allegra point their guns at a man who had been part of their earlier eXistenZ game: the man who asks "Are we still in the game?" As film scholar Adam Lowenstein explains, "'Are we still in the game?' is a question that cannot be answered by anyone within eXistenZ because Cronenberg recognizes how it ultimately addresses the audience outside the film ... It is toward them (us) that the guns are pointed."[12]

Attentive viewers are thus forced to contemplate how they temporarily kill elements in their own existence when they enter the game-like Narcissus trance of film, choosing to believe in the existence of virtual characters and adventures—as in eXistenZ. We must therefore ask ourselves how characters' responses to disturbing elements in eXistenZ might parallel our responses to disturbing elements in the film that contains them: *eXistenZ*. For example, one key scene shows Ted avidly slurping the slimy skin off of mutant amphibians. Eating voraciously, Ted tells the appalled Allegra, "I find this disgusting but I can't help myself!" Then, as he gnaws the gooey flesh off the slippery creatures, Ted assembles their bones into a gun that he aims at Allegra—anticipating the moment he aims a gun at us. Significantly, the mutant amphibians have been served to him by the same man Ted and Allegra attempt to shoot at the end of the film. Hence, when the film closes with their guns aimed at viewers, Cronenberg forces us to consider how certain movies kill abhorrence to disgusting images that we ingest without thinking, making us hungry for more and more mutant deformations of existence. The medium is about its own power to "deform reality."

This, then, becomes the point of breaking the fourth wall: not in order to transcend the medium but to see how the medium itself explores the relationship between existence and transcendence. Like *eXistenZ*, the following films question the existence of a divinity that shapes our ends, rough hew them (into guns) as we will.

The Mission: To Break the Fourth Wall

Winning multiple international awards, Roland Joffé's 1986 film *The Mission* breaks the fourth wall at the beginning. We see, in extreme close-up, a dour male face look us in the eye while speaking, "Your Holiness, the little matter that brought me here to the furthest edge of your light on earth is now settled. And the Indians are once again free to be enslaved by the Spanish and Portuguese settlers." His reference to "the furthest edge of your light" helps explain why the filmmakers have him break the fourth wall. Viewers in a darkened theater indeed recognize his place on screen to be the furthest edge of their light: an entirely different realm, both in space and time, than their own. Soon learning that the speaker has traveled from Europe to South America, viewers sense that he looks out of the screen at the vast dark seas that separate him from a culture that he regards as the source of light: somewhat like the projection booth that is the source of light at the back of the theater in which we sit.

But then the man on screen blinks, shifting his eyes away from the camera while commenting, "I don't think I set the right note. Begin again." With a close-up on his hands tearing paper, followed by a shot of a scribe writing with a quill, it soon becomes apparent that the speaker, a Cardinal, is dictating a letter to the Pope. When the Cardinal begins again, he states, "Your Holiness, I write to you in the year of the Lord 1758 …" In a far more benevolent tone he proceeds to describe the South American natives as "noble souls" with "nimble and gifted hands," his commentary delivered in voice-over as idyllic images of the Indians fill the mise-en-scène.

The contrast in the Cardinal's two letters—the first about Indian enslavement, the second about Indian nobility—is reinforced by the lighting. The first dictation is shot in low-key lighting, emphasizing the dark complicity of the Church with slavery. But when the voice-over describes the gifted hands of the converted natives, the camera reveals a beautifully crafted mission in the high-key lighting of golden sunlight. In the first several minutes of *The Mission*, then, we are given a visual synecdoche of its diegesis. For the film focuses on the tension between the redemptive motives of Jesuit missionaries who supervise the sun-blessed mission and the darkly mercenary motives of Spanish and Portuguese colonists, who desire not only Indian acreage for cultivation but also Indian slaves to work the land. Furthermore, as becomes evident later, European Church leaders are inclined to side with the colonists over the Jesuits. Because the latter have been challenging the Church hierarchy in Europe, it is in the Church's interest to win favor (and hence power) from Spanish and Portuguese settlers—and their European monarchs—by disbanding the Jesuit missions.

So why start the synecdoche (and the film) by breaking the fourth wall? After all, the distance between European "enlightenment" and dark South American jungles, between political power-plays and Christian charity, between darkness and light, could have been established without the Cardinal looking straight into the camera as he dictates his first letter. The answer comes at the end of the film. The very end.

After the closing credits, when many viewers will have exited the theater or shut down their computer or television screens, the Cardinal once again breaks the fourth wall, creating a framing device. The symmetrical structure is reinforced by the fact that, at the film's start, the Cardinal appears on the left side of our screen, slightly facing right, while in the closing shot he appears on the right side of our screen, slightly facing left. In between, we have seen Church-condoned imperialists wipe out the missions, European Jesuits (played by Jeremy Irons, Liam Neeson, and Robert De Niro) dying side by side with Indian converts, all of whom seek to protect their sacred work from violent settlers.

Significantly, when the Cardinal breaks the fourth wall at the end of the film, he says nothing. No longer dictating his letter, his eye contact seems all the more focused on us, the viewing audience. Implicating us in what we have just seen, his stare penetrates our psyches like a bullet, as though to ask, "How about you? Might you condone violence to protect the institutional dominance of your religion, or would you exercise sacrificial love? Is your status tied to wealth and power, or does love of God enable you to renounce things of this world, to the point of death itself?" This, one of the most chilling moments in the history of film, is missed by viewers who leave during the credits—and is usually overlooked by theology/religion scholars who write about *The Mission*.[13]

Other Missions: *Whatever Works*

The Mission, of course, is about Christian missions, making the tension between Christ-like love and self-serving religious practices natural to both its message and its medium. Other films deliver the same message in more subtle terms. Take, for example, *12 Years a Slave*, directed by the first African American to win the Oscar for Best Picture (Steve McQueen, 2013). Based on a memoir, the film follows the travails of Solomon (Chiwetel Ejiofor), who is kidnapped from a respectable life in 1841 New York and sold into slavery. In the midst of Solomon's horrendous experiences, McQueen inserts a full-frame medium shot of Solomon breaking the fourth wall. Like the Cardinal at the end of *The Mission* he wordlessly stares out at us, as though questioning how we would have behaved in the antebellum South, either as black victim or white observer. Though most contemporary Americans want to believe they would have supported the abolitionist cause, it is highly unlikely. The majority of antebellum Christians—in both the North and the South—did nothing to eliminate slavery, many, in fact, quoting the Bible in order to justify it. By having a nineteenth-century character stare out of his 2013 film, McQueen prods viewers to consider how they respond to human trafficking in their own twenty-first century society.[14]

By breaking the fourth wall, then, both *The Mission* and *12 Years a Slave* force attentive viewers to consider a highly religious issue: the relationship between lived existence and transcendent righteousness, between eXistenZ and transCendenZ. How then might comedies, which tend to break the fourth wall merely for laughs, elicit the same reflections? We have already seen how Woody Allen transforms comedy into a self-referential medium in *Annie Hall*. The next two examples explore how he breaks the fourth wall in order to question the very existence of God.[15]

In the first example, *Whatever Works* (2009), the message of the medium is considerably more profound than that of the story. Allen's film begins with a fifty-something man named Boris (Larry David) talking to friends about the beautiful teachings of Jesus and Karl Marx. Boris explains that they are "all based on the fallacious notion that people are fundamentally decent," that "they're not stupid, selfish, greedy, cowardly, short-sighted worms." In contrast, Boris asserts, "We're a failed species."

Boris, of course, misrepresents Christian doctrine, which establishes that salvation is necessary precisely because we are "a failed species." According to the concept of "original sin" exfoliated by Augustine (354–430 CE), humans are indeed selfish, greedy, cowardly, and short-sighted. Whether Boris's doctrinal misunderstanding reflects his own prejudices or those of Woody Allen does not matter as much as the fact that *Whatever Works* presents a fundamental theological issue in its very first scene: human depravity. This, then, is the context in which Allen has Boris break the fourth wall.

As Boris despairs over moral turpitude, he subtly starts looking in the direction of the camera. When I first saw the movie I thought, "What bad acting! Larry David relies too heavily on his cue cards." I was disabused of this notion several minutes later. After stating to his friends, "My story is whatever works, as long as you don't hurt anybody," Boris gestures toward the camera and refers to "an audience full of people" watching them.

When Alvy Singer breaks the fourth wall in *Annie Hall*, no one else in the scene notices him doing so, except for the arrogant academic, who, significantly enough, is a pontificating professor at Columbia—as is Boris. In *Whatever Works*, however, Boris's friends are incredulous, looking beyond the screen frame (but not directly into the camera) as they try to see what Boris sees, ultimately dismissing Boris's actions as signs of mental instability. Meanwhile, Boris leaves them, walking down the sidewalk in order to talk more intently with us, the viewing audience. Employing an unusually long take, Allen has Boris pontificate about the way people cover up the meaninglessness of life through their children, their financial portfolios, their big houses, their fancy cars, their omega-three vitamins, etc. But, in spite of all these comforts, he notes, "You'll still die." After revealing that his father committed suicide due to depressing stories in the newspaper, Boris states, "'The Horror,' Kurtz said at the end of *Heart of Darkness*, 'The Horror.'" Without some kind of salvation, in other words, life has horror at its heart due to the narcissistic self-interest of most humans. By breaking the fourth wall, Boris thus seems to imply that a remedy can only come from a realm beyond that which breeds dark hearts: salvation from beyond the fourth wall of existence.

Boris then starts talking about his own suicide attempt: an attempt to escape hopelessness and despair by breaking the wall that frames existence. At this point, Allen inserts a flashback: we see Boris run down the inside stairs of his luxurious Manhattan apartment yelling "I'm dying." When his wife challenges this statement, he says "Eventually," followed by "I'm the only one who sees the whole picture actually for what it is." An argument ensues, Boris yelling,

> I married you for all the wrong reasons. You're brilliant. I wanted someone to talk to. You love classical music. You love art. You love literature. You love sex. You love me ... On paper we're ideal. But life isn't on paper.

And then he throws himself out the window, quite literally breaking through a transparent wall in their well-appointed apartment.

As in *Annie Hall*, this scene subverts the fantasy that concludes most romantic comedies, in which one attains happiness by finding a person who satisfies all one's sexual, intellectual, and emotional needs. Boris had everything our culture, and most movies, establish as fulfilling: he was a Nobel Prize-nominated scientist teaching at Columbia, with an "ideal" wife in a sophisticated Manhattan apartment and a son at Yale. But, like most Woody Allen protagonists, he wasn't satisfied, sensing that there has to be something more to existence than exciting sex, bountiful money, and elevated prestige.

After we see Boris break through the wall of his apartment, the shot cuts back to Boris breaking the fourth wall with us. He states, "I hit the canopy" and hence did not die. But his life does indeed change, as we soon discover. No longer teaching at Columbia, he now lives alone in a tiny apartment, where we see him discover a girl hiding under cardboard in the alley. Begrudgingly, Boris offers shelter to the girl, Melodie (Evan Rachel Wood), who slowly worms her way into his affections. Though they have nothing in common—she an optimistic dimwit, he a downbeat intellectual—the two eventually marry.

This is not the first time Allen has symbolized the search for satisfaction by way of a male protagonist switching his affection from an intellectually and culturally sophisticated beauty to an uneducated but sweetly spontaneous earth-mama (or vice versa). One woman provides the satisfaction of intellectual companionship, while the other offers escape from thinking about all the unanswered questions about life. In films like *Interiors* (1978), *Manhattan* (1979), *Stardust Memories* (1980), *Broadway Danny Rose* (1984), *Hannah and Her Sisters* (1986), *Match Point* (2005), and *Midnight in Paris* (2011), male protagonists go after "whatever works" to provide emotional satisfaction at a particular moment. However, "whatever works" usually does not last.

Indeed, in *Whatever Works*, the charmingly vapid Melodie tells Boris, after only several months of marriage, that she has fallen in love with a handsome younger man. The aging husband, who has a limp from his first suicide attempt, tells her he understands. But not long afterwards we see him obsessively wash his hands, as he does periodically throughout the film, and then throw himself out the window, again breaking through the transparent wall of an apartment. Why wash one's hands before a suicide attempt? It's as though Allen wants to indicate the impossibility of removing the bacteria of doubt and despair that unsettle the life of a thinking person.

Christian viewers may think that Woody Allen would benefit from the Gospel message. But he does not take Christianity seriously, due to his existentialist philosophy and his Jewish heritage: a double inheritance that he explores in several films. In his award-winning *Hannah and Her Sisters* (1986), for example, he plays Mickey, a Jew in despair over the meaninglessness of life. At one point, we see Mickey empty contents of a bag onto a table: a close-up displays a beatific picture of an Anglo-Saxon Jesus, followed by a loaf of white bread. The implication is clear: following Jesus is a non-Jewish "white bread" solution to the agonies of existence.

Whatever Works gets downright offensive in Allen's depiction of Christianity. Though at the start of the film Boris praises the teachings of Jesus, Allen presents Melodie's dysfunctional parents as Fundamentalists who spout superficial Christian clichés. Both parents are miserable until they abandon their faith and find satisfaction through "whatever works" to provide sexual contentment: the mother in a *ménage à trois*, and the father with a gay lover. Boris similarly achieves satisfaction through sex, but only by way of luck when he survives his second suicide attempt. This time, rather than a canopy, a woman walking her dog breaks the fall, giving him another chance at life.

To symbolize new chances, the film ends with a New Year's party in which everyone joyfully celebrates with their new companions: Melodie with her handsome young man, Melodie's mother with her two lovers, Melodie's father with his gay partner, and Boris with the woman who broke his fall—both literally and figuratively: she provided a satisfying fall-back relationship after the one with Melodie ended. It would seem that, as in most romantic comedies, we are left with that same old clichéd ending: happiness depends upon finding a satisfying lover.

But Allen's medium subverts this generic storybook message. At the New Year's party, Boris breaks the fourth wall as he did at the start of the film. Moving toward the camera as his lover enters the mise-en-scène, he tells us "I totally lucked out. It just shows what meaningless blind chance the universe is. Everybody schemes and dreams to meet the right person, and I jump out a window and land on her." Then, as his friends look at a television screen to the side of our screen in order to count down the seconds to a new year, Boris again looks at us in order to pronounce the philosophy that recurs in Woody Allen movies:

> Celebrate what? A step closer to the grave? That's why I can't say enough times: whatever love you can get and give, whatever happiness you can filch or provide, every temporary measure of grace: whatever works. And don't kid yourself. It is by no means all up to your own human ingenuity. A bigger part of your existence is luck than you'd like to admit.

Rather than accept the possibility of eternal grace, Boris settles for "temporary" grace mediated through luck.[16] It is "Death to transCendenZ" in another voice. Significantly, *Whatever Works* does not end with this speech by Boris. For, just as at the film's start, Boris's friends ask him to whom he is speaking. They quizzically look in our direction as Melodie asks, "Does anybody see anybody out there?" Someone repeats "Out there?" before we hear reiterated the word "no." Boris smiles at us through the fourth wall and states, "See? I'm the only one who sees the whole picture": the same phrase he used at the start of the film.

By placing scenes that mirror each other at the start and end of his film, Allen shapes his medium to create a nearly symmetrical framing device. It can be charted something like this:

Start of *Whatever Works*
Boris converses with a group of friends
Boris states, "My story is whatever works, as long as you don't hurt anyone"
Boris breaks the fourth wall to talk about the horrors of existence
Boris admits to us "I was pretty lucky" to fall *for* an "ideal" woman
Boris tells his wife, "I'm the only one who sees the whole picture"
Boris throws himself out a window after the demise
of a once satisfying relationship
Center: Boris meets, marries, and is rejected by Melodie
Boris throws himself out a window after the demise
of a once satisfying relationship
Boris admits to us "I was pretty lucky" to fall *on* an "ideal" woman
Boris continues to break the fourth wall to talk about
the meaninglessness of existence
Boris says, "Celebrate what? A step closer to the grave? ... Whatever works"
Boris tells us, "I'm the only one who sees the whole picture"
Boris turns back to converse with his group of friends
End of *Whatever Works*

With Melodie as the central fulcrum, Allen has created an ending that mirrors the beginning. This framing device suggests that the pattern will be repeated, thus implying erotic love to be only a "temporary" answer to life's quandaries. Furthermore, when Boris breaks the fourth wall to say "I'm the only one who sees the whole picture," his friends, hemmed in by the movie screen that contains them, watch a very small picture on a tiny television screen. Allen thus implies that seeing the big picture entails awareness that something huge may very well exist beyond the small, screened-in frame of existence: transCendenZ exceeds eXistenZ.

Allen's breaking of the fourth wall is therefore charged with theological meaning: only something beyond the confines of everyday life can give meaning to existence. Indeed, as Allen admitted in an interview long before *Whatever Works*, "I think the only thing, or the best thing, that gives you a chance to triumph in life is religious faith. It surpasses even earthly love between a man and a woman."

Though it "works" for many people, faith in someone "out there" watching (over) us is not an option for Allen: "I feel that faith is blind. It will work, but it requires closing your eyes to reality." Allen is commenting upon his film *Crimes and Misdemeanors* (1989), which ends with a blind rabbi.[17] However, *Whatever Works*, made twenty years later, suggests that Allen still desires a transcendent principle or person that might give meaning to the small screen of existence.

Breaking the fourth wall, then, is a good metaphor for what it means to be a person of faith. Most people go through life believing that existence is limited to the stage of empirically verifiable human action. But believers—from multiple religions—look beyond the small screen of everyday reality whenever, through prayer or meditation, they seek connection with someone or something that transcends lived experience. Christians believe, in addition, that a transcendent someone broke through the fourth wall in the opposite direction: from transcendence onto the stage of earthly existence. Walking and talking with people in first-century Palestine, Jesus offered not a "temporary measure of grace" but grace everlasting. Allen's hunger for such a miracle is apparent in one of his best films: *The Purple Rose of Cairo* (1985), in which a character literally breaks through the fourth wall.

Hope beyond the Fourth Wall: *The Purple Rose of Cairo*

Set in Depression-era New Jersey, *The Purple Rose of Cairo* focuses on Cecilia (Mia Farrow), who tries to make ends meet while her cad of a husband dissipates their money on gambling and adultery. Cecilia seeks relief from her bleak existence by going to the movies, where she enters a Narcissus trance as she watches happy-ever-after stories. Woody Allen thus reflects actual history: during the Great Depression, movie attendance was at an all-time high as people sought momentary relief from their bleak lives.

After discovering her husband in their bedroom with another woman, Cecilia escapes once again to the theater, where she watches repeat showings of a brand-new movie called *The Purple Rose of Cairo*. In order to emphasize her Narcissus trance, Allen intercuts scenes from the black-and-white movie Cecilia views with full-frame close-ups of her wide-eyed face, which is lit up (both literally and figuratively) by the fantasy on screen.

And then something amazing happens: Tom Baxter (Jeff Daniels), the handsome lead of the film she has watched multiple times, suddenly begins to break the fourth wall of the movie that contains him, looking out toward her in the audience. However, unlike Alvy in *Annie Hall* and Boris in *Whatever Works*, who address their entire movie audience, Tom addresses only one person, saying to Cecilia, "Boy, you must really like this film." Then Tom literally breaks the fourth wall by stepping off of the screen of the black-and-white movie watched by Cecilia and into the color movie that contains her. We see him, now in color, take Cecilia's hand and run with her out of the theater.

Woody Allen thus alludes to the fantasy of all filmgoers who have wished their lives to be as thrilling or romantic or happy-ever-after as those depicted on movie screens. Indeed, Tom Baxter treats Cecilia like the most important woman in the world, giving her a wonderful night of dinner and dancing, ending with a romantically chaste kiss. Handsome, attentive, courageous, sensitive, loving, and faithful, Tom Baxter fulfills the ideals scripted for him, telling Cecilia these characteristics are "written into my character." Or, as another actor in the black-and-white movie puts it, "Tom is perfect." Cecilia realizes this as well: "I've met the perfect man! Of course, he's only fiction, but you can't have everything." Indeed, the fantasy of perfection cannot function in the real world. When Tom tries to pay a dinner bill, Cecilia tells him that his money is fake "movie" money. When he tries to start a getaway car after they dash from the restaurant, he discovers that real cars need keys. When he kisses Cecilia, he is shocked to discover that there isn't a "fade-out" to darkness, as in 1930s movies.

Allen puts the kissing scene in an amusement park that has closed for the season: an apt metaphor. Having entered a movie theater as a form of distracting amusement, Cecilia now sits inside another location designed for amusement, kissing a leading man in what looks like a roller-coaster car—as though in anticipation of her roller-coaster emotions with Tom. The scene also adumbrates a moment later in Allen's film when Tom takes Cecilia back to the theater showing *The Purple Rose*, where he pulls her onto the screen, breaking the fourth wall in reverse. Cecilia, though now appearing in black and white, has a fantastic night on the town, experiencing the "mad-cap Manhattan weekend" she repeatedly saw movie characters enjoying. Drinking and dancing with Tom to her heart's content, Cecilia does what many filmgoers wish they could do: escape real life by entering the roller-coaster fantasy world of film.

To symbolize their all-night escapade, Allen uses techniques from 1930s films: a black-and-white montage of blinking cabaret signs, full-frame close-ups on overflowing champagne glasses, clips of samba dancing, etc. Allen thus employs his medium to deliver his message about the black-and-white fantasies of 1930s movies. And he implies that they are indeed black-and-white when Cecilia notices that the champagne at the Copacabana is only fizzy water. Furthermore, Cecilia's very presence changes the script. The Copacabana singer who is supposed to marry Tom in the last reel of the film faints when she realizes that Tom has fallen for a woman from the "real world." And when a waiter discovers that the script has been changed, he refuses to do his job, breaking into a dance routine in order to fulfill his own desires. In this scene, then, Allen explores a theological conundrum: the relationship between free will and determinism.

We know Allen was thinking theologically due to a scene in a church, which begins with a full-frame close-up on a sculptured image of Jesus hanging from a cross. Cecilia explains the crucifix to the baffled Tom: "It's about the meaning of life, the reason for everything."[18] Allen then has Cecilia's husband, Monk, enter the church and pick a fight with Tom in front of the cross. Knowing Allen's suspicions about Christianity, we sense that the fight might symbolize the religious wars that have marred Christianity through the centuries—reinforced by the fact that Allen chose the name *Monk*. More significant, however, is the fact that Tom suffers no damage from being struck down in the fight. Because he is a fictional character he cannot suffer harm unless his screenwriter "creator"—a word repeatedly used in the film—wills it.

Tom nevertheless rebels against the life his creator scripted for him by walking off the screen. We are reminded of Adam and Eve, who rebelled against the script written by their Creator. Though I strongly doubt Allen intended *Purple Rose* to be a biblical allegory, it is clear that Tom's life is determined for him, written by his creator. If he follows his scripted lines, life will be perfect. But instead he rebels, wanting something beyond the fourth wall of his determined environment: a life of free will, which is fulfilled in the act of leaving the screen. However, when he leaves his paradise he discovers the effects of free will: the pain and suffering of the real world.

Free will is represented by Gil Shepherd, the "real world" actor who plays Tom Baxter. We see Gil freely choosing scripts for roles he wants to play, if even having to negotiate the politics of Hollywood—much as any human chooses "real-world" roles in life (career, marriage, parenting, etc.) while having to negotiate impediments and disappointments. However, when Gil discovers that a character he "fleshed ... out," Tom Baxter, has left the screen, he is horrified. Traveling to New Jersey to rein Tom in, Gil runs into Cecilia, who swoons over him, never having met a real movie star before. Flattered, Gil asks her to go back to Hollywood with him.

Cecilia thus has to make a choice between the "perfect" Tom or the "real" Gil. When she chooses Gil, the dejected Tom climbs back into the screen for a life of determined bliss. His dejection illuminates the religious problem with determinism: an unchanging script predetermined by a good creator might eliminate evil, but it also eliminates what makes us human. As one character on the black-and-white screen puts it, "The most human of all human characteristics is the ability to choose." But that means humans can choose self-interest over the good, as illustrated by Gil Shepherd. Basically a likeable self-aggrandizing actor, Gil thinks primarily of his own best interests. Fearing that Tom's antics off-screen might ruin his reputation as an actor, Gil wants to destroy the film character. Hence, as soon as Tom goes back onto the screen, movie theaters are instructed to burn all copies of *The Purple Rose of Cairo*, so that Tom cannot exit paradise again: a Hellish ending for the man who defied his creator.

But we viewers don't mind, knowing that Cecilia will be happy. Escaping her brute of a husband, Cecilia will live with a celebrity actor in a Hollywood heaven. However, as she waits at their determined rendezvous spot, Gil never shows up. Instead, the film cuts to Gil sitting alone in an airplane, headed back to Hollywood, having saved his career by getting Tom to re-enter the black-and-white film. The realm of free will, Allen shows, is the realm of self-serving behavior that leads to human suffering.

Used to romantic comedies ending happily—as determined by genre convention—viewers are dismayed. Their response illustrates a pronouncement made by one of the characters in the black-and-white movie: "The real ones want life fiction and the fictional ones want life real." This statement reveals the significance of Woody Allen's title, *The Purple Rose of Cairo*, which names not only the

1985 film and the 1930s movie within the film, but also an object described in the black-and-white movie. At the start of the black-and-white film that initially contains him, Tom Baxter searches inside an Egyptian tomb for the so-called "purple rose of Cairo." Originally painted by a pharaoh, the rose "now grows wild under the tomb." In other words, a created artifact has magically transformed into a living reality, as Tom himself will do when he steps off the screen of a black-and-white movie called *The Purple Rose of Cairo*.

But the "reality" he steps into is also called *The Purple Rose of Cairo*, which is the name of the film we watch, containing Cecilia. Like her, we want to escape into a "purple rose" ending in which a handsome, rising star would carry a poor working woman back to Hollywood with him. We want to believe Gil Shepherd's proclamation of love to Cecilia: "I know this is the real thing." However, his "real thing" is as fictional as the inner film and the framing film we have been watching. The Hollywood star is more a shooting star, something beautiful but temporary, like the experience of a movie itself. Significantly, as the attentive viewer may have noticed, Allen names the amusement ride in which Tom kisses Cecilia "The Shooting Star."

Hence, just as Tom summarizes his *Purple Rose* movie with "I search in vain for the legendary purple rose," we might summarize our *Purple Rose* movie with "Cecilia searches in vain for the purple rose." Jilted by Gil, she returns, suitcase in hand, to the theater where she saw *The Purple Rose* only to find it no longer there. Instead she watches *Top Hat*, an actual 1935 musical in which Fred Astaire sings to Ginger Rogers "I'm in heaven." Cecilia wipes her tear-stained face and slowly raises her face to the screen, her countenance soon lit up in hope.[19]

Woody Allen thus signals several things. First, skeptical of religion, he implies that "heaven" is a fictional hope as outrageous as the song-and-dance routine of Rogers and Astaire. But perhaps it is a necessary hope, generated to alleviate the pain and suffering caused by human free will. Many who do not believe in the "purple rose" of heaven therefore lose themselves in the Narcissus trance engendered by media fictions. Indeed, Allen begins his Oscar-nominated 1987 film *Radio Days* with a narrator describing his awe, as a child in the 1930s, over Radio City Music Hall: "It was like entering heaven." It's as though *Radio Days* begins where *The Purple Rose of Cairo* ends: with a sense that the Narcissus trance entices viewers with a fake purple rose. Perhaps it is no coincidence that the flower known as Narcissus was named after the Narcissus myth. *The Purple Rose of Cairo*, however, breaks us out of our Narcissus trance by refusing to give us the "purple rose" of an artificially happy ending.

Allen also, even if unwittingly, provides a profound answer to people who blame God for evil in the world. *The Purple Rose of Cairo* explicitly argues that free will defines what it means to be human. Without the ability to choose, we are merely puppets of a creator, following a script that protects us from evil. And there is the conundrum: those who unquestioningly follow a determined script have lost their free will and hence are no longer human; but as soon as we posit free will we allow for the fact that humans can choose to act selfishly rather than for the good of others.[20]

Back to the Beginning

Like Tom Baxter, who returns to the predictability of his black-and-white film, this chapter ends by returning to the predictability of Marshall McLuhan, who relegated cinema to an easy distinction between "hot" and "cool" medium. Both Baxter and McLuhan, serving as characters in Woody Allen films, prove that the wall separating fiction from reality is permeable, undermining easy assessments of "hot" versus "cool," of "inside" versus "outside," of eXistenZ versus transCendenZ. Though breaking the fourth wall does not always signal a realm of transcendence that gives meaning to existence, the technique nevertheless gestures toward an interdependence of medium and message that mimics—if only artificially, like a painted purple rose—the interplay of transcendence and immanence found in multiple religions.

Notes

1 Marshall McLuhan, *Understanding Media: The Extensions of Man* (New York: McGraw-Hill, 1964), 23, 292–3.
2 Annie Murphy Paul, "Your Brain on Fiction," *New York Times*, March 17, 2012.
3 Ibid. The Emory study, published in *Brain and Language*, focused on verbal clichés like "She had a nice voice" versus brain-activating metaphors, like "She had a velvet voice." Since, as film theorists have long proclaimed, film is a kind of language, I feel comfortable making the parallel.
4 As Stephen Heath famously argues, conventional films "suture" viewers into the illusions they watch, such that they forget what is outside the frame of the screen. See *Questions of Cinema* (London: Macmillan, 1981), 76–112.
5 Stig Björkman, *Woody Allen on Woody Allen* (London: Faber & Faber, 1995), 75. Significantly, Godard made a short film about Woody Allen called *Meetin' WA* (1986).
6 Film theorist David Bordwell identifies explicit "references to previous films" as one of the signs of artistic cinema. See "The Art Cinema as a Mode of Film Practice," in *Film Theory and Criticism: Introductory Readings*, 6th edn, ed. Leo Braudy and Marshall Cohen (New York: Oxford University Press, 2004), 778.
7 The Godard quotation is from a 1962 interview in *Cahiers du cinéma*, trans. Tom Milne, reprinted in the booklet accompanying the Criterion Collection DVD of *Breathless* (2007): 42.
8 *Tombstone* (George P. Cosmatos, 1993) begins with several clips from *The Great Train Robbery*, obviously gesturing toward the history of "the western." The term New Hollywood is used to describe films, produced after the demise of the Hays Code, that bear the influence of the French New Wave.
9 Ironically, or perhaps appropriately, one of the actors looking us in the eye at the end of *Balanta* is Maia Morgenstern, the Romanian actor who played the mother of Jesus in Mel Gibson's *The Passion of the Christ* (2004), a film that will be discussed in Chapter 7.
10 Robert K. Johnston and Brian Godawa both parallel sex and violence in film with that found in the Old Testament, quite rightly assessing disturbing images according to a story's "larger moral and religious framework." Robert K. Johnston, *Reel Spirituality: Theology and Film in Dialogue* (Grand Rapids: Baker Academic, 2006), 218–19; Brian Godawa, *Hollywood Worldviews: Watching Films with Wisdom and Discernment* (Downers Grove: IVP, 2009), 32–8.
11 Quoted in Richard von Busack, "Pod Man Out," metroactive.com, April 22–8, 1999, accessed 18 October 2014.

92 Theories of Film Salvation

12 Adam Lowenstein, "Interactive Art Cinema: Between 'Old' and 'New' Media with *Un Chien Andalou* and *eXistenZ*," in *Global Art Cinema: New Theories and Histories*, ed. Rosalind Galt and Karl Schoonover (New York: Oxford University Press, 2010), 102.

13 Though Roy Anker mentions a "solitary figure looking intently into the camera" at the start of the film, he does not analyze the implications of the shot, focusing primarily on "the larger tragic story that the film will describe." See *Catching the Light: Looking for God in the Movies* (Grand Rapids: Eerdmans, 2004), 177. Peter Fraser, though helpfully drawing attention to several cinematic techniques, does not mention breaking the fourth wall in *Images of the Passion: The Sacramental Mode in Film* (Westport: Praeger, 1998), 79–89. Also overlooking the technique while discussing *The Mission* are Margaret R. Miles, *Seeing and Believing: Religion and Values in the Movies* (Boston: Beacon, 1996), 56–9; and Anthony J. Clarke and Paul S. Fiddes, eds, *Flickering Images: Theology and Film in Dialogue* (Oxford: Regent's Park College, 2005), 233–40.

14 For Christian complicity with slavery, see Mark A. Noll, *The Civil War as a Theological Crisis* (Chapel Hill: University of North Carolina Press, 2006). For the epidemic of slavery today, and people who are doing something about it, visit the website of the International Justice Mission at www.ijm.org.

15 For Woody Allen's interest in theological issues, see *The Films of Woody Allen: Critical Essays*, ed. Charles L. P. Silet (Lanham: Scarecrow, 2006), especially Gary Commins, "Woody Allen's Theological Imagination" (34–49); Maurice Yacowar, "The Religion of *Radio Days*" (250–5); Mark W. Roche, "Justice and the Withdrawal of God in Woody Allen's *Crimes and Misdemeanors*" (268–83); and Paul Nathanson, "Between Time and Eternity: Theological Notes on *Shadows and Fog*" (284–98).

16 Boris's comments echo those of a Jewish philosopher, Professor Levy, in Woody Allen's brilliant film *Crimes and Misdemeanors* (1989): "It is only we, with our capacity to love, that give meaning to the indifferent universe. And yet, most human beings seem to have the ability to keep trying, and even to find joy from simple things." Significantly, like Boris's father, Professor Levy commits suicide by jumping out a window. For an extended discussion of the philosophical and theological implications of the earlier film, see Crystal Downing, "Woody Allen's Blindness and Insight: The Palimpsests of *Crimes and Misdemeanors*," *Religion and the Arts* 1 (1997): 73–92.

17 Woody Allen, with Stig Björkman, "Woody Allen on Woody Allen," in *The Religion and Film Reader*, ed. Jolyon Mitchell and S. Brent Plate (New York: Routledge, 2007), 243.

18 Immediately before this scene, Cecilia gives Tom a tour of life outside his film, explaining how things in the "real" world work. Because Tom was designed for a script about the Manhattan elite, he has never seen bread lines or a pregnant woman. Allen films Cecilia's explanations of these phenomena without speech, her gestures and Tom's amazed face signaling all we need to know. The absence of speech serves to emphasize the noisy scene inside the church to follow.

19 Much of this paragraph was borrowed from Crystal Downing, "Broadway Roses: Woody Allen's Romantic Inheritance," *Literature/Film Quarterly* 17.1 (1989): 13–17. In the essay I explore Allen's flower imagery in several films, aligning it with the "blue flower" idealized by Novalis (1772–1801) and his Romantic followers.

20 For a different religious approach to the film, which reads Tom Baxter as a "supernatural" Christ-figure who concretizes Cecilia's "mystical experience," see Irving Singer, *Reality Transformed: Film as Meaning and Technique* (Cambridge: MIT Press, 1998), 52–78.

Part II
Salvation from Film Theory

5 Enlightenment as Mass Deception
Certain Tendencies in Film Theory

Pious people are not the only ones to have established opposite meanings for "salvation from cinema." In the first half of the twentieth century, secular humanists demonstrated as much religious zeal as the Catholic Legion of Decency in their denunciations of Hollywood products, similarly concerned about their adverse effects on human integrity. As film scholar Robert Stam notes, "From the beginning, there were simultaneous tendencies to either over-endow the cinema with utopian possibilities, or to demonize it as a progenitor of evil."[1] The primary difference is that the devout tended to ask of films "Where is the transcendence, the hard-earned hope?" whereas secularists queried "Where is the art, the hard-earned craft?"[2] Focusing on the secular domain, this Chapter looks at competing definitions of "salvation from cinema" in order to explore not only the relationship between medium and message but also the relevance of film theory to religion.

Let There Be Lumière

In Chapter 1, I briefly outlined the material origins of cinema, Edison attempting to embellish his phonograph for consumer enticement. This chapter takes us to Europe, where Edison's peep-box viewing-machines inspired two brothers to invent their own filmmaking devices. Operating a factory that produced photographic equipment in Lyon, France, Auguste and Louis Lumière had the knowledge and the incentive to devise a machine that might do the work of Edison's kinetograph (camera) and kinetoscope (projector) combined. Their apparatus, which they called a *cinématographe*, had the advantage of being portable. Because the kinetograph weighed several hundred pounds, filming was limited to the confines of a small studio. In contrast, the *cinématographe*, weighing less than sixteen pounds, could be carried to diverse locations, not only for filming purposes, but also for projection. The Lumières therefore hold a position in film history as the first inventors to screen a movie *for a group* (in Paris on March 22, 1895). It was a shot of workers leaving the Lumière factory.

Even though Lumière projections were no more than brief documentary clips of everyday life (called "*actualités*"), viewers saw them infused with redemptive significance. Spectators seemed to recognize, from the very start, deep symbolism to the filmmakers' name, since Lumière means "light." One reporter noted, after attending the first Lumière screening for a *paying* audience (December 28, 1895):

> When these apparatuses are made available to the public, everybody will be able to photograph those who are dear to them, no longer as static forms but with their movements, their actions, their familiar gestures, capturing the speech on their very lips. Then, *death will no longer be absolute*.[3]

Salvation from the *cinématographe*!

Ironically, the very same historical moment led to a different definition of "salvation from cinema." One of the *actualités* that the Lumières projected on that historic December day showed a train pulling into a station. Later, a story developed that viewers were so startled by seeing a locomotive barreling toward them that some screamed and jumped out of the way, fearfully seeking salvation from cinematic realism. Film historian Martin Loiperdinger calls this story the "founding myth" of cinema, as though echoing Joseph Gaer's argument that "fear of the unknown or the unpredictable and, above all, the fear of death had, and has, its part in the architecture of religion."[4] The fear shaping the founding myth of cinema, of course, arose from what Stephen Bottomore calls "discomfort about a new and uncomfortably realistic ... *medium*."[5] The Lumière medium thus became a message about salvation in more ways than one.

Salvation as the Resurrection (of) Story

Inventors in Germany and England were also developing their own apparatuses, producing, like the Lumières, single-shot films lasting only one or two minutes. Because tension from take-up reels tended to break longer strips of film, narrative cinema, as it is now called, was impossible. Hence, the device that enabled celluloid to tell stories energized "salvation from cinema," especially for those who believe that "in film, story reigns supreme."[6]

Credit for the saving device takes us to New York City, where an American Civil War veteran and his two sons, the Lathams, operated a kinetoscope parlor and started their own studio. In order to produce movies that lasted longer than the shorts viewed through kinetoscope peep-holes, Latham studio personnel created a device, patented in 1896, that briefly diverted film above and below the projector lens, taking tension off the celluloid strips as they went from reel to reel. Now called the Latham Loop, the tiny little device had huge aesthetic implications. For with the possibility of longer films came the possibility of resurrecting stories important to various religions. As silent film director Abel Gance proclaimed in 1927, "All legends, all mythologies, and all myths, all the founders of religions, indeed, all religions ... await their celluloid resurrection."[7] The Latham Loop enabled the salvation of religion: a holy calling. Indeed, two years later, French playwright Alexandre Arnoux summarized the possibilities of film with religious awe: "Do not all the bold descriptions we have given amount to a definition of prayer?"[8]

Not all, of course, have been so sanguine. In 1930, French author Georges Duhamel denounced narrative cinema as

> a diversion for uneducated, wretched, worn-out creatures who are consumed by their worries ..., a spectacle which requires no concentration and presupposes no intelligence ..., which kindles no light in the heart and awakens no hope other than the ridiculous one of someday becoming a "star" in Los Angeles.[9]

Marxist cultural critics echoed Duhamel's suspicions about cinema. In 1944, German-trained philosophers Max Horkheimer and Theodor Adorno published *The Dialectic of Enlightenment*, containing a famous chapter entitled "The Culture Industry: Enlightenment as Mass Deception." Written not far from Hollywood (Adorno and Horkheimer moved to the area after Hitler's rise to power), the essay's subtitle implies its thesis: as a dominant part of the capitalist culture industry, cinema deceives viewers into assuming that movies enlighten them about reality. In actuality, films inculcate "promulgation of the status quo,"[10] lulling viewers into what Marshall McLuhan would later called a Narcissus trance. Indeed, sounding like Marxist theorists who preceded him, the Roman Catholic McLuhan considered popular cinema as a "monster ad for consumer goods."[11]

There is legitimacy in the Marxist critique. While it is easy to recognize dehumanizing sex and violence on film, far more insidious is cinema's complicity with what Tom Wolfe, in 1986, called *plutography*: "the graphic depiction of the lives of the rich."[12] Similar to how pornography generates sexual lust, plutography entices viewers with artificially slick images of expensive dwellings, designer clothing, and high-end cars, along with the surgically enhanced bodies that consume them: Narcissus with a facelift. People become identified not by their commitment to social justice, but through commodities they have purchased.

For Adorno, then, the medium must deliver a different kind of message. This led him to collaborate on another book, one that reflected his lifelong study of music: *Composing for the Films* (1947).[13] His co-author was an Austrian musician, Hanns Eisler, whose 1930s accompaniments to Bertolt Brecht's subversive theatrical productions were banned by the Nazi Party. When Eisler moved to Los Angeles in 1942, he composed music for eight Hollywood films, two of his scores receiving Oscar nominations.[14] *Composing for the Films*, then, advocates for movies that call attention to their construction through discontinuities between sound and image. In contrast to most Hollywood movies, which lull viewers into thoughtless emotion through their soundtracks, self-consciously artistic films generate engaged reflection. Adorno and Eisler thus argue for "salvation from cinema" in both senses of the term: the need to be saved from the bourgeois complacency of standard Hollywood fare, a salvation that comes from attentiveness to cinema artistry.

Salvation from Sergei Eisenstein

Adorno and Eisler discuss only one canonical film theorist in *Composing for Cinema*, Soviet filmmaker Sergei Eisenstein (1898–1948). However, they indict Eisenstein's "error," "inadequacy," and "fundamental misconceptions" when it comes to cinematic music.[15] This may explain why film scholars focus on *visual* discontinuities in Eisenstein's films: discontinuities Eisenstein both practiced and preached. Committed to Marx's dialectical materialism, Eisenstein believed that artistic filmmaking relied not on compelling stories but on *dialectical montage*: the cutting together of discontinuous shots, creating a "collision" between them that "shocks" viewers into thought.

Take, for example, his famous *Battleship Potemkin* (1925), which he based on an historical incident twelve years before the Bolshevik Revolution. In what has been called "the single greatest and most influential montage sequence in the history of the cinema,"[16] Eisenstein intercuts shots of Czarist soldiers marching in a line down steps leading to the Odessa Opera House with discontinuous close-ups on the horrified faces of innocent bystanders. To emphasize their innocence, Eisenstein next intercuts a baby plummeting down the steps in an abandoned carriage with shots of the dying mother, an outraged woman wearing pince-nez, and an incredulous young man with wire-rim glasses. The shots seem to randomly "collide" with each other such that the linearity of action is unclear, undermining viewer confidence in the order of events. For Eisenstein, the continuity of action is not as important as the shock viewers get from close-ups on horrified faces. Soon to follow is a classic example of symbolic (rather than dialectical) montage: after the Potemkin fires its guns on the Odessa Opera House, Eisenstein inserts three still shots of different lion statues, starting with one at rest, the next lifting its head, and the third partially standing. Looking like three black-and-white photographs spliced together, the montage symbolizes how the Russian people will rise up to overthrow a despotic Czarist government. *Potemkin* thus functioned as an apologetic for the Communist Revolution.

Nevertheless, by the 1930s Soviet leaders were denouncing dialectical and symbolic montage as signs of capitalism. As a decadent focus on the *medium* of film, emphasizing formal structures on the screen, montage distracted from the salvation *messages* a film might deliver. Rather than "formalism," Stalinist officials demanded "socialist realism," which required that movies be windows through which the blessings of Stalinism could be viewed. For them, a good film, like a clear window, does not draw attention to itself as medium. Moviegoers should think about Communism, not cinematic techniques like those generated by Eisenstein. Rather than dialectical montage, socialist realism requires continuity editing: cuts that maintain a coherent sense of time and space. The medium, in other words, is a message that must be destroyed: salvation from cinematic manipulation.

The ironies, of course, are obvious. First, socialist realism presented not realism but artificial pictures of a Stalinist state filled with happy, thriving workers. Second, the realism of continuity editing (also known as invisible editing) is one of the hallmarks of classic Hollywood cinema, which is a bastion of capitalist interests. Continuity editing contributed to a Narcissus trance valued by both Western capitalists and Eastern Communists.[17]

The ironies intensified for Hanns Eisler not long after he indicted Eisenstein's approach to music. Having fled Nazi-era Europe due to his anti-fascist compositions, Eisler was blacklisted by Hollywood studio bosses for his Communist connections. Undergoing two interrogations by the House Committee on Un-American Activities, Eisler was finally deported in 1948, despite support from actor/director Charlie Chaplin and composers Igor Stravinsky, Aaron Copland, and Leonard Bernstein. During the "Red Scare" following World War II, "salvation from cinema" took on a whole new meaning as numerous talented contributors to Hollywood cinema were "blacklisted," no longer allowed to participate in filmmaking.

Salvation from Cinema Montage: André Bazin

Eisenstein's emphasis on montage generated a reaction in more than the Soviet politburo. Whereas French novelist André Malraux argued in 1940 that montage (which is merely the French word for editing) turned cinema into an art form,[18] André Bazin sought to save cinema from dependence on montage. Preferring the "objective nature of photography" to manipulation of the celluloid medium, Bazin believed that a realistic mise-en-scène encouraged "a more active mental attitude on the part of the spectator."[19] He therefore advocated, among other things, (1) deep focus, in which objects in both the foreground and the background of the mise-en-scène are clearly depicted; (2) wide shots that include far more objects in the mise-en-scène than do medium shots; and (3) long takes that give viewers time to assess everything in the mise-en-scène. Elevating as exemplars the Italian neorealists that followed World War II, Bazin steered filmmakers away not only from "tricks of montage" but especially from the fanciful sets and unrealistic lighting that marked German expressionism, a movement after World War I that produced silent film classics like *The Cabinet of Dr. Caligari* (Robert Weine, 1919), *Nosferatu* (F. W. Murnau, 1922), and *Metropolis* (Fritz Lang, 1927).[20] Believing such films control viewer perception, he advocated salvation from celluloid artifice. At the same time, as Robert Stam notes, he used explicitly religious language—"real presence, revelation, faith in the image"—to celebrate the sacramental nature of mise-en-scène. Bazin, in other words, preached salvation from cinema in both senses of the phrase.[21]

The French New Wave and Truffaut's Auteur: *400 Blows* to Cinema

Bazin's writings were so influential—due in part to an extremely important journal he co-founded called *Cahiers du cinéma*—that he helped inspire a new kind of filmmaking. Later dubbed *Nouvelle Vague* [New Wave], several French filmmakers followed the example of Bazin's favored Italian neorealists by going into the streets, where they filmed un-choreographed, un-scripted scenes for their movies.[22] Rather than slavishly capturing a pre-established text on film, they "wrote" a movie as they filmed it. Doing so, they instantiated Bazin's proclamation in 1950 that "the director writes in film."[23]

Bazin and his disciples thus fulfilled what is now considered one of the founding manifestos of the *Nouvelle Vague*. In an essay entitled "Birth of a New Avant-Garde: The Camera Pen," French novelist Alexandre Astruc (who later became a filmmaker) argued that directors, not screenplay writers, are the actual authors of film. Their pen is the camera, which moves in and around the mise-en-scène the way authors' pens move on paper. Because the French term for "camera pen" is *caméra-stylo*, Astruc's original French title implied a pun: the caméra-*stylo* is manifest in the *style* of a director. (The word *style*, in both French and English, originates from *stilus*, Latin for the sharpened instrument employed by the ancients to mark on wax tablets. Significantly, the Greek word for *stylus* is *graphion*, as in cinemato*graphy*.)

Several years after Astruc's celebration of *caméra-stylo*, an upstart 21-year-old named François Truffaut intensified the importance of directorial style through a notorious essay published in *Cahiers du cinéma*. Called "A Certain Tendency in French Cinema," Truffaut's 1954 piece attacked France's "Tradition of Quality" in which directors use "scholarly framing, complicated lighting effects, [and] 'polished' photography" while transposing literate scripts onto film. As far as Truffaut was concerned, this tradition is inimical to "an 'auteur cinema.'"[24] (*Auteur*, of course, is French for *author*.) While screenwriters in the "Tradition of Quality" adapt texts for the screen, an auteur director *composes*, like an author, a uniquely cinematic work of art. Truffaut, in other words, demanded salvation from cinema as currently practiced in France.[25]

In order to incarnate his message, Truffaut became a filmmaker, his *Les quatre cents coups* (*The 400 Blows*, 1959) energizing the French New Wave. The film's thirteen-year-old protagonist, Antoine (Jean-Pierre Léaud), rebels against the rules of both home and school, much as Truffaut rebelled against the rules of the well-crafted French "*cinéma de papa*" that preceded him.[26] Early in *400 Blows*, for example, a teacher writes a poem—a text *de papa*—on the blackboard, expecting his students to slavishly copy it into their notebooks. Antoine, however, having been sent to the corner of the classroom for misbehaving, writes his own poem on the wall, establishing himself as original auteur in defiance *de papa*. Significantly, Truffaut starts the sequence with a medium long shot, so that when we see Antoine sent to the corner, he disappears behind a free-standing blackboard that mimics the shape of a cinema screen. Hence, while the *papa*-teacher writes on a traditional blackboard at the center of the room, Antoine is behind a screen inscribing his own unique statement.

The medium delivers a similar message not much later. As Antoine and a friend enter a building, Truffaut tilts the camera in order to focus on the word "CINE" above the door. Inside, Antoine takes a ride on a whirling machine that holds bodies on its barrel-like wall through centrifugal force. The scene cuts back and forth between shots of Antoine plastered against the wall and his point of view (POV shots) as he sees people watching him from above. Because the faces he views are separated by bars on the whirling machine, the POV shots make the swiftly moving images look like frames of film moving through a projector.[27] Antoine then defies the rules of the game: held by centrifugal force to the spinning wall, he crawls so that his body is positioned nearly upside down, a POV shot turning the viewers upside down. Thus challenging the way the swirling apparatus has traditionally been ridden, Antoine parallels Truffaut, who challenged the way cinema had traditionally been written, turning cinema upside down.

Truffaut's connection to André Bazin reinforces this interpretation. While the entrance to the centrifugal-force machine is preceded by the sign "CINE," so viewer entrance to *400 Blows* is preceded by a sign: "Dedicated to the memory of André Bazin." And, as Truffaut surely knew, Bazin argued that "the space of the screen is centrifugal."[28] Unlike the centripetal force of theater, which pulls all fictional action onto center stage, cinema often forces the action off the screen where viewers still assume the fiction continues even when they do not see it: as when Antoine disappears behind the screen-shaped blackboard where his rebellious actions continue. Not coincidentally, one of the other riders on the centrifugal-force machine is Truffaut himself, who makes a brief cameo upon exiting the apparatus. This not only reinforces the parallel between filmmaker and protagonist, it also alludes to the work of Alfred Hitchcock, who, famous for making cameo appearances in his films, helped inspire New Wave directors. By placing himself in the film, then, Truffaut establishes his presence as auteur.[29]

Truffaut's presence in the film is intensified by the way Antoine's life parallels his own. Both were illegitimate until "given a name" by the men who married their mothers. Like Antoine, Truffaut lived with his grandmother until, around age ten, he moved in with his mother and her new husband. Also like Antoine, he escaped both home and school by sneaking into movies, until his rebellious behavior landed him in military school, just as Antoine's petty thievery lands him in a juvenile detention center. A friend who tries to visit Antoine at the center is turned away, just as Truffaut's friend—though much older—was turned away from visiting him at military school. In Truffaut's case, the friend sent away was André Bazin, with whom the young cinephile had established a relationship after writing Bazin about his views on film.[30]

Significantly, Antoine goes into juvenile detention because he stole the writing implement *du papa*: his stepfather's typewriter. And just in case viewers miss the significance of this theft, Truffaut reinforces the point in two other scenes. In the first, Antoine's stepfather queries him about a new pen (*stylo*) he holds—presumably another writing implement Antoine has stolen. Later, during an English lesson at school, Antoine watches as a fellow student has trouble repeating the English phrase, "Where is your father?"

Not coincidentally, when Truffaut defied his cinematic fathers in "A Certain Tendency in French Cinema," he was forced into a type of detention, being banned from attending the Cannes Film Festival. Not much later he was celebrated at Cannes due to accolades generated by *The 400 Blows*. The film, after all, fulfilled the rallying cry of Bazin: to elicit "a more active mental attitude on the part of the spectator." Indeed, even though it tells an identifiable tale, *400 Blows* also includes random, unexplained scenes that the spectator must work to understand. At the detention center, for example, three little girls are shut into a large dog cage immediately before delinquents come outside to play ball. The camera lingers on the innocent faces peering through the chain-link barrier—reminding us of earlier shots when Antoine peers less innocently through the bars of jail cages. In a more baffling scene, we see Antoine and his friend holding the hand of an unidentified little girl before the shot cuts to a room containing scores of children watching a puppet show. Because Truffaut lingers on the faces of the enchanted children with long takes in multiple shots, we are forced to question the scene's significance, perhaps concluding that Truffaut wants us to think about our own watching, about what enchants us.

As with several other seemingly random scenes, attentive viewers are forced out of their Narcissus trance by questioning what they see. As though this were the point, Truffaut ends *400 Blows* with a famously ambiguous image. After throwing a soccer ball onto the detention center field, Antoine turns his back on the game and runs through a hole in a chain-link fence, escaping his confinement (unlike the caged girls). Multiple tracking shots follow Antoine as he darts through woods and fields until he finally runs onto a beach and into the waves. The film suddenly ends with a freeze-frame on Antoine, the camera zooming to a close-up on his expressionless face. What is he thinking? Is he worried or at peace? Spectators are forced to draw their own conclusions.

One conclusion is that Antoine has escaped the detention center the same way Truffaut escaped the rules for "quality" cinema. Indeed, as waves lap at Antoine's feet, those familiar with Bazin may remember words that follow his reference to "centrifugal" cinema: "On the screen man is no longer the focus of the drama, but will become eventually the center of the universe. The impact of his action may there set in motion an infinitude of waves"[31]—like those set in motion by the French New Wave. It is thus no coincidence when later films about rebels—like *Butch Cassidy and the Sundance Kid* (1969) or *Thelma and Louise* (1991)—end with a freeze-frame on protagonists escaping their cultural prisons. The films are quoting the ending shot of *Les quatre cents coups*, the title of which is based on a French idiom meaning rebellious excess.

A year after *400 Blows*, Jean-Luc Godard would celebrate rebellious excess in *Breathless* (1960), turning a sexist thieving murderer into a charmingly sympathetic protagonist. Like Truffaut, Godard had contempt for *cinéma de papa*, defiantly telling his story-telling predecessors, "you don't know how to create cinema because you no longer even know what it is."[32] Like Truffaut's Antoine, who steals his stepfather's typewriter after being questioned about his new pen, Godard stole authorship, and artistic authority, from his cinematic stepfathers. Hence, using the camera-pen, *Nouvelle Vague* directors wrote, often quite spontaneously, the screen's mise-en-scène with camera angle, pan, deep focus, and tilt. Even their hired actors seemed to give up control over their craft, improvising on the spot as though indifferent toward any kind of plot trajectory. Reviling well-crafted stories, New Wave directors considered mise-en-scène, written with the camera-pen, "primarily responsible for giving meaning and structure to a work."[33] For them, the medium was the message.

In 1962 American film critic Andrew Sarris dubbed analysis of camera-pen style "auteur theory," defining an auteur with three basic characteristics: (1) "technical competence"; (2) a recurring visual style that expresses "distinguishable personality"; and (3) something that Truffaut called "the temperature of the director on the set."[34] Hence, whereas Bazin generated a binary opposition between montage and mise-en-scène, the French New Wave generated a binary opposition "between auteur cinema (worthy of interest) and popular genre cinema (beneath contempt)."[35]

Many filmmakers in the developing world, however, decided that viewers need salvation from both.

Salvation from Hollywood and Auteurism: Third Cinema

"Third Cinema" is the most famous film theory not originating in Euro-American contexts. The term, inspired by a 1969 manifesto called "Towards a Third Cinema," alludes not only to three kinds of cinema but also to the revolutionary potential of filmmaking in the Third World.[36] Written by Argentine filmmakers Fernando Solanas and Octavio Getino, "Towards a Third Cinema" echoes other militant 1960s manifestos that privilege feisty political values over flashy production values.[37]

The consumerist model that dominates Hollywood, which spends obscene amounts of money to generate viewer contentment, constitutes "first cinema," while the distinctively defiant style of auteur film shapes "second cinema." For Third Cinema theorists, however, first and second cinema differ very little, for both encourage a bourgeois mystification of autonomy. Whereas first cinema celebrates the on screen protagonist who doesn't play by the rules, second cinema celebrates the off-screen director who doesn't play by the rules, both benefiting from their individualistic pursuits.[38] Hollywood protagonists get rewarded with happy endings *in* their films, while auteur directors get rewarded with accolades for the originality *of* their films.

Renouncing both first and second "*cinéma de papa*," Third Cinema focuses on groups of people—in several different ways. Rather than employing close-ups that cause viewers to identify with autonomous protagonists, Third Cinema employs long and wide shots in order to capture collectives working together for a cause, no individual standing out from the rest. Second, rather than elevate an autonomous director, Third Cinema highlights the collaborative nature of filmmaking, a type of creative socialism that renounces the huge salaries of mainstream cinema. Finally, Third Cinema makes its movies available to the masses, screening its films outside of theaters so that even the poor can participate in the viewing experience. In fact, the most radical Third Cinema films are often shown in secret, not only to avoid government censorship but also to inculcate a sense of risk in spectators. Rather than generating a Narcissus trance, then, Third Cinema is meant to incite political action, encouraging collaborative revolution instead of individualistic evolution.[39]

As theologians and religion scholars will recognize, Third Cinema bears a striking resemblance to liberation theology. Both got their start in Latin America with a focus on the suffering of the disaffiliated poor, and both became famous through manifestos written within several years of each other: A *Theology of Liberation* by Peruvian priest Gustavo Gutiérrez (1971) follows "Towards a Third Cinema" by only two years.[40] Influenced by Marxian rhetoric about class struggle, both Third Cinema and liberation theology encourage resistance to unjust institutions that oppress those outside corridors of power. And both movements, encouraging the sword rather than the plowshare, spread with crusader zeal into Third World countries around the globe.

The term Third World, coined in the 1950s as an allusion to the "Third Estate" igniting the French Revolution, was nevertheless denounced by the 1980s as homogenizing and imperialist.[41] Third Cinema has similarly been denounced. Noting that class struggle is a limited lens through which to view the world, feminist theorists have challenged the problematic sexism of Third Cinema, some declaring it dead.[42] Nevertheless, there is no denying the influence Third Cinema continues to exercise on filmmaking in developing countries. *Bamako*, a 2006 release by Abderrahmane Sissako, provides an intriguing example. Most of the film's action takes place in the crowded courtyard of a house in Mali's capital, Bamako, where African lawyers and judges have gathered to hold court. Denouncing injustices perpetuated by the International Monetary Fund, they proceed to sue the World Bank. Rather than employ actors, Sissako recruited local citizens as well as legal professionals, who, playing themselves, helped script their powerful speeches.[43] Defying the autonomy celebrated by first and second cinema, the film is a collaborative construction about collaborative action, signaled by its opening shot: a four-story high scaffold stands out against an evening sky, the silhouettes of multiple humans working on its construction.

To emphasize that the film celebrates a politically inspired collectivity rather than individual prowess, Sissako draws attention to the cinematic medium in other intriguing ways. Most obviously, he puts cameras into the mise-en-scène. Indicating that the legal arguments are being filmed, the visible cameras self-reflexively allude to the potential for political change through cinema. Ironically, during the evenings when the court is no longer in session, we see locals sitting in courtyard chairs while watching a cheesy movie on a small television screen, as though signaling the much smaller perspective of first cinema cameras. Indeed, the film the locals watch, called *Death in Timbuktu*, mimics classical Hollywood westerns that glorify autonomous cowboys whose gunshots seem more exciting than camera shots of brilliant legal speeches. Significantly, Sissako places in the fake western movie individuals famous in non-Western filmmaking, such as the Palestinian Elia Suleiman, the Congolese Zéka Laplaine, and himself, as though to say first cinema celebrity is small compared to the political potential of Third Cinema.

Indeed, like the cowboys in the small-screen western, the celebrity status inflecting first and second cinema seems to be under attack. Sissako even put a famous Hollywood star, Danny Glover, into the small televised movie. Meanwhile, in the larger framing movie he literally marginalizes a gorgeous Senegalese woman (Aïssa Maïga) who plays a nightclub singer.[44] While Hollywood often makes a beautiful woman's story central to the political message—like Julia Roberts in *Erin Brockovich* (2000)—Sissako shows the singer to be indifferent to the court proceedings, impatiently standing in doorways at the margins of the action while seeking someone to help dress her, moving around the courtyard only to serve her individual needs. The first time we see the woman, right after the opening scaffold shot, she sits alone, facing a mirror. In her last appearance she cries while singing, having decided to leave her husband, who proceeds to kill himself. Ironically, despite the fact that her fictional story is marginal compared to *Bamako*'s Third Cinema message—delivered by actual people proclaiming real political concerns in a Bamako court(yard)—the woman's stunning image appears on the DVD box, evidence of first cinema marketing ploys.

Though defying auteurism, Third Cinema nevertheless echoes Bazin and the French New Wave by perpetuating a view of salvation dependent upon binary oppositions. In the case of Third Cinema, salvation relies on community action rather than autonomous efforts, Third World struggle rather than First World privilege, political messages rather than compelling stories.

Salvation from Binaries and Nazis: Structuralism and *John Rabe*

Ironically, just as Third Cinema was quenching the thirst for political agency among "Third World" filmmakers in the 1970s, a different kind of binary theory was intoxicating "First World" cinephiles: an approach to cinema that questioned the very possibility of political agency altogether. Rather than denouncing *cinéma de papa,* this movement adopted a different *papa*: Ferdinand de Saussure (1857–1913), a Swiss linguist.

Saussure established a binary between the old-fashioned "diachronic" study of language—changes through time—and his preferred "synchronic" analysis of meaning at particular moments in history. For him, each linguistic sign, composed of a signifier and a signified, has value according to the particular *system*, or *langue*, that generates its meaning. For example, the sign "gay" has different synchronic value when describing lovers in 1950s romantic comedies than it does when used in films today. Hence, the connection between signifier and signified is "arbitrary," entirely dependent upon the *langue* in which a sign is embedded. People don't create meaning; the system does.

Saussure's disciples applied his theory about signs, or semiology, to cinema. Russian linguist Roman Jakobson, who coined the word *structuralism* in 1929 to explain Saussure's theory, wrote an essay four years later addressing the semiology (often translated "semiotics") of cinema.[45] More famous in film studies, however, is structuralist Roland Barthes, who demonstrated how visual signs, though arbitrary, attain mythic power within their cultural contexts. For example, seventeenth-century Christians, influenced by Talmud scholars, regarded Alpine peaks as signifiers of the fall and hence perceived them as warts and pimples on the face of the earth, whereas today most Christians regard the Alps as signifiers of God's glorious creation and hence perceive them to be sublimely beautiful.[46] In other words, the structural relationship of signifier and signified within a particular *langue* controls the way people actually *see* reality: mountains as ugly versus mountains as beautiful. For Saussure-influenced structuralists, then, Bazin's belief in "the essentially objective character of photography," and hence of mise-en-scène, would seem like the ultimate naiveté.[47] When Bazin argues that "Photography affects us like a phenomenon in nature, like a flower or a snowflake whose vegetable or earthly origins are an inseparable part of their beauty," the structuralist would retort that even signs of nature are not natural; they are culturally informed by synchronic relations between signifier and signified, as in the so-called "beauty" of the Alps.[48]

A sign's synchronic value can be illustrated with *John Rabe* (Florian Gallenberger, 2009), a film set during the infamous Rape of Nanking in 1937. Based on published diaries, the German–Chinese–French collaboration focuses on Rabe (1882–1950), a German businessman who supervised a factory in Nanking for nearly three decades. Though a Nazi party member, Rabe saved his Chinese workers from Germany's Axis allies, the Japanese, when they started strafing his factory. In the film we see him unfurl a huge Nazi flag at ground level, instructing his workers to hide under it. Filmed via crane shot, as though from the bombers' point of view, the red and white flag with its huge black Swastika fills the mise-en-scène as Chinese workers stretch it out above their heads. The image therefore creates discomfort in spectators who have been molded to see the swastika as a sign of death. A signifier that has signaled genocide in almost every film in which it has appeared since 1945 suddenly has a different signified: it is a sign of salvation. Ironically, of course, Rabe regarded the swastika as a sign of salvation from the start. Like the director of a film, his direction of Chinese behavior reflects his own embeddedness in the Nazi *langue*.

Rather than dialectical montage, then, *John Rabe* explores the dialectics of the sign itself—a dialectic that John Rabe, the man, experienced after returning to Germany. Titles at the end of the film explain that Rabe, first detained by Hitler's Gestapo for defying the Japanese invaders, was denounced after the war for his Nazi affiliations, forcing him into poverty—until citizens of Nanking started sending him care packages in gratitude for saving over 200,000 Chinese lives. As a signifier, John Rabe himself signified different things in different contexts.

Death of the Auteur

Just as structuralism undermines Bazin's belief in the objectivity of photography, it also subverts auteur theory. Neither authors nor auteurs create meaning, leading Roland Barthes to hyperbolically proclaim "the death of the author." By this Barthes signaled his sense that authors—like all humans—don't autonomously generate thoughts that they subsequently write up, whether on the page or with a camera-pen. Instead, the signs of a culture precede and hence constitute thought:

it is "language which speaks, not the author."[49] A culture's *langue* generates particular signs at particular times. This, then, would explain why manifestos for Third Cinema and liberation theology appeared within two years of each other: they were synchronic signs developing out of a South American *langue*.

Structuralism also explains why movies about the exact same topic often appear around the same time. Two films about Snow White premiered in 2012: *Mirror Mirror* was released in March, *Snow White and the Huntsman* in June. *Capote*, a film about Truman Capote's writing of *In Cold Blood*, appeared in 2005 while *Infamous*, a film about the exact same topic, was still in production. In 1998, two films about asteroids rocketing toward earth entered theaters within two months of each other (*Deep Impact* then *Armageddon*), while a year earlier two volcano disaster movies appeared on screen (*Dante's Peak* and *Volcano*). In 1997, two films depicting the Tibetan childhood of the Dalai Lama (*Seven Years in Tibet* and *Kundun*) were released within a few months of each other. And, most amazing of all, in 2011 two adapted versions of the same 1912 novel, *War of the Buttons*, premiered on French screens *the very same week*. Ironically, of course, filmmakers want to generate something strikingly original (or at least deliver a unique take on a popular genre) in order to titillate audiences and tilt box-office earnings in their favor.[50] But it would seem that a synchronic system of possibilities (i.e. *langue*) often influences the not-so "original" films Hollywood produces. As Barthes might put it, it is the language preceding film that speaks, not the auteur. Indeed, whereas Truffaut and other New Wave auteurs considered themselves "original" in their rebellion, their defiance of established tradition merely conformed to high modernist belief in the autonomy of the artist. Their so-called new wave in cinematic language reflected the eternally recurring waves of *langue*.

Structuralism influenced several schools of film theory, all of which include an emphasis on binary oppositions. While Laura Mulvey's feminist theory (discussed in Chapter 3) sets up an opposition between object of the gaze and subject of the gaze, genre criticism focuses on binaries visualized on the screen: an opposition between civilization and the wild west in the classic western, an opposition between innocence and guilt in film noir, an opposition between male and female in romantic comedies.[51] Echoing Barthes's idea that language speaks, not the auteur, genre critics assess how genre speaks, analyzing a film's "structure of oppositions."[52] In other words, genres like the western, film noir or the romantic comedy have structural conventions that precede, like *langue*, any one filmic example.

Exceedingly more influential than genre criticism, however, has been an approach to cinema developed by a disciple of Barthes: Christian Metz (1931–93).

Christian Metz and the Semiotics of Cinema: *I Confess* to *The Butler*

In his collection of groundbreaking essays, *Film Language: A Semiotics of the Cinema*,[53] Metz argues that film is not a *langue* in Saussure's sense. In other words, there is not an identifiable system that generates meaningful cinematic signs.

Instead, cinematic meaning reflects a different binary established by Saussure: the paradigmatic versus the syntagmatic relationship between signs.

While the paradigmatic function refers to choosing one sign over another, like choosing a Nazi flag rather than a Chinese flag, the syntagmatic function concerns the way one sign succeeds another, as in the syntax of a sentence. For example, "hunter kills tiger" means something radically different than "tiger kills hunter," even though each sentence is composed of the exact same linguistic signs. The syntactic order creates different meanings. In film, then, the splicing together of shots creates meaning, returning us to the importance of montage.[54] Indeed, Eisenstein reports that before *Battleship Potemkin* was screened in Sweden, authorities re-cut it, rearranging various shots in order to transform a pro-Bolshevik film into a "counter-revolutionary" movie.[55]

In response to Bazin, therefore, Metz argues that the "isolated shot is not even a small fragment of cinema; it is only raw material ... Only by montage can one pass from photography to cinema, from slavish copy to art." However, he also cautions against the "fanaticism" and "ingenious manipulation" of Eisenstein, as though seeking to strike a balance between the problematic binary reinforced by Bazin: the opposition between mise-en-scène and montage.[56] Indeed, Metz emphasizes the importance of the photographed image like Bazin, but he describes it in structuralist terms: "The image is first and always an image. In its perceptual literalness it reproduces the signified spectacle whose signifier it is, and thus it becomes what it shows." Nevertheless, what is *done to* the image (framing, lighting, camera angle, dissolve, tracking shot, etc.) is "the heart of the semiological dimension of film": the medium becomes a message only through "human intervention."[57]

Metz therefore outlines how different kinds of syntagma, the splicing together of shots, communicate different kinds messages. Take, for example, *alternating syntagma*: the cutting back and forth between images, for which he identifies three "cases." The first case is most common, Metz giving the example of "two tennis players framed alternately, at the moment each one is returning the ball."[58] The second case is commonly known as *crosscutting*, wherein "the alternating of the signifiers corresponds to a simultaneity of the significates."[59] In other words (and Metz often needs other words), while the first case signals temporal *succession*—one moment following another as in a tennis match—the second usually indicates temporal *simultaneity*.

For a good example of effective crosscutting, consider *The Butler*, a 2013 film based upon an African American who served as White House butler, starting with Eisenhower's administration, until he finally met the first black man to become President of the United States. In one sequence, the butler Cecil (Forest Whitaker) serves food to well-appointed guests at a lavish presidential dinner party. Meanwhile, his son joins other blacks at a "whites only" café counter in an act of civil disobedience. The camera cuts back and forth between the two very different dining experiences, signaling not only simultaneity of action but also simultaneity of very different attitudes about race: a father accepting his servitude to the white elite, a son protesting the elitist racism of lower-class whites. While the black father pours expensive liquids into crystal goblets for people of privilege, the black son has cheap liquids poured over his body by racist trash. The crosscutting is the message.

The third case of alternating syntagma is more symbolic than temporal and might be illustrated by the intriguing opening sequence from Alfred Hitchcock's *I Confess* (1953). After starting with an establishing shot of the iconic Château Frontenac—signaling a Quebec City location—Hitchcock cuts to a close-up on the Château, shot at an oblique angle (often called a Dutch shot or canted shot) as though to communicate that the story will be about off-kilter human behavior, as in most Hitchcock movies. Indeed, after the canted shot, we are given a long shot of Hitchcock walking across a plaza at the top of stairs: a cameo like those that appear in most of his movies. And then, in a type of pun on this signature, the shot cuts from the image of Hitchcock, the director, to a close-up on a street sign that says "DIRECTION" with an arrow pointing right. With this "sign" the alternating syntagma begins, cutting back and forth between close-ups on DIRECTION signs and shots of different Quebec City locations. After the fourth close-up on DIRECTION, however, the camera pans right, as though following the "direction" of the sign, moving into an open window where we see a murdered body, and moving out again to see a priest running down the street. Employing no dialogue, the medium is the message: under the "direction" of Alfred Hitchcock, which is as much a presence in the film as is the body of the director, the film directs viewers' attention to an off-kilter Quebec City, destabilized by a sordid murder with dark religious associations. Indeed, while the murdered body is shot in high-key lighting, the priest running away is filmed in chiaroscuro. It's all about reading the *signs* of direction.

Metz outlines, among other techniques and devices, eight different kinds of syntagma within the "grammar" of cinema. Rather than perpetuate binaries like that between montage and *mise-en-scène*, or between *auteur* and Hollywood cinema, he thus focuses attention on the relationship between signifier and signified. Doing so, he challenges film analysis where the "discussion is centered around the plot and the human problems it implies," arguing that such analysis examines the signified "without taking the signifiers into consideration."[60] Believing that plot is merely one cinematic "code" among many, Metz focuses on the medium to the near exclusion of story, rarely analyzing at length particular films that might helpfully illustrate the shaping of meaning by cinematic codes.[61] The inverse of scholars who privilege story over medium, Metz hides the light of story under a bushel of semiotic devices.

Metz and Lacan: *Breaking the Waves* of Spectator Psychology

When Metz does look beyond semiotic coding, he merely transfers his attention to spectator psychology, analyzing how cinema parallels dreams and inculcates narcissism.

In 1975, Metz published "The Imaginary Signifier" to highlight three kinds of machines that manipulate film viewers: (1) industrial machines that manufacture movies as profitable commodities; (2) the mental machines of consumers, who are trained to identify with the camera's perspective; and (3) advertising machines, including the film reviews that "vaunt" particular movies. Metz then outlines ingredients that lubricate these various machines, such as viewers' "voyeuristic" satisfaction of being "all-perceiving" without being seen, and reviewers' "fetishism" of the "machinery that is carrying them away."[62]

Metz's terminology sounds much like that of Laura Mulvey, whose discussion of "the male gaze" was explored in Chapter 3 above. This is because both were influenced by Jacques Lacan, who applied Saussure's semiology to psychoanalysis.[63] Believing that a sense of identity is energized by visual images—first through a baby's identification of self in a mirror—Lacan argues that identity is completed only when one enters into the realm of "the Symbolic": the realm of culturally shaped signifiers that create signified reality in people's minds. As he puts it, "perception is not in me," but rather "on the objects that it apprehends."[64] For example, when mountains generate emotions of uplift and awe, people assume those emotions express their individualized perceptions of what is beautiful. In actuality, their "reality" of emotional uplift has been culturally constructed—as is the "reality" mirrored on any cinema screen. Culturally contingent signifiers explain why monsters that genuinely terrified viewers in 1950s movies elicit laughter when seen today: contemporary psyches have been shaped by machines generating more digitally enhanced, albeit similarly fantastical, signifiers. For Lacan, then, "reality" is what people get in exchange for entering the realm of the Symbolic.[65]

Lacanian structuralism might be illustrated through Lars von Trier's 1996 film *Breaking the Waves*. Bess McNeill, played by the amazing Emily Watson, lives in a remote Scottish village in the 1970s. Several times we see her kneel in prayer. As she unfolds her heart to God, suddenly she starts speaking in a stern lower register, as though channeling God's response. The severe voice, duplicating the austere piety (and Scottish brogue) of the church elders, tells her what to do. In structuralist terms, Bess has absorbed the realm of the Symbolic, what Lacan calls "*le nom du père*," or "the name of the father."

Significantly, in Lacan's original French, *le nom du père* sounds like *le non du père* or "the no of the father." Employing this pun, Lacan makes a structuralist point: individuals' understanding of reality arises from the signifiers of the discourse in which they are embedded. Bess's pysche, then, has been formed by the religious laws (the various "No's") of the church fathers, evident when a clergyman chides her from the pulpit: "No woman speaks here!" Lars von Trier seems to channel Lacan, in fact, when he says of his movie, "The priest talks about loving the Word and the Law ... That's what would make a person complete."[66] Bess, however, develops a different understanding of love, telling the priest, "You can't love the Word. You can only love a person." After her beloved husband, Jan (Stellan Skarsgård), is paralyzed in an oil rig accident, she encounters a radically different Symbolic language. Jan tells her to have sex with other men and then to describe it to him, saying "It will feel like you and me being together again. And that, that will keep me alive." Though made miserable by this idea, as well as by the abusive practice, Bess offers her body to total strangers. Scholars have therefore suggested that Bess represents Christ-like sacrificial love.[67]

Astutely challenging such scholars, Alyda Faber cites a feminist theorist influenced by Lacan: Julia Kristeva. As Faber puts it, Kristeva regarded "transgressive sexuality as a practice that constitutes hierarchy *within patriarchal orders*."[68] Or, to put it in Lacanian terms, Bess merely transitions from one oppressive *nom du père* to another, as reflected in another prayer. This time, after asking God, "Am I going to go to Hell?" Bess channels a response that sounds more like Jan than the church elders. Missing the denunciatory austerity and the Scottish brogue, Bess channels the words "Whom do you want to save? Yourself or Jan?" This implied parallel between the voice of God and the voice of Jan is reinforced by the medium. As Faber notes, "The aerial view above the action of the film, implied as the God's-eye-view, is inhabited by Jan in one shot as he returns via helicopter to the oil rig after his marriage to Bess."[69]

Some might invoke this parallel in order to denounce religion in its entirety, arguing that religious vocabularies endorse a transcendent "name of the Father" that monitors behavior. Kristeva is not so simplistic. In 1979 she argued that "Feminist ideology leaves the door open to the return of religion, whose discourse, tried and proved over thousands of years, provides the necessary ingredients for satisfying the anguish, the suffering, and the hope of mothers."[70] This assumption harmonizes with Lacan, who posited a "Real" that transcends *le nom du père* of "reality," a "Real" that exceeds a principle of exchange between signifier and signified: a "Real" that some people align with God, others with Nirvana.[71] Nevertheless, as soon as people name the "Real" as God, or Allah, or Yahweh, or Nirvana, they must employ signifiers instituted by the *nom du père* of the religion with which they identify.

This might explain why religion, like sex, operates all too often according to principles of exchange. While Calvinist elders teach Bess that good behavior gets heaven in exchange, Jan convinces Bess that seducing strangers will get his healing in exchange: opposite sides of the same coin.[72] In contrast, "real" love is a gift, which by its very definition requires nothing in exchange. As Bess tells God in one of her early prayers, "I thank you for the greatest gift of all—the gift of love." Significantly, Lacan uses the phrase "active gift of love" to endorse a stance that looks "towards the being of the loved subject, towards his particularity," as opposed to seeing the "other" according to the "screen" of culturally endorsed signifiers.[73] It seems perfectly appropriate, then, that Lars von Trier directs Bess to look beyond the screen on which she is placed, having her break the fourth wall twice in the film. The device implies that Bess looks beyond the "reality" framed by patriarchy, looking out of the screen to a "Real" that exceeds culturally constructed signifiers.[74]

Salvation in *Breaking the Waves* therefore occurs not when Bess offers her body to strangers who share the screen with her, but when she asks forgiveness of people who do not deserve it, looking to a "Real" beyond their denunciatory signifiers. Hospitalized after a beating during one of her brutish sexual encounters, Bess expresses only tender love to her judgmental mother, saying

"I am sorry." And though her grandfather refuses to visit her and bans her from the church, Bess offers him an unwarranted gift: "Tell him that I love him." Hence, the church bells welcoming Bess to heaven in the last shot of the film celebrate an "active gift of love" that rises above the manipulative "reality" of each *nom du père*.

Lacan, Althusser, and *Screen* Theory: *Titanic* Delusions

While *Breaking the Waves* illustrates *le nom du père* imposed on Bess, most film theorists interested in Lacan explore *le nom du père* imposed on movie spectators. Indeed, in conjunction with Metz, Lacan powerfully influenced the apparatus theory introduced in Chapter 1, whereby the cinematic apparatus manipulates viewers to identify with their protagonists, encouraging belief that the characters act and talk the way actual people would in similar situations. As Kent Brintnall summarizes, "the spectator is not a person, but rather a site of identity generated through the interaction of the film and the viewer's unconscious fantasies, desires, and wishes."[75] Like prisoners in Plato's allegory of the cave, spectators are thus oblivious to the apparatus that generates false images of "reality."

This assumption was given a Marxist twist by film theorists publishing in the British journal *Screen* during the 1970s. They viewed Lacan through the lens of Louis Althusser, a Marxist structuralist who argued that signs generated by multiple institutions—religion, cinema, politics, education, art, etc.—reinforce values buttressing capitalism. Calling these institutions Ideological State Apparatuses, Althusser asserts that they control not only the way people act but also how they think about their very identities.[76] For *Screen* theorists, then, film spectators are manipulated by signs of an exciting "reality" coded with *le nom du père* of capitalism, reinforcing a principle of exchange by which protagonists are rewarded with personal gain, whether through money, romance, or admiration. These protagonists, with whom viewers identify, usually break rules in order to preserve (rather than transform) society, thus maintaining an oppressive status quo.[77]

Titanic provides a good example. The winner of numerous Academy Awards, including Best Picture and Best Director (James Cameron), the 1997 release was the highest-grossing film in history until supplanted in 2010 by James Cameron's *Avatar*. Leonardo DiCaprio plays Jack, a young man who wins passage on Titanic's 1912 voyage in a poker game. Onboard ship, he meets the charming Rose (Kate Winslet), whose mother plans to marry her off to the wealthy but despicable Cal. As Rose falls in love with Jack, she discovers that the poor people in steerage have much more fun than the rich snobs luxuriating on decks above. We see the laborers dancing and partying together in class solidarity, while the wealthy passengers look bored to death as they eat off expensive china and engage in stultifying small talk. Then, after the *Titanic* hits an iceberg, the wealthy Cal—who almost always wears black—cheats his way onto a lifeboat, whereas the poor Jack—who almost always wears white—risks his life to save others, ultimately dying so that Rose might live. All the signifiers point to wealthy capitalists as bad, poor laborers as good.

Having been influenced by *le nom du père* of Lacan, Althusser would most likely respond that these apparently "subversive" signifiers in *Titanic* actually reinforce capitalist ideology. For by showing those in steerage to be happier and to have more integrity than the wealthy people above, the film maintains *le nom du père* of capitalism by eliminating any motivation for revolt. Why would the proletariat down below seek to overthrow a system that keeps them happier than those with capital above? The filmmakers, it would seem, have been so molded by bourgeois ideology that even when they attempt to be subversive they end up perpetuating the status quo.[78]

Though some might justly scoff at this reading of James Cameron's film, there is no denying the complicity of capitalism with Hollywood. After *Titanic* became titanic in its financial returns, stores all across America sold reproductions of Rose's expensive diamond necklace—the signifier motivating much of the action in *Titanic*—thus undermining the potential for any subversive film message about the marginalized poor. Romance, it would seem, is purchasable. Like Rose's sparkling diamond, then, Hollywood films become identified with a "glossiness" in which multiple signifiers "are arranged together as a single object of consumption by the camera lens," as Marxist critic Fredric Jameson puts it.[79] Especially insidious are merchandise tie-ins with children's movies, reducing signifiers within film to purchasable (and hence disposable) commodities.

The word *insidious*, however, could also describe the apparatus and *Screen* theorists who turned semiology into a *nom du père* as oppressive as those in *Breaking the Waves*. They regarded film spectators as passive recipients of capitalist ideology, internalizing arbitrary "truths" that reinforce their "subject-positions" within society. For these scholars, the word *subjective* no longer signified autonomous opinion; it referenced *subjection* to semiotic apparatuses. As film theorist Stephen Heath succinctly puts it, "the subject is an effect of the signifier."[80] Not surprisingly, many Marxist scholars became concerned about the loss of human agency such subjection implied, for it undermined any possibility of reform or revolt. They therefore helped ignite, in response, the academic discipline known as cultural studies, which looks beyond economic issues in order to assess other elements of culture that shape identity. Considering how race, class, ethnicity, nationality, gender, sexuality, and religion affect perception, cultural studies influenced the development of reception studies in film. It is no wonder that scholars in religion and film picked up on this trend, some turning away from religious messages on the screen in order to emphasize the religious implications of viewer response, as discussed in Chapter 1.[81]

Nevertheless, by ignoring the artistry of medium-specific devices, scholars interested in audience reception ended up mimicking the psychoanalytic structuralists they were reacting against. Both approaches impose theoretical/religious paradigms on cinema rather than allowing individual films to speak for themselves. As a result, true believers in both groups tend to find what they are looking for, identifying capitalist or racist or (hetero)sexist or imperialist assumptions—much like people who see Christ-figures every time actors die with outspread arms. By the mid 1980s, a reaction had set in, film specialists suggesting the need for an entirely different approach to cinema, one that emphasized active viewer cognition over the passivity implied by ideological and cultural control.

Post-Theory: Cognitivism

By the end of the twentieth century, philosopher Noël Carroll and film professor David Bordwell had ignited "cognitivism," an approach to cinema that defies "Grand Theory": their term for paradigms influenced not only by Saussure, Lacan, and Althusser, but also by the cultural studies movement that rose up in response. In contrast to the psychoanalytic bent of Grand Theory, which emphasizes unconscious processes manipulated by multiple linguistic and/or cultural apparatuses, cognitivism argues for *conscious* analysis of screen signifiers and their emotional effects. As part of their "inductive" approach to cinema, Bordwell and Carroll also advocate "empirical" research about the historical development of cinema technology, exhibition, and aesthetics.[82] Nevertheless, even though they titled a collaborative book *Post-Theory*, Bordwell and Carroll do not dismiss film theory in its entirety. Instead, using terminology like "belief system," "doctrine," and "high-church Structuralism" to describe aspects of Grand Theory, they challenge an approach to cinema that echoes religious certitude. As Carroll colorfully puts it, "To stamp one's feet and to insist that every dimension of film must have an ideological dimension ... is simply dogmatic."[83]

The word *dogma* comes from a Greek word—*dokein*—meaning "to believe." Religious dogma is made up of communally shared beliefs inspired by revelations from prophets like Moses, Isaiah, Buddha, Confucius, St. Paul, Muhammad, and Joseph Smith. Taken by faith, dogma is verified by its transformative power in believers. Dogmatism, in contrast, parallels what Umberto Eco calls the "Fundamentalist Fallacy," which is "instantiated when one assumes that his/her own philosophy is the only valid philosophy ... (and demands a universal agreement on such a statement)."[84] It is this fallacy that Bordwell and Carroll see operative in Grand Theory.

Many people respond to the fundamentalist fallacy—in both religion and film—by preaching tolerance for all positions. As a universal panacea, however, "tolerance" differs little from an Ideological State Apparatus, for it discourages critical thinking and hence motivation for reform and revolt. After all, many abusive practices done in the name of God/Yahweh/Allah should *not* be tolerated. Carroll takes a similar perspective when it comes to film theory. Though advocating plural approaches to the study of cinema, he also "hopes that some [theories] will be eliminated through processes of criticism and comparison in light of certain questions and the relevant evidence."[85] In other words, rather than starting with an overriding theory about (or theology of) cinema—and then finding filmic examples to verify that theory or theology—viewers should consider the cognitive power of visual art, not in search of transcendence, but in order to appreciate the immanence of cinematic technique, an immanence that may well speak to the culturally constructed biases of religion. Nevertheless, the *semiotics of cinema*—generated by signs on the screen—communicates first: the medium is the message.

At this point, some cognitivists might protest, arguing that "semiotics" should not sully a paragraph discussing Noël Carroll. Like Christians who protest the practice of Yoga because of its association with Asian religions, such cognitivists think semiotic analysis should be avoided because of its association with Grand Theory. However, just as Yoga (as a technique rather than an ideology) can help Christians meditate on their relationship with God, so semiotics (as a technique rather than an ideology) can help cognitivists analyze the relationship between mental processes and screen devices. This, in fact, is the tack taken by film scholar Warren Buckland. In *The Cognitive Semiotics of Film* Buckland argues that, unlike Anglo-American cognitivists, European film specialists have synthesized cognitivism with semiotics to achieve a productive "balance," one that considers not simply cognitive processes but also the body and its relation to language.[86]

As with multiple religions, then, cautions against dogmatism are as relevant to Post-Theory as they are to Grand Theory. The fundamentalist fallacy tempts anyone who defines their approach to cinema in contradistinction to that of their predecessors, from the *cinéma de papa* denounced by Truffaut to the *nom du père* descried by Lacan. Not coincidentally, one film scholar names his discussion of film theory with a phrase lifted directly from the Hebrew Scriptures: "The Sins of the Fathers."[87] The next Chapter of *Salvation from Cinema*, in contrast, explores the forgiveness of sins. It does so with the aid of Jacques Derrida, who exposed the limitations of structuralism decades before Bordwell and Carroll challenged Grand Theory. Doing so, Derrida helped initiate "the religious turn" in philosophy, making him relevant, on several different levels, to the field of religion and film.[88]

Notes

1 Robert Stam, *Film Theory: An Introduction* (Malden: Blackwell, 2000), 25.
2 I lifted the phrase "Where is the transcendence …?" from Craig Detweiler, *Into the Dark: Seeing the Sacred in the Top Films of the 21st Century* (Grand Rapids: Baker, 2008), 69. Though Detweiler is not talking about early twentieth-century attitudes toward film, his phrase captures the response of many thoughtful Christians toward film.
3 Quoted in David A. Cook, *A History of Narrative Film*, 2nd edn (New York: Norton, 1990), 13, emphasis mine.
4 Martin Loiperdinger, "Lumière's *Arrival of the Train*: Cinema's Founding Myth," *The Moving Image* 4.1 (2004): 89–118; Joseph Gaer, *What the Great Religions Believe* (New York: Signet, 1963), 23.
5 Stephen Bottomore, "The Panicking Audience? Early Cinema and the 'Train Effect'," *Historical Journal of Film, Radio and Television* 19.2 (1999):186, emphasis mine. Seeds for the founding myth were planted by Maxim Gorky, who published his response to seeing *L'Arrivée d'un train*: "It darts like an arrow straight towards you—watch out!" But rather than saying people jumped out of the way, he notes that "this, too, is merely a train of shadows." Quoted in Gerard Loughlin, *Alien Sex: The Body and Desire in Cinema and Theology* (Malden: Blackwell, 2004), 101n. 76. Perpetuating the myth are André Bazin, *What Is Cinema?*, trans. Hugh Gray, vol. 1 (Berkeley: University of California Press, 1967), 45; and Christian Metz, *The Imaginary Signifier: Psychoanalysis and the Cinema*, trans. Celia Britton, Annwyl Williams, Ben Brewster, and Alfred Guzzetti (Bloomington: Indiana University Press, 1977), 73.

6 The phrase "In Film, Story Reigns Supreme" comes from a Chapter title in Robert K. Johnston, *Reel Spirituality: Theology and Film in Dialogue* (Grand Rapids: Baker Academic, 2006).
7 Quoted in Walter Benjamin, "The Work of Art in the Age of Its Technological Reproducibility," *The Norton Anthology of Theory and Criticism*, 2nd edn, ed. Vincent B. Leitch, et al. (New York: Norton, 2010), 1054–5. Benjamin's essay is considered canonical in film theory.
8 Ibid., 1059.
9 Ibid., 1068.
10 Max Horkheimer and Theodor W. Adorno, *Dialectic of Enlightenment*, trans. John Cumming (New York: Continuum, 1972), 140. Theodor Adorno and Hanns Eisler, *Composing for the Films* (1947; Oxford: Oxford University Press, 1969).
11 Marshall McLuhan, *Understanding Media: The Extensions of Man* (New York: McGraw-Hill, 1964), 294. Mark K. Stahlman considers McLuhan "one of the most profound Catholic intellectuals of the modern era." See "The Place of Marshall McLuhan in the Learning of His Times," *Renascence: Essays on Values in Literature* 64.1 (Fall 2011): 5.
12 Tom Wolfe, "Snob's Progress," *New York Times*, June 15, 1986.
13 As recounted by Graham McCann, Adorno's name did not appear as co-author of the first edition, published by Oxford University Press, "in order to avoid being implicated" in Eisler's communist associations. Adorno was first acknowledged on the cover in a 1969 edition. Graham McCann, "New Introduction" to Theodor Adorno and Hanns Eisler, *Composing for the Films* (New York: Continuum, 2007), xxx–xxxi.
14 The award-nominated scores were for *Hangmen Also Die!* (Fritz Lang, 1943) and *None but the Lonely Heart* (Clifford Odets, 1944).
15 Adorno and Eisler, *Composing for the Films*, 52, 104, 107. They cite Eisenstein's book *The Film Sense* (New York: Harcourt, Brace, 1941), which discusses music in a Chapter entitled "Form and Content: Practice" (157–216).
16 Cook, *A History of Narrative Film*, 162–3. Cook provides a shot-by-shot reproduction of the Odessa Steps sequence (166–75).
17 See Gilles Deleuze, *Cinema 2: The Time-Image*, trans. Hugh Tomlinson and Robert Galeta (Minneapolis: University of Minnesota Press, 1989), 162–3.
18 André Malraux, *Outlines of a Psychology of the Cinema*, first published in *Verve* 8.2 (1940), was later reprinted in Susanne K. Langer, ed., *Reflections on Art: A Source-Book of Writings by Artists, Critics, and Philosophers* (New York: Oxford University Press, 1961), 317–27.
19 Bazin, *What Is Cinema?*, vol 1, 13, 35–6. Bazin's assumptions about viewer engagement have long been challenged. Charles Affron, for example, argues, contra Bazin, that the "processes of Eisensteinian montage force the viewer to create the film." See *Cinema and Sentiment* (Chicago: University of Chicago Press, 1982), 76.
20 Bazin, *What Is Cinema?*, vol 1, 27, 26. Roberto Rossellini, praised by Bazin for energizing Italian neorealism, once said "Things are. Why manipulate them?" Quoted in Christian Metz, *Film Language: A Semiotics of the Cinema*, trans. Michael Taylor (Chicago: University of Chicago Press, 1974), 36.
21 Stam, *Film Theory*, 76.
22 *Nouvelle Vague* was coined in 1957 by journalist François Giroud to describe the current generation exuberantly rising from the ashes of World War II. The term was appropriated not much later to describe the new generation of filmmakers. See Genette Vincendeau, "Fifty Years of the French New Wave: From Hysteria to Nostalgia," in *The French New Wave: Critical Landmarks*, ed. Peter Graham (New York: Palgrave Macmillan, 2009), 6. Vincendeau's superb overview captures the political and aesthetic nuances of the movement, as well as of scholarly responses to it.
23 Bazin's statement was first published in *Cahiers du cinéma*, and republished in Bazin, *What Is Cinema?*, vol 1, 39.

24 François Truffaut, "A Certain Tendency of the French Cinema," in *The Film Studies Reader*, ed. Joanne Hollows, Peter Hutchings, and Mark Jancovich (New York: Oxford University Press, 2000), 59, 62.
25 The term *auteur* long preceded the French New Wave. Jean Epstein described filmmakers as auteurs in 1921. See Stam, *Film Theory*, 33, 85.
26 Vincendeau explains that "Truffaut's insolent oedipal rebellion against the '*cinéma de papa*' attacked the hegemonic 'well-made films' that displayed the craft of the French film industry" ("Fifty Years of the French New Wave: From Hysteria to Nostalgia," 3). The phrase *cinéma de papa* seems to have been coined by French actor Jean Narboni in the March 1967 issue of *Cahiers du cinéma*.
27 The image is also reminiscent of the zoetrope, a spinning toy with slots at the top through which pictures are viewed. Film historians often identify the zoetrope, invented in 1834, as a precursor of movies. See Cook, *A History of Narrative Film*, 2.
28 Bazin, *What Is Cinema?*, vol 1, 105.
29 As has been said of Hitchcock, "the director authenticates the fact that it is indeed he who is making the film, claiming it as his own." Peter Brunette and David Wills, *Screen/Play: Derrida and Film Theory* (Princeton: Princeton University Press, 1989), 123.
30 Biographical details come from the commentary by Glenn Kenny, film critic for *Premiere* magazine, that are included on the 1999 Fox Lorber DVD of *400 Blows*.
31 Bazin, *What Is Cinema?*, vol 1, 106.
32 The comment appears in an article published in an April 1959 issue of *Arts*, and is reprinted (trans. Tom Milne) in a booklet included with *The Criterion Collection DVD of* Breathless (2007): 28.
33 Ronald Abramson, "Structure and Meaning in the Cinema," in *Movies and Methods: An Anthology*, vol. 1, ed. Bill Nichols (Berkeley: University of California Press, 1982), 561.
34 Andrew Sarris, "Notes on the *auteur* theory in 1962," in *The Film Studies Reader*, 69.
35 Vincendeau, "Fifty Years of the French New Wave: From Hysteria to Nostalgia," 13.
36 Fernando Solanas and Ottavio Getino, "Towards a Third Cinema," in *Reviewing Histories: Selections from New Latin American Cinema*, ed. Coco Fusco (Buffalo: Hallwall's, 1987), 56–81.
37 For the multifaceted development of Third Cinema, see Ella Shohat and Robert Stam, *Unthinking Eurocentrism: Multiculturalism and the Media* (London: Routledge, 1994).
38 Consider this comment by Jean-Luc Godard: "The cinema is not a craft. It is an art. It does not mean teamwork. One is always alone on the set as before the blank page." Quoted in Dudley Andrew, "*Breathless* Then and Now," the Criterion DVD booklet, 19.
39 As Philip Rosen summarizes, second cinema "auteurs and films remain subordinated to the tradition of aesthetics, that is, bourgeois notions such as beauty and universality, rather than functionality in a sociopolitical struggle." See "Notes on Art Cinema and the Emergence of Sub-Saharan Film," *Global Art Cinema: New Theories and Histories*, ed. Rosalind Galt and Karl Schoonover (New York: Oxford University Press, 2010), 255.
40 Helping ignite Third Cinema was Brazilian director Glauber Rocha's manifesto "Aesthetics of Hunger" (1965). For discussion of liberation theology related to film, see Christopher Deacy, "From Bultmann to Burton, Demythologizing the Big Fish: The Contribution of Modern Christian Theologians to the Theology–Film Conversation," in *Reframing Theology and Film: New Focus for an Emerging Discipline*, ed. Robert K. Johnston (Grand Rapids: Baker Academic, 2007), 239–42. For the imbrication of Third Cinema and religion, see Antonio D. Sison, "Perfumed Nightmare: Religion and the Philippine Postcolonial Struggle in Third Cinema," in *Representing Religion in World Cinema: Filmmaking, Mythmaking, Culture Making*, ed. S. Brent Plate (New York: Palgrave Macmillan, 2003), 181–6.

118 Salvation from Film Theory

41 Stam, *Film Theory*, 92–3, 281–7.
42 Glen M. Mimura, *Ghostlife of Third Cinema: Asian American Film and Video* (Minneapolis: University of Minnesota Press, 2009), 55–8. See also Ella Shohat, "Post-Third-Worldist Culture: Gender, Nation, and the Cinema," in *Rethinking Third Cinema*, ed. Anthony R. Guneratne and Wimal Dissanayake (New York: Routledge, 2003), 51–78.
43 Details about the making of *Bamako* come from Rachel Gabara, "Abderrahmane Sissako: Second and Third Cinema in the First Person," *Global Art Cinema*, 329–31.
44 Danny Glover helped produce the movie. Ibid., 330.
45 Roman Jakobson, "Is the Cinema in Decline?" trans. E. Sokol, in *Russian Formalist Film Theory* (Ann Arbor: University of Michigan Press, 1981), 161–6. The essay, originally published in 1933, defended the advent of sound in cinema.
46 Roland Barthes, *Mythologies*, trans. Annette Lavers (New York: Hill & Wang, 1972). Though Barthes does discuss the nineteenth-century craze for "picturesque" mountains (74–5), the example of the Alps is my own, based on the work of Marjorie Hope Nicholson, *Mountain Gloom and Mountain Glory: The Development of the Aesthetics of the Infinite* (New York: Norton, 1963). See pp. 35, 42, 62, 76, and 116 for pre-nineteenth-century denunciations of mountains.
47 As Stephen Heath put it in 1973, "there is a crucial and urgent necessity to finish with the flow of (ideologically complicit) drivel that currently and massively passes as 'film-criticism.'" See "Introduction: Questions of Emphasis," *Screen* 14.1/2 (Spring/Summer 1973): 9.
48 Bazin, *What Is Cinema?*, 13. Daniel Morgan argues that Bazin's thought is more complex than dismissive structuralists made it out to be. See "Rethinking Bazin: Ontology and Realist Aesthetics," *Critical Inquiry* 32 (Spring 2006): 443–81.
49 Roland Barthes, *Image—Music—Text*, trans. Stephen Heath (London: Fontana, 1977), 143. For his views on cinema, see Roland Barthes, "Towards a Semiotics of Cinema," interview with Michel Delahaye and Jacques Rivette, tr. Annwyl Williams, in *Cahiers du Cinéma, Volume 2, 1960–1968: New Wave, New Cinema, Reevaluating Hollywood*, ed. Jim Hillier (Cambridge: Harvard University Press, 1986), 276–85. Barthes also discusses cinematic signs in *Mythologies* (39–40, 94–6).
50 "A study of studio publicity materials" established that, rather than "familiarity," it was "difference and newness that studios employed in order to sell their products." Azadeh Farahmand, "Disentangling the International Festival Circuit: Genre and Iranian Cinema," in *Global Art Cinema*, 265.
51 According to *The Film Studies Dictionary*, by Steve Blandford, Barry D. Grant, and Jim Hillier (London: Arnold, 2001), the romantic comedy "operates almost exclusively with respect to heterosexual relationships" (202).
52 Joanne Hollows, Peter Hutchings, and Mark Jancovich, "Genre Criticism," in *The Film Studies Reader*, 85. The most famous structuralist approach to genre is that by Thomas Schatz, *Hollywood Genres: Formulas, Filmmaking, and the Studio System* (Philadelphia: Temple University Press, 1981).
53 The book was first published in 1971 as *Essais sur la signification au cinéma*. The English translation, as noted above, was published in 1974. The translator's use of the word "semiotics" in the title reflects how scholars replaced Saussure's term *semiology* with the word *semiotic*, borrowed from American philosopher Charles Sanders Peirce, who will be discussed in Chapter 7. (The "s" was added to semiotics by anthropologist Margaret Mead.)
54 My analogy implies that a "shot" is comparable to a "word" in a sentence, but Metz argues against this common idea of cinema language. For him, each "filmic shot is of the *magnitude of the sentence*." For Metz, even a close-up on a revolver is not a cinematic "word"; it is a sentence stating "Here is a revolver!" Hence "the smallest filmic unit is the 'sentence'." Metz, *Film Language*, 86, 67, 84, emphasis his.

55 Johannes Ehrat, *Cinema and Semiotic: Peirce and Film Aesthetics, Narration, and Representation* (Toronto: University of Toronto Press, 2005), 416.
56 Metz, *Film Language*, 32, 33. Bazin perpetuates binary thinking when he refers to the "long-standing opposition between realism and aestheticism on the screen." See *What Is Cinema?*, vol. 2, trans. Hugh Gray (Berkeley: University of California Press, 1971), 16.
57 Metz, *Film Language*, 75–6, 101, 98.
58 Ibid., 105.
59 Ibid., 103. Unfortunately, as my quotation illustrates, Metz's vocabulary is not that helpful, largely due to the "scientific" pretensions of semiotic theory, which is rife with neologisms.
60 Ibid., 143.
61 Christian Metz introduced the idea of "codes" in *Language and Cinema*, trans. Donna Jean Umiker-Sebeok (The Hague: Mouton, 1974). As he puts it, "the specificity which interests semiotics is the specificity of codes, not the 'crude' specificity of physical signifiers" (219).
62 Christian Metz, "The Imaginary Signifier," *Screen* 16.2 (1975): 14–76. I quote from its reprint in Christian Metz, *The Imaginary Signifier: Psychoanalysis and the Cinema*, trans. Ben Brewster (Bloomington: Indiana University Press, 1982), 49, 14, 63, 48, 74. Metz also invokes Freudian distinctions between "primary" and "secondary" psychical processes and between "condensation" and "displacement" in the dream-work in order to align them with various structuralist binaries: paradigm/syntagm from Saussure; imaginary/symbolic from Lacan; metaphor/metonymy from Jakobson. "The Imaginary Signifier" includes over fifty binary oppositions in its index.
63 See, especially, Jacques Lacan, "The Mirror Stage as Formative of the Function of the 'I' as Revealed in Psychoanalytic Experience," in *Écrits: A Selection*, trans. Alan Sheridan (New York: Norton, 1997), 1–7.
64 Jacques Lacan, *The Four Fundamental Concepts of Psycho-Analysis*, trans. Alan Sheridan (New York: Norton, 1978), 80.
65 Many film theorists who appropriate Lacan discuss ways that the cinematic medium "sutures" various "lacks": viewers, sensing their lack of viewing omnipotence, are sutured into the film through sutures of montage, such as shot/reverse shot, which enable them to identify with protagonists' points of view. For a lucid summary of suture theory, see Kaja Silverman, *The Subject of Semiotics* (New York: Oxford University Press, 1983), 194–236. For an application of suture theory to religion and film, see Steve Nolan, *Film, Lacan and the Subject of Religion: A Psychoanalytic Approach to Religious Film Analysis* (London: Continuum, 2009), 80–154. Rather than reiterating what Nolan has done so thoroughly, I relegate suture theory to this footnote.
66 Lars von Trier, with Christian Braad Thomsen, "Trier on von Trier," in *The Religion and Film Reader*, ed. Jolyon Mitchell and S. Brent Plate (New York: Routledge, 2007), 232.
67 See James M. Wall, "Paradoxical Goodness," *The Christian Century* 114 (February 1997): 115. Loughlin says of Bess, "She is simply a saint who loves as Christ loves" (*Alien Sex*, 178). To his credit, Loughlin also acknowledges feminist critique of this interpretation (195n. 15).
68 Alyda Faber, "Redeeming Sexual Violence? A Feminist Reading of *Breaking the Waves*," *Literature and Theology*, 17.1 (March 2003): 63, 65, emphasis hers.
69 Ibid., 70.
70 Julia Kristeva, "Women's Time," in *Critical Theory since 1965*, ed. Hazard Adams and Leroy Searle (Tallahassee: Florida State UP, 1986), 482. See also C. W. Maggie Kim, Susan M. St. Ville, and Susan M. Simonaitis, eds, *Transfigurations: Theology and the French Feminists* (Minneapolis: Fortress, 1993).
71 Assessing film and other media through the lens of the Lacanian "Real," Slavoj Žižek writes "What lies beyond is not the symbolic order but a real kernel." See *The Sublime Object of Ideology* (New York: Verso, 1989), 132.

72 An economy of exchange is reflected when Bess tells Jan's doctor, "I don't make love with [the stranger], I make love with Jan and I save him from dying."
73 Jacques Lacan, *The Seminar of Jacques Lacan, Book I: Freud's Papers on Technique, 1953–54*, trans. John Forrester (Cambridge: Cambridge University Press, 1988), 276. Lacan employs the term "screen," rather than "mirror," to describe how identity is molded by the "gaze" of culture, in *Four Fundamental Concepts of Psycho-Analysis*, trans. Alan Sheridan (New York: Norton, 1978), 67–119.
74 Greg Watkins similarly argues that, by looking into the camera, Bess "apparently sees God in a way no other character in the film does and apparently has an intimacy with God no other character has." Greg Watkins, "Seeing and Being Seen: Distinctively Filmic and Religious Elements in Film," *Journal of Religion and Film* 3.2 (October 1999): 3.
75 Kent Brintnall, "Psychoanalysis," in *The Routledge Companion to Religion and Film*, ed. John Lyden (London: Routledge, 2009), 302. Brintnall adeptly summarizes psychoanalytic film theory.
76 Joel W. Martin and Conrad E. Ostwalt Jr. provide a lucid, though brief, summation of Althusser in their introductions to essays in *Screening the Sacred: Religion, Myth, and Ideology in Popular American Film* (Boulder: Westview Press, 1995), 3, 120–1, 173n. 8.
77 Some argue that *Screen* theorists misunderstood Lacan. See Julie Kelso, "Gazing at Impotence in Henry King's *David and Bathsheba*," in *Screening Scripture: Intertextual Connections between Scripture and Film*, ed. George Aichele and Richard Walsh (Harrisburg: Trinity, 2002), 165–71; and Nolan, especially 173n. 1.
78 I have adapted these last two paragraphs from my *Changing Signs of Truth* (Downers Grove: IUP Academic, 2012), 149.
79 Fredric Jameson, *Signatures of the Visible* (New York: Routledge, 1990), 135.
80 Stephen Heath, *Questions of Cinema* (Bloomington: Indiana University Press, 1981), 14. Heath discusses the influence of Saussure on cinema on pp. 194–9.
81 For an astute assessment of cultural studies and film, see Stam, *Film Theory*, 223–9. For the applicability of cultural studies to religion and film, see Gordon Lynch, "Cultural Theory and Cultural Studies," in *The Routledge Companion to Religion and Film*, 275–91.
82 David Bordwell, "Contemporary Film Studies and the Vicissitudes of Grand Theory," in *Post-Theory: Reconstructing Film Studies*, ed. David Bordwell and Noël Carroll (Madison: University of Wisconsin Press, 1996), 23, 25, 28.
83 Noël Carroll, "Prospects for Film Theory: A Personal Assessment," in *Post-Theory*, 47, 51. The phrase "high-church Structuralism" comes from Bordwell, "Contemporary Film Studies and the Vicissitudes of Grand Theory," 13. Similarly, Jean Mitry indicts the "choking dogmatism" of Metz's followers for the demise of film semiotics in *Semiotics and the Analysis of Film*, trans. Christopher King (London: Athlone, 2000), 259.
84 Umberto Eco, "Semiotics and the Philosophy of Language," in *Reading Eco: An Anthology*, ed. Rocco Capozzi (Bloomington: Indiana University Press, 1997), 7.
85 Carroll, "Prospects for Film Theory: A Personal Assessment," 63.
86 Warren Buckland, *The Cognitive Semiotics of Film* (Cambridge: Cambridge University Press, 2000). See especially pp. 2–3 and 31–2. Buckland, like the "cognitive film semioticians" he celebrates, appeals to the semiotic theory of Charles Sanders Peirce, the focus of Chapter 7 herein.
87 Victor F. Perkins, *Film as Film: Understanding and Judging Movies* (New York: Penguin, 1972).
88 See John D. Caputo, *The Prayers and Tears of Jacques Derrida: Religion without Religion* (Bloomington: Indiana University Press, 1997); Hent de Vries, *Philosophy and the Turn to Religion* (Baltimore: Johns Hopkins University Press, 1999); and Yvonne Sherwood and Kevin Hart, eds, *Derrida and Religion: Other Testaments* (New York: Routledge, 2005).

6 The Gift of Salvation
Derrida and Holocaust Cinema

A little over a decade after François Truffaut published "A Certain Tendency in French Cinema," Jacques Derrida challenged a certain tendency in French semiology.[1] Reviled like Truffaut, who helped ignite a "New Wave" in filmmaking, Derrida helped ignite a new wave in structuralism called post-structuralism. Though his contribution, known as *deconstruction*, was not about cinema, by the early 1970s the term *deconstruction* was appearing in *Cahiers du cinéma*: the journal that published Truffaut's famous essay in 1954, and later printed an interview with Derrida in 2001.[2] In this and other interviews, Derrida explains that even though he has "seen many films," he feels "more at ease with philosophical and literary texts."[3] Nevertheless, as this chapter will demonstrate, Derrida's deconstruction of philosophic and literary texts might inspire a new approach to religion and film. Like Derrida, who once said that "to turn to religion is also to turn religion around,"[4] I argue that to turn to the field of religion and film is also to turn it around.

Defining Deconstruction in Religion and Film

To understand Derrida's deconstruction, we must re-turn to Saussure, the father of structuralism and hence of the Grand Theory indicted at the end of the preceding chapter. For Saussure, "the entire mechanism of language ... is based on oppositions."[5] This is because the signifier as "sound-image" can only be defined by what it is not: a *pit* is not a *pin*, and a *pin* is not a *bin*. Saussure's emphasis on oppositions led to the "consistent binarism"[6] of his followers, which might be illustrated as follows:

signified	*natural*	*spoken*	*message*	*spirit*
signifier	cultural	written	medium	body

People perpetuate these binaries when they regard terms above the line as more authentic and/or closer to ideal truth than the ones paired with them below the line. In other words, they assume that a *natural* understanding of truth is most authentically *signified* through *spoken messages*. Plato certainly believed this, elevating the spoken word to such an extent that he banished the written signifiers of poets from his ideal Republic. His elevation of *spirit* over *body*, in fact, banished belief in the hypostatic union of divine-and-human for those Christian gnostics who followed in his footsteps. Indeed, binary oppositions seem to drive numerous religions:

soul	*divine grace*	*determinism*	*Heaven*	*saved*	*the enlightened*
body	human works	free will	Hell	damned	the deluded

Derrida deconstructed structuralist binaries by arguing for both/and thinking: both parts of each binary need their other halves for self-definition. In relation to the oppositions in the first chart above, we cannot understand the *significance* of *nature* apart from the *signifiers* our *culture* has *written* on our minds, as when Alps *signified*, for seventeenth-century viewers, warts and pimples on the face of the earth.[7] Deconstruction, then, can be defined as the destabilization of problematic binaries—like the one perpetuated by religion and film scholars who emphasize message to the near exclusion of the cinematic medium.

In addition to deconstructing the message/medium binary, *Salvation from Cinema* seeks to deconstruct the binaries presented in the preceding chapter on film theory:

art	*montage*	*auteur/foreign*	*semiotics*	*apparatus control*
commerce	mise-en-scène	Hollywood	story	viewer agency

The both/and thinking reflected in such deconstruction encourages analysis of montage as well as mise-en-scène, of foreign as well as Hollywood films; it recognizes the semiotic manipulations, both good and bad, of story, while encouraging viewers to exercise agency by actively assessing how the cinematic apparatus controls their perception.[8] In fact, the very title of this book encourages both/and thinking when it comes to "salvation from cinema" itself:

- We can save our sensibilities—and time—by avoiding movies that offer trite and/or outrageous stories filled with titillating cliches and little art.
- We can be saved from the consumer-oriented banality of quotidian existence by paying attention to artistry in the cinematic medium.

Or, as film scholar William Rothman puts it, "whether a film's ideological project is *successful*—whether a viewer will actually submit to a film designed to tyrannize—depends in part on the attitude of the viewer."[9] It depends, in other words, on whether or not viewers understand that medium and message are interdependent: an issue close to the heart of Derrida. As French professor Ellen S. Burt notes of his thought, "the content is not the matter, it is not just that the medium is the message, but that the medium affects and finds itself implicated in the developments that the content can take in ways that are very revelatory to us." Significantly, Burt made this statement to filmmaker Joanna Callaghan, who was constructing a 2014 film inspired by Derrida's famous book *The Post Card* (1980). Derrida's face and words—the embodied medium of his verbal messages—both appear and speak in Callaghan's *Love in the Post*, as they do in several other films.[10] Hence, even though Derrida commented very little about cinema in his work, cinematic works have captured Derrida commenting, as though gesturing toward the signifier used to address him, his parents naming him "Jackie" after the movie character Jackie Coogan in Charlie Chaplin's *The Kid* (1921).[11]

Just as Derrida changed the signifier that named him, from *Jackie* to *Jacques*, so he changed the signifier for *deconstruction*—several times. This is because many of his followers, demonstrating the fundamentalist fallacy discussed in Chapter 5, became rabidly dogmatic about deconstruction. As theologian Mark C. Taylor stated in his obituary for Derrida (October 14, 2004), "Betraying Mr. Derrida's insights by creating a culture of political correctness, his self-styled supporters fueled the culture wars that have been raging for more than two decades and continue to frame political debate."[12] In order to deconstruct deconstruction, then, Derrida developed new terms, several of which help illuminate both cinema and religion.

Signs of Derrida in Film: Exchangism and *The Forgiveness of Blood*

As part of his critique of structuralism, Derrida employs the term "exchangist."[13] This is because, in Saussure's system, signifiers are *exchanged* for signifieds, as when speakers in the eighteenth century exchanged the signifier *tan* for a concept signifying "ugliness," a tan associated with peasants whose sun-burnished skin indicated they had to work outdoors. Two centuries later the exact same signifier, *tan*, was exchanged for "attractiveness," since people with leisure and money had the luxury to "work on" their tans. In the realm of cinema, Grand Theory took "exchangism" one step further, arguing that spectators received capitalist ideology in exchange for cinematic signifiers, the eyes of beholders manipulated by the apparatus of movie production and distribution. When Derrida deconstructed structuralism, then, he implicitly questioned the exchangism that drove Grand Theory, as well as the exchangism that drives many film narratives.

Mafia films make exchangism obvious: you insult my people, I take revenge; you betray the business, you suffer in exchange; you kill my kindred, I kill yours in return. Such attitudes and behaviors were common to gangster movies of the 1930s, influencing the film noir of the 1940s and 1950s. Though film noir challenged the binary opposition between "good guys" and "bad guys" by presenting ethically ambiguous protagonists—think of Humphrey Bogart in *The Maltese Falcon* (1941)—a more dramatic change came in 1972 with the premiere of

Francis Ford Coppola's *The Godfather*, which the American Film Institute ranks only after *Citizen Kane* as the greatest American movie of all time. Offering more psychologically complex mobsters than those depicted in earlier cinema, *The Godfather* provided a model for powerful Mafia films to follow: Coppola's *Godfather Part 2* (1974) and *Godfather Part 3* (1990), of course, but also Martin Scorsese's *Mean Streets* (1973), *GoodFellas* (1990), and *Casino* (1995), all of which deconstruct a clear-cut binary between good and evil.[14] Nevertheless, most characters in these films are driven by principles of exchange, whether for good or for ill.

Exchangism shapes foreign-language films as well, many of which explore similar issues to Hollywood productions while often avoiding their spectacular special-effect violence. For example, *The Forgiveness of Blood*, a 2011 Albanian/American collaboration, focuses on a twenty-first-century Albanian village that employs an exchangist paradigm dating back to an ancient religious code called *Kanun*, the word related to *canon*, as in *canon law* and the *canon* of the Bible.

The blood feud signaled by the film's title arises after two middle-age brothers kill a man in a dispute over land rights. The murderers' relatives meet to discuss how to protect the family from Kanun rules of revenge—traditional rules they take for granted even as their progeny send text messages and play video games in adjacent rooms. The tension between the ancient exchangist code and contemporary high-tech culture (predicated, of course, on its own binary codes) is captured in the difference between the son and daughter of Mark, one of the murderers. Because the Kanun code dictates that all male children are legitimate targets for blood revenge, Mark's teenage son, Nik, is told he can no longer leave the house. Meanwhile, Nik's sister Rudina must take over Mark's bread delivery business to generate income while her father goes into hiding. Driving Mark's primitive horse-drawn cart, Rudina must bargain with clients while avoiding threatening gestures from the murdered man's family.

The opening and closing shots of the film visually capture the paradoxes of the family's exchangist existence. A long take of a long shot begins *Forgiveness of Blood*, a distant stone building framed by purple mountains and golden fields. Reinforcing a sense of untainted agrarian beauty, a handmade box on wheels enters the high-angle shot from the left, a horse pulling it through the golden field. This idyllic pastoral moment, however, inculcates violence when the owner of the land later protests the cart's passage. Unlike American Mafia films, however, viewers never see the violent act that kills the landowner, thus imputing greater value to the psychological effects of the exchangist code.

The film shows the consequences of exchangism in its closing sequences. Rudina must sell the horse to feed the family, while Nik must leave the town where he wanted to open an internet café, both forced to exchange something they value to honor Kanun. Not needing words, the last two shots symbolize the binary oppositions of the siblings' positions. A close-up tracking shot follows Nik from behind, showing his back as he walks away from the life he has known, while the final shot of the film shows the opposite: a close up on Rudina's face as she hopelessly watches, from the rooftop, Nik's retreat. Thus visualizing leaving home versus staying, back versus front, change versus tradition, the medium encapsulates the message. Furthermore, by refusing to end the film with Hollywood happiness or even narrative closure, *The Forgiveness of Blood* implies that only forgiveness can subvert the exchangist blood feud.

Religion and the Gift of Forgiveness

Many religions inculcate, if even unwittingly, some form of exchangism: do these works, you receive salvation; perform this rite, you become redeemed; behave this way, you attain Paradise; believe this doctrine, you escape damnation; follow these principles, you achieve Nirvana; kill these infidels, you enjoy the pleasures of heaven; say these words, you become born again. It is no wonder, then, that theologians and religion scholars often assess salvation from cinema in terms of exchange: transcendence or valuable insight received in exchange for attentive viewing. Some, in fact, endorse religious exchangism in cinematic narratives, as exemplified by responses to the film discussed in my introduction: Scorsese's *Raging Bull*. For example, Christopher Deacy asserts that "the violence [boxer Jake LaMotta] inflicts upon himself in the cell constitutes a spark of redemption." He thus echoes film scholar Laurence Friedman, who asserts that Jake "atones for his sin by absorbing vicious punishment in the ring."[15] Problematically, endorsement of redemption through violence—whether to self or to others—has marred religion for millennia.

In defiance of what he calls an "an economy of exchange,"[16] Derrida advocates, instead, "the gift," noting that Jesus repeatedly teaches against an economy of exchange: "You have heard that it was said, 'An eye for an eye and a tooth for a tooth.' But I say to you, Do not resist an evildoer. But if anyone strikes you on the right cheek, turn the other also. ... For if you love those who love you what reward do you have? Do not even the tax collectors do the same?" (Matthew 5:38–9, 46).[17] Derrida's commentary on these Bible verses is relevant to all religions:

> If you love only those who love you and to the extent that they love you, if you hold so strictly to this symmetry, mutuality, and reciprocity, then you give nothing, no love, and the reserve of your wages will be like a tax that is imposed or a debt that is repaid, like the acquittal of a debt. In order to deserve or expect an infinitely higher salary, one that goes beyond the perception of what is due, you have to give without taking account and love those who don't love you.[18]

Whereas Derrida, a Jewish atheist, cites the example of Jesus, other religions offer similarly profound examples of "the gift." As discussed in Chapter 2, Mahayana Buddhism celebrates bodhisattvas who delay their entrance into Nirvana in order to help others attain it, without any notion of self-serving benefit. Muslims regard the Third Pillar of Islam to be charity, which means helping the needy and practicing hospitality without expecting anything in return. And Jews regard the Ten Commandments not as a legalistic code for attaining salvation but as a gift from the Creator of humanity, who knows what is best for human flourishing. Unfortunately, like those Christians who reduce the gift of salvation to something received in exchange for sacraments and/or belief, people of other religions often bypass their own fundamental doctrines about "the gift" in favor of more archaic notions of retribution and exchange.[19]

Because tensions between exchangism and "the gift" inform multiple religions, the field of religion and film might be fertilized through the exploration of movies that deconstruct economies of exchange by offering images of unearned, unmerited, unanticipated gifts of salvation.[20] As famous Derrida scholar John D. Caputo astutely summarizes, "A gift is a gift for Derrida when it is removed from the circle or circulation of giving in return or paying back (remuneration, retribution), of action and proportionate reaction, when we let the gift be."[21]

Significantly, Derrida's suspicions about exchangism may have been ignited by his experience as an ethnic Jew during the rise of Nazism. Though saved from Holocaust ovens because his family lived in French Algeria, the twelve-year-old Derrida was nonetheless expelled from school in 1942 due to his Jewish heritage. The Holocaust, one of the most despicable and far-reaching forms of exchangism in modern times, has provided subject matter for numerous cinematic investigations of exchangism—as well as salvation from it.

Exchangism, the Holocaust, and Film

Ambivalence over economies of exchange may explain the fascination viewers have with Holocaust films. Most believe, quite rightly, that a nation's vitality depends on healthy economies of exchange in financial and judicial spheres. At the same time, informed viewers know that exchangism fed antagonism toward European Jews. In exchange for the aggressions of World War I, the Treaty of Versailles punished Germany, generating resentments that Hitler nurtured while encouraging Germany to exchange its marginalized status for new territory. In the process, Hitler enabled Germans to exchange their sense of inferiority for superiority by demonizing an entire people group that had garnered far greater wealth than they. The nation thus transformed Jews into signifiers of its own degradation, degrading them in exchange. As a result, Jews were forced to exchange their homes and possessions for squalid quarters in quarantined areas, followed by the exchange of life in the ghetto for concentration camps that separated them from their families. And, as the Final (Exchangist) Solution, millions were forced to exchange their lives for German notions of Aryan supremacy.

Significantly, some of the most famous names in the so-called Golden Age of Hollywood (late 1920s to early 1960s) witnessed Holocaust depravity. George Stevens, later winning awards for *A Place in the Sun* (1951), *Shane* (1953), and *Giant* (1956), was ordered by General Eisenhower to document the massacre at Dachau only several hours after its discovery. His footage was shown at the Nuremberg Trials (1945–6), which were themselves filmed by navy photographer John Ford, the famous director of *Stagecoach* (1939), *The Grapes of Wrath* (1940), and *How Green was my Valley* (1941). Billy Wilder, a Jew who fled Nazi

Germany only to become the famed director of *Double Indemnity* (1944) and *The Lost Weekend* (1945), was recruited by the US Department of War in 1945 to make a documentary about Holocaust atrocities for compulsory viewing by Germans. The following year some of those horrific documentary images entered a *fiction* film when Orson Welles made *The Stranger* (1946), thus instantiating his belief that Holocaust footage "must be seen" to communicate the "putrefaction" and "spiritual garbage" generated by Fascism.[22] Although the cinematic transformation of Shoah atrocities into consumer entertainment is legitimately controversial, scholars who specialize in cinema and the Holocaust nevertheless regard the *visual medium* as essential to the historical message.[23]

Perhaps not coincidentally, George Stevens, the first to film Dachau horrors, directed *The Diary of Anne Frank* (1959), based on a play about several Jewish families in Amsterdam who hide from the Nazis in a cramped attic space.[24] Though the film won acclaim and three Academy Awards, Bruno Bettelheim, who had been interred at Buchenwald, denounced the movie for failing to adequately *visualize* Holocaust horrors. Achieving international fame as a child psychologist after he immigrated to America, Bettelheim argues that "The universal success of *The Diary of Anne Frank* suggests how much the tendency to deny the reality of the camps is still with us."[25] Rather than Holocaust horror, *Anne Frank* merely communicates what Bettelheim regards as Jewish passivity during the Holocaust, victims contributing to their own genocide by failing to resist the Nazis.

This may explain why *Schindler's List* (Steven Spielberg, 1993) garnered overwhelming attention and seven Academy Awards. Unlike *Anne Frank*, it presents intensely horrific images of Holocaust atrocities, employing black-and-white cinematography reminiscent of the documentary footage taken by George Stevens and John Ford. Spielberg may even allude to a canonical film about totalitarian abuse when he adds one bit of color to his movie: the reddish-pink dress of a young Jewish girl. In 1925 Sergei Eisenstein added red Communist flags to his black-and-white *Battleship Potemkin*, having them hand-tinted in every frame of the original prints in which they appear. Both reddish images are signifiers of hope: for Eisenstein, a Communist, the red flags symbolized faith in a revolution that would overthrow Tsarist oppression, while for Spielberg, a Jew, the reddish dress symbolized childlike purity in the midst of Nazi depredations. For both, the tinted medium is the message.

Nevertheless, some contend that *Schindler's List*, like *Life is Beautiful* (Roberto Benigni, 1997), offers only "unforgivable distortions of what happened to the vast majority of Jews."[26] Judaic scholar Judith Doneson, in fact, argues that *Schindler's List* perpetuates Bettelheim's disturbing paradigm:

> Because there are no references in the film to resistance and organization within the ghetto, the Jews remain the perfect victims—weak, ineffectual, incapable of helping themselves, the stereotype of women. If someone strong, fearless, and virile—an Oskar Schindler—does not act on their behalf, they are doomed.[27]

One could argue in defense of Spielberg's film that Nazi brutality made organized resistance nearly impossible, as symbolized by one of its most wrenching scenes: children jump into latrines to hide from camp guards, suggesting that immersion in putrid human waste was preferable to vile German treatment.[28]

More problematic than Bettelheim's critique is the fact that *Schindler's List* reinforces the economy of exchange that generated Holocaust atrocity in the first place. Oskar Schindler (Liam Neeson) originally protected his Jewish factory workers for financial reasons: they were cheap labor. Successfully bribing SS officers to protect his investment, Schindler took advantage of exchangism even after he began to care for Jews as human beings. This perhaps explains the most unconvincing scene in the movie: Schindler, in a fit of agony while fleeing advancing Allied Forces, despairs that he could have sold his wedding ring and his car to save more Jews. Though his desire to rescue Jews for their own sake is admirable, Schindler still remains embedded in an economy of exchange: money for Jews. And exchangism perpetuates either/or binaries: good versus evil, Jew versus German, the drowned versus the saved.

In *The Drowned and the Saved*, Auschwitz survivor Primo Levi indicts such binary oppositions, aligning them with Manichaeism, a Persian religion that perpetuated gnostic binaries:

> Popular history, and also the history taught in schools, is influenced by this Manichaean tendency, which shuns half-tints and complexities: it is prone to reduce the river of human occurrences to conflicts, and the conflicts to duels—we and they, … winners and losers, … the good guys and the bad guys, respectively, because the good must prevail, otherwise the world would be subverted.[29]

"Popular history," of course, includes the history taught in film, which helps explain Doneson's dissatisfaction with *Schindler's List*: "the film solidifies a phenomenon that historians often fear but that nonetheless is increasingly becoming the reality—the learning of history through the popular media," a history that reinforces Bettelheim's binary construction of viciously strong Germans in opposition to weakly passive Jews.[30] In contrast, the following films, discussed in chronological order, deconstruct the Manichaean tendency to reduce Holocaust horror to simplistic binaries. They thus offer a "salvation from cinema" that differs from the emphasis on "meaning-making" and "transcendence" that often informs scholarship on religion and film.

The Pianist: Defying an Economy of Exchange

Winning numerous awards, including three Oscars and the Palme d'Or at Cannes, *The Pianist* (Roman Polanski, 2002) focuses on a wealthy Polish Jew who goes into hiding after Nazis send his family to the Warsaw Ghetto and then to an extermination camp. Based on the autobiography of pianist Władysław Szpilman, the film shows the degradation Szpilman (Adrien Brody) experiences as he seeks to escape Nazi forces.

In order to emphasize what Szpilman has lost, the film takes us into the elegantly appointed living space of his family, who, at the start of the film, take their creature comforts for granted. The mise-en-scène showcases the home's richly colored fabrics, gleaming grand piano, and tasteful décor: an elegant and comfortable space. Viewers are therefore struck by the contrast when the Szpilmans are forced into the Warsaw Ghetto: bleak browns and grays fill a mise-en-scène in which all creature comforts have been eliminated. Whereas despicable Nazis gunning down innocent Jews is common Hollywood fare, *The Pianist*'s emphasis on mise-en-scène seems closer to home, quite literally. By drawing viewers into a lovely and loving family space at its start, the early mise-en-scène reminds viewers of their own homes, with décor reflective of their personal lives and loves. Hence, images of a family forcefully evicted from a place filled with memory and sentiment helps viewers identify with their pain, generating despair when the displaced Jews comfort each other with statements about the temporary nature of their evacuation. For isn't that how we would feel? Wouldn't we have trouble believing that our government would force innocent citizens to abandon everything they own, forever? After all, these abject horrors occurred during *my parents'* lifetime!

Later in *The Pianist*, the mise-en-scène of another abandoned home summarizes the trajectory of the entire film. Szpilman, defying Nazi exchangism, takes a chance to escape, eventually hiding in an attic space that contains nothing, not even plaster on the walls. On the floor below, however, stands a grand piano, representative of Szpilman's former life as a well-paid musician. Unfortunately he cannot touch that symbol of his identity because any music he produces will identify his location: piano music, in other words, identifies him in both senses of the word.[31] As far as the Nazis are concerned, Szpilman's identity is only that of a despised Jew—at least until a Wehrmacht officer, Wilm Hosenfeld (Thomas Kretschmann), discovers the starving Szpilman desperately trying to open a can of food in the kitchen below his hiding place.

When the emaciated Jew tells Hosenfeld that he is a pianist, the officer asks him to play the grand piano in the adjacent room. Profoundly moved by Szpilman's performance, Hosenfeld not only allows the Jew to stay in hiding, but also provides him with food and clothing. Rather than spoken language, it is the medium that communicates this message. Hosenfeld does not comment on Szpilman's music and says nothing about saving the accomplished artist. Instead, mise-en-scène and montage break down the Manichaean distinction between German and Jew. First we see Szpilman seated before the piano, one hand enfolding the other, as though to crack his knuckles. When he starts to play, the shot cuts to a full-frame side view of the piano, Szpilman seated at its left, Hesenfeld's military coat lying across its harp at the right. In between, a light shines through the window behind, falling upon the keys like the Shekinah glory described in Hebrew Scripture. Seeming to proclaim the glory of Szpilman's performance, the light washes out the remaining colors in the scene, such that Hosenfeld's crisp new coat now matches in color the frayed coat worn by Szpilman. The shot then cuts to a full frame of the officer in a chair, one hand enfolding the other, mirroring

Szpilman's gesture before the piano. By effacing visual differences between the two men, mise-en-scène and montage deconstruct the opposition between them. Furthermore, rather than establish an economy of exchange by verbalizing something like "I will save you because you are a great artist" or "I'll keep you alive if you play for me," Hosenfeld offers a gift of salvation with no words, no strings attached. Indeed, Szpilman never again plays for Hosenfeld, despite the salvation from starvation the officer provides. In fact, *The Pianist* shows that while Szpilman survived the war, enabling him to perform Chopin to an elegant crowd in an ornate theater space, Hosenfeld died in Soviet captivity. We see that the gift of salvation does not operate according to an economy of exchange, wherein Jews are rewarded for their faithfulness to God or Hosenfeld is rewarded for his salvation of Szpilman. This, of course, does not exonerate Hosenfeld for his complicity with the Nazis. Instead, the only way to escape an economy of exchange is with the gift of forgiveness. As Derrida scholar John Caputo beautifully puts it in his award-winning book *The Weakness of God*,

> if we are not simply giving back to repentant sinners what they have earned and deserve, then it is the sinner qua sinner, the sinner who is still sinning, whom we must forgive, who, in a certain sense, is the only one we can "forgive" if forgiveness is a gift and not an economic exchange.[32]

Caputo also makes clear, however, that forgiveness does not mean forgetting. Holocaust films help us remember the vile atrocities that exchangism—an attitude perpetuated by many religions—can incite. Revenge merely duplicates attitudes made extreme by the Nazis. Only "the forgiveness of blood" can deconstruct exchangism.

Unfortunately, even forgiveness easily falls into an economy of exchange: I forgive you because I need your love or I forgive you in order to free myself from anger. In *The Gift of Death*, Derrida describes such forgiveness as counterfeit:

> The moment the gift, however generous it be, is infected with the slightest hint of calculation, the moment it takes account of knowledge [*connaissance*] or recognition [*reconnaissance*], it falls within the ambit of an economy: it exchanges, in short it gives counterfeit money, since it gives in exchange for payment.[33]

Derrida thus suggests that a *pure* gift is impossible, because, as soon as someone consciously offers a gift, she reinforces an economy of exchange through the satisfaction garnered by offering it.

There is perhaps one Holocaust film that gets close to a pure gift as Derrida limns it: *Perlasca: The Courage of a Just Man* (Alberto Negrin, 2002). The film, divided into two episodes for Italian television, visualizes the tactics of Giorgio Perlasca, an actual historical figure who saved five thousand Jews from the Nazis, often without "the slightest hint of calculation." At one point in the film, a fellow Italian asks Perlasca why he risks his life to save Jews, and all Perlasca can answer is "I don't know": his motivation falls outside "the ambit of an economy." Significantly, Derrida once defined deconstruction as an affirmative "I don't know": "it is an affirmation that is very risky, uncertain, improbable; it entirely escapes the space of certainty." The phrase "I don't know," in other words, is a matter of stepping out in faith as though in response to "a call." As Derrida puts it, the affirmative *I don't know* "doesn't just result from ignorance, or skepticism, or nihilism, or obscurantism. This nonknowledge is the necessary condition for something to happen, for responsibility to be taken, for a decision to be made, for an event to take place."[34] Significantly, Perlasca's "I don't know" was so powerful that he never talked about his salvation of Jews, his heroism kept hidden for 45 years, even from his family.

Compared to Perlasca, Schindler seems to offer "counterfeit money." Nevertheless, when it comes to the Holocaust, better counterfeit money than none at all: a point suggested by *The Counterfeiters* (Stefan Ruzowitzky, 2007), an Austrian–German production.

The Counterfeiters: Financial Exchange

Winner of the 2008 Oscar for Best Foreign Language Film, *The Counterfeiters* is a fictional movie based on the memoir of Adolf Burger, a Slovak Jew placed in a special ward of the Sachsenhausen concentration camp in 1942. Along with other Jews who had paper-making, engraving, banking, or printing-press skills, Burger was compelled to manufacture counterfeit American dollars and British pounds that the Germans planned to drop on Allied countries in order to devastate their economies.

Granted special favors in exchange—healthy food, comfortable beds, hot showers, fresh toiletries—these Jews aided an enemy destroying their race. Thus "counterfeiting" in more ways than one, they illustrate what Primo Levi called "the gray zone" of collaboration. In *The Drowned and the Saved* Levi says of his Auschwitz experience, "the enemy was all around but also inside, the 'we' lost its limits."[35] *The Counterfeiters*, then, is about the complexity of defining the "we." Focusing on tensions among the counterfeiting Jews themselves, it deconstructs the binary between victims and perpetrators of evil. Doing so, the film avoids the "Manichaean tendency," identified by Levi, "which shuns half-tints and complexities."

Significantly enough, *The Counterfeiters* opens with a scene shot in half-tints. In the muted tones of twilight, a man dressed in black sits on dark gray stone, watching a gray-blue sea beneath a light gray sky. Picking up a black briefcase and walking by newspaper debris announcing the end of the war, the man enters a Monte Carlo casino, where bright lights and garish colors contrast dramatically with the previous subdued tones. Donning a black-and-white tuxedo bought with money pulled from the briefcase, the man proceeds to the gaming tables, where he gambles and wins—repeatedly. The next morning, after bedding a gorgeous woman in an opulent hotel room, he sits on a luxurious patio, where he is served a bottle of champagne in a silver bucket.

The shot dissolves into a graphic match: in the exact same spot on the screen a champagne bucket is placed on a rustic table from an earlier time—1936 Berlin—implying a causal connection between the two incidents: the medium is the message. We see the same black-clad man managing a squalid bar radically different from the glossy casino bar. He jokes with his sleazy customers and roughs up thugs who fail to deliver what they owe him. Just as we decide this man, called "Sally" (Karl Markovics), warrants little respect, we are given a new scene. In a room above the bar, Sally counterfeits passports to help Jews escape Germany. Our positive opinion is subverted, however, when Sally hesitates to make a passport for a beautiful woman until she offers to sleep with him.

In other words, Sally, a Russian Jew originally named Salomon Sorowitsch, operates according to a sordid economy of exchange, counterfeiting not out of compassion but in order to serve his own best interests. He replies to adulation for counterfeit passports with "Our people? I'm me and the others are others": a Manichaean binary between self and other. When a German officer bursts into the room and sends Sally off to prison, it therefore seems like a bit of poetic justice. After all, an economy of exchange is necessary not only for a state's economic health but also within its justice system: criminals must be justly punished. What Holocaust films challenge, however, is our Manichaean tendency to adjudicate justice in black-and-white terms. When implemented by unjust governments, ostensibly legal exchangism is counterfeit justice.

Ambiguities in Sally's character, deconstructing an easy distinction between "the good guys and the bad guys," adumbrate the ethical ambiguities of the rest of the film. For example, as Sally enters a concentration camp, he witnesses a Jewish prisoner ferociously pummel a new arrival, while a German guard encourages the brutality. The shot—like much of movie—is filmed in tones of gray, as though alluding to Primo Levi's "we" losing its limits. Sally must negotiate this "gray zone" when taken, five years later, to the Sachsenhausen camp to aid the Nazi counterfeiting scheme. Another Jewish prisoner, Dr. Viktor Hahn, is appalled that he must work with a famous criminal, telling Sally that he preferred it when the only "professional criminals" in the camp were Nazi guards. When Sally retorts, "So it besmirches your honor" to work with a "jailbird," Hahn replies with dismayed dignity, "If honor is all you have left!" Just as our heart goes out to Hahn—a former banker seeking to hold on to a bit of honor—the camera cuts to an inmate telling Sally, "The true criminals are the capitalist exploiters who made Fascism possible." Delivered with a searing glare at the banker, this line references another gray zone of collaboration: criminality, no longer rendered in Manichaean black and white, marks legal as well as illegal tender.

Of course, there's no denying or excusing the despicable criminality of the Nazis. But the film even turns this into a gray zone. The officer in charge of the operation, Herzog, treats the counterfeiting Jews gently, limiting his exchangism to benevolent rewards for good work rather than harsh punishments for bad. While another officer, Holst, contemptuously abuses the counterfeiters, Herzog never once lifts a finger against what he calls "my Jews." In fact, when Holst starts to beat Sally for standing around, Herzog violently stops him, disdainfully telling his fellow Nazi, "Thinking can also be work, Holst! Try it yourself sometime." Even when he discovers that Sally has lied to protect some other inmates, Herzog does not punish the Jew, instead exhorting him with the words "We're on the same side now." This very statement, of course, highlights the gray zone of collaboration: the upright Herzog collaborates with a professional criminal, and the Jewish Sally collaborates with an SS officer.

There is only one Jew in the film who refuses to collaborate: Adolf Burger, the collotype expert who wrote the memoir inspiring the film. While all the other counterfeiters abet the Nazi cause in order to save their own skins, Burger refuses complicity by unabashedly sabotaging their efforts. In fact, the first time we see him, he refuses to wear the clothes taken off the bodies of dead Jews, eliciting condemnation from others who worry that such defiance will threaten the lives of them all.[36] Viewers therefore assume early on that Burger, refusing complicity, is the film's hero. But such an assumption reflects Primo Levi's "popular history," in which "the good must prevail." *The Counterfeiters*, refusing to shun half-tints, sets up Burger as a hero in order to deconstruct either/or definitions of heroism. For example, when Sally asks him why he looks so healthy having just arrived from Auschwitz, Burger explains that his job was to sort luggage on the train platform as Jews arrived for the gas chambers. He therefore had access to food scavenged from Jewish suitcases. We cannot help wondering how eating the food of deported Jews differs from donning the clothes of dead Jews. Furthermore, even as Burger contemptuously disparages a fellow Jew (Hahn the banker) for collaborating with capitalism, he is at that very moment collaborating with the enemy by counterfeiting the British pound. It is only later, during the counterfeiting of the American dollar, that he sabotages the machines.

As Burger tries to escape the gray zone of collaboration, viewer ambivalence increases. For his sabotage puts the lives of his Jewish colleagues at risk. Herzog tells the counterfeiters that if American bills are not produced in one month, five Jews, including Burger, will die. Though we admire Burger's willingness to sacrifice himself and four others in order to slow down Germany's destruction of millions, we feel sorry for those four who had no say in the matter. The gray grows murkier when Burger proclaims why he defies his captors—"It's the principle"—and one of his fellow Jews responds, "Nobody's prepared to die for a principle." Significantly, screenwriter/director Stefan Ruzowitzky juxtaposes Burger's commitment to well-being of the majority with Nazi actions based on the same "principle": Holst, upon discovering that one of the counterfeiters has tuberculosis, shoots the sick man in the head, stating that the sacrifice is necessary to protect the lives of the majority. This "principle"—exchanging one life for the good of the majority—functions as a synecdoche for the Final Solution, when millions were killed in order to protect the health of the Aryan state.

Burger also fails to rise above such exchangism when he identifies himself with Communism, the "principles" of which led to Stalin's destruction of millions to make Communism work for the majority: a connection made explicit early in the film. After Sally tells a thug that repayment of a loan (economic exchangism) "is a matter of principle," someone later says to Sally, "I hope you're not a Communist." We should take note, then, when Sally abandons his principles to protect the lives of his fellow counterfeiters. Sally's exchangist principles, of course, were problematic to begin with: "Our people? I'm me and the others are others." But this makes his transformation in Sachsenhausen all the more interesting. While at first motivated solely by his own survival, Sally eventually takes personal risks to save the lives of "others," taking and giving blood when necessary. He stops a guard from beating a bloody prisoner; he covers up—in several senses—the man with tuberculosis, cutting his own finger to rub blood on the pallid man's cheeks to disguise the illness; he prevents another man from committing suicide, inadvertently smearing his own face with the prisoner's blood; he defends Burger from the attacks of other prisoners, though Burger has called him a "cheap whore." When Burger continues to sabotage the counterfeiting machines, Sally stays up all night rectifying the subversion so that no one—including Burger—will get killed. Sally has thus deconstructed his original Manichaean principles by learning to put others before himself. Significantly, Derrida defines deconstruction as "an openness toward the other."[37]

The deconstruction of clear-cut boundaries between good and evil intensifies with the advance of Allied forces. After German guards abandon the concentration camp, gaunt dirt-covered prisoners break through the boundary that separated the healthy counterfeiters from the rest of the imprisoned Jews. Wielding guns abandoned by German guards, the malnourished prisoners threaten to kill the counterfeiters, assuming that such clean, well-fed men could not be part of the abused "we." Thus, as Jew threatens Jew with Nazi weapons, we get a visual metaphor for the gray zone of collaboration. Only when counterfeiters roll up their sleeves to show numbers tattooed on their arms do the malnourished prisoners lower their weaponry.

The camera then cuts to a chilling shot: healthy counterfeiters cower against a wall as the incredulous walking dead wander through the collaborators' tidy dormitory, touching clean sheets and thick mattresses with stupefied amazement. To ease guilt over their privileges, a counterfeiter points to Burger, saying "He's a hero." As one of the drowned adoringly touches the saved "hero," tears flow down Burger's cheeks, generating another gray zone of ambiguity. Why does he cry? Because he is embarrassed by his creature comforts? Because he didn't do enough to sabotage the Nazi cause? Because his principles nearly got five Jews killed unnecessarily? Then, to intensify the gray, we see Burger and Sally smile at each other, like comrades who have fought side by side. Perhaps, then, Burger cries because he is still alive—thanks to an unwarranted "gift" from Sally, a criminal he despised.

The Counterfeiters ends by returning us to Sally in the casino, establishing an interesting framing device. While at the start of the film a chilled champagne bucket mediates the transition of Sally from 1945 Monte Carlo to 1936 Berlin, a more chilling image brings him back to the Monte Carlo scene. After destruction of the boundary separating the drowned from the saved in the concentration camp, Sally discovers the suicide of one of his "mates": a lad who counterfeited knowledge of engraving to get out of Auschwitz and therefore contributed little to the Nazi counterfeiting scheme. As Sally carries the body though a corpse-lined area of the camp, he moans "Where do I take him? He's dead." And we hear a voice answering "full house," as though in reference to the piles of bodies that fill the camp. But then "full house" is repeated again as the shot cuts to a close-up on four aces in a five-card hand: cards that trump a full house in poker. Nevertheless, the man holding the winning hand—Sally—folds to the player with the full house. By connecting camp with casino, the phrase "full house" implies that one must sometimes fold one's principles when it comes to life and death, even when those principles seem like the winning hand. After all, good and evil cannot always be reduced to easily identifiable categories of "we and they, ... winners and losers, ... the good guys and the bad guys."

Significantly, *The Counterfeiters* closes in the same tones with which it began, the screen divided into three horizontal strips of differing grays: the sky above, the sea in the middle, the pebbles below. We see the figure of Sally filling the middle strip of gray—like the letter S filling a space on lined paper. Dancing with him is a woman who watched him in the casino folding his hand multiple times, until he lost all his counterfeit money. She joins Sally, as did Burger, in a gray zone of collaboration: a zone viewers enter as they sympathize with a Jewish criminal who aided Nazi counterfeiting. We as viewers thus collaborate in a counterfeiting scheme—history counterfeited by cinema—as we watch a movie, filmed mostly in shades of gray, challenging easy economies of exchange.

Watching *In Darkness*

While the medium of *The Counterfeiters* opens and closes in shades of gray, appropriate for a message about the "gray zone of collaboration," *In Darkness* (Agnieszka Holland, 2011) opens with impenetrable darkness punctuated with small moving lights, as though referencing the opposition between light and darkness key to Manichaeism.[38] In fact, when Primo Levi indicts the "Manichaean tendency ... to reduce the river of human occurrences to ... we and they, ... winner and losers," he offers an image relevant to *In Darkness*, where people slog through rivers of human waste in order to escape the Nazis. Based upon historical figures and events in Lwòw, Poland, Holland's Polish film traces the story of Jews who hid for eighteen months in city sewers. Its protagonist, proclaimed by Jews to be one of the "Righteous Among the Nations," is Catholic sewer inspector Leopold Socha (Robert Wieckiewicz), who, like Schindler, initially saved Jews for financial reasons. His slow transition from an economy of exchange to the gift of salvation drives the film, but not without visualizing disturbing Manichaean tendencies along the way.

The clear-cut distinction between light and darkness in the film's opening shot turns out to be flashlights illuminating various household objects that two burglars discuss stealing. At one point, the light shines on a child's train running on its track, one of the men watching it with fascination. When two adolescents turn on the room's lights, the burglars make their escape into the darkness of the surrounding woods. There they see in the distance what looks like lights of a train moving through the trees, accompanied by the screech of its horn. The extreme long shot, however, cuts to a much closer image of terrorized naked women running through the woods, their white bodies and screams explaining the train-like effects. As German soldiers shoot them dead, we realize that the burglars' criminal activity, like the toy train, is mere child's play compared to the mass murder of innocent women.

After this horrific scene, In Darkness takes us into the darkness of the city sewer system, where the burglars hide their precious stolen goods—preparing us for the fact that the same men will hide precious human beings in the same locale. And for the same reason: to serve their own economic interests. Indeed, when Socha, the head thief, discovers Jews digging an opening into the sewer from their cramped room in the ghetto above, he blackmails them, saying he will help them hide in the underground system in exchange for large sums of money. And even then he refuses to hide more than a few, fearing that too many bodies will risk detection.

This decision, like his decision of what to steal in the opening scene, is made in darkness, the mise-en-scène communicating a message almost as chilling as Nazi brutality. Surrounded by dozens of desperate Jews in the dark sewer space, Socha selects a wealthy professor who can pay him, as well as the man's family, and only seven others. Holland follows the selection of "the saved" with a montage of shots, each of which shows one Jewish face lit up in the darkness. But then the light slowly fades on each morose face, representing how the light of their lives will slowly be snuffed out because there is no room for them in the sewer inn.

In fact, much of the film is shot in darkness, making the timid flashlights and lanterns in the Jews' sewer retreat seem all the brighter. Sometimes a light shines directly into the camera, blinding viewers from seeing anything but the surrounding darkness. The medium thus seems to ask us how we have been blinded by Manichaean versions of the Holocaust in which good and evil seem exceedingly clear-cut: aggressive Germans versus compliant Jews. In contrast, In Darkness is excruciating to watch because it presents Manichaean distinctions between light and darkness, "good guys and bad guys," only to subvert them. We shudder while watching Jews fight and claw each other to get into the sewer; we wince at the vile behavior of one Jew, who lustfully commits adultery in the presence of his wife and daughter, threatens to shoot the professor's children for making too much noise, and robs his compatriots, leaving them to care for his now-pregnant "mistress." In Darkness thus captures the Holocaust as Primo Levi experienced it: "the enemy was all around but also inside, the 'we' lost its limits."[39]

In Darkness, in other words, deconstructs a binary opposition between good and evil, between "we" and "they." When Socha talks to his wife, Wanda, about the Jews hiding in the sewer, she expresses concern for them, saying "the Jews are the same as us." When he angrily retorts that the Jews deserve their persecution because they killed Jesus (thus endorsing an economy of exchange), Wanda responds that "Jesus was a Jew." Socha, who had earlier called the Jews "lice," "vermin" and "Yids" to their faces, is clearly flabbergasted. And when he later shares Wanda's revelation with his partner in crime, the younger man repeats several times "Jesus was a Jew?": a phrase that subverts the opposition between Christian and Jew.[40]

The mise-en-scène reinforces the connection between Jews and Christians when, during two separate dark scenes, the only thing lit up is a symbol of faith: a golden cross that Socha refuses to steal in the first burglary scene, and a golden Menorah that he steals from somewhere else. Both, of course, are emblems of God's gift of salvation, the seven-branched Menorah transported by Moses as he led the Jews out of Egyptian captivity to the Promised Land.[41] Not coincidentally, the Jews in the sewer call Socha their "Polish Moses" as he leads them through the underground system to a promised safe place, where he later gives them the stolen Menorah. Socha's "we," then, begins to lose "its limits" due to his role as Polish Moses. When, early in the film, Socha tells a score of Jews that he can only successfully hide ten or eleven of them, several plead for him to make it twelve: after all, they note, there were "twelve apostles" (and we can't help thinking of the twelve tribes of Israel led by Moses). After Socha retorts that there were only eleven disciples after Judas betrayed Jesus, a Jew notes that Judas was replaced by the apostle Matthias (Acts 1:26). Nevertheless, Socha holds his ground, insisting that only eleven can cross the river of sewage into the promised space, which is situated under his church. However, as the film proceeds, we realize that Socha, himself, is the twelfth, for we see him spending more time with the Jews than with any other group of people in the film. At first, then, Socha functions like Judas, who exchanged Jesus for thirty pieces of silver. Indeed, when the Jews can no longer pay him, Socha tells them "I'm not coming back. ... You'll die like dogs."

Fortunately, *In Darkness* is about salvation—not only of the Jews from exchangist Nazis, but also of Socha from exchangist Christianity. Slowly transforming from Judas to Matthias, Socha is saved through the innocence of children. Early in the film we see the tenderness with which Socha tucks in his sleeping daughter, so when he later finds the professor's young children wandering lost in the sewer, we are not surprised when he treats them tenderly, leading them back to their parents with no expectation of reward. The camera, in fact, gives us an extreme close-up on Socha's hand extended to the Jewish girl, who takes it in her own. When he returns them to their mother, he reverses his earlier comment—"I'm not coming back"—by telling her he "will continue," obviously with no hope of economic benefit.

Later, when a baby is born in the hiding place, with no place to lay its head, the first thing Socha says is "Jesus!": an oath we have not heard him utter before. The significance of "Jesus" being pronounced at the birth of a baby is reinforced by the comment of one of the eight remaining Jews: that the baby is "all of ours." In fact, when Socha's wife hears of the baby, she suggests that they adopt him, once again destabilizing the boundaries between "us" and "them," between Jew and Christian. But before Socha can retrieve the helpless infant, its unwed mother ends up killing it to save the rest of the Jews, worried that its piercing cries might reveal their location. From this moment, when an innocent babe dies to save the lives of others, Socha treats the Jews as friends, bringing them literal gifts for Hanukkah. Ironically, he tells the professor to pretend to pay him, knowing that most people take comfort from an economy of exchange.

Socha finally offers salvation as a gift during a deluge that floods the sewer where the Jews are hidden: a sanctuary directly below the Roman Catholic church where Socha attends his daughter's first communion. In other words, the space where Polish Christians celebrate Eucharist is built upon a space where Polish Jews light their Menorah, as though to reinforce the religious binary originally assumed by Socha:

Christians above, freely seeing the light

Jews below, imprisoned "in darkness"

As the waters advance, however, the medium itself deconstructs this binary. After a shot of the Jews praying in darkness, lit only by their Menorah, the camera ascends, as though on an elevator, cutting through the street above the Jews' heads, lifting the shot into the candle-lit service in the Catholic Church. By joining two worshipping groups in one continuous take, Holland visually eliminates the boundary between them—her medium's message inspired, perhaps, by her own birth to a Roman Catholic mother and Jewish father. Once inside the church, Holland's camera takes the priest's point of view as children kneel at the altar railing, opening their mouths to receive the Host. After this clear symbol of Christ's sacrifice, we see Socha leave the ceremony in the pouring rain, sacrificing his wife's good graces and his own safety to enter the sewer tomb to rescue the Jews. The shot cuts back and forth between Jews swimming at the top of their alcove, with only several inches of air to breathe, and Socha scrambling to their rescue. As he makes his way to their hiding place, we hear him pray "Our Father, who art in Heaven." Then, in a profound bit of filmmaking, the first statement we hear after this prayer is a proclamation by one of the Jews: "It's a miracle." The flood waters, as they later recount to Socha, suddenly receded without drowning them: a miraculous gift of salvation from "*Our Father.*" The "we" is losing its limits. It's as though *In Darkness* seeks to capture the significance of Primo Levi's *The Drowned and the Saved*. Viewers familiar with the Hebrew Scriptures also cannot help thinking of the miraculous parting of the Red Sea when God saved Moses-led Jews from drowning (Exodus 14). Indeed, after the flood, Socha discovers the body of a Polish officer who had entered the sewer to kill the Jews—drowned like Pharaoh's officers who chased the Hebrews into the Red Sea.

Once the Russians liberate Poland, Socha can elevate the Jews to street level. We see him standing in the middle of a cobbled road, where he opens a manhole, rolling away the cover like the stone of a tomb. Then the camera focuses, once again, on Socha's hand, this time extended to all the Jews, not just the children. The film then cuts to a POV shot: the perspective of the Jews as they look up to the light framing Socha's hand over the sewer opening. As townspeople watch Socha pull each Jew up to the street, we hear a Pole exclaim

"Jesus Christ!" When another asks "Where did you come from?" a Jew answers, "From the dead, sir. From the dead." The medium thus encapsulates the message of Exodus 15, after the passage through the Red Sea: "The floods cover them; / they went down into the depths like a stone. / Thy right hand, O Lord, glorious in power, / thy right hand, O Lord, shatters the enemy" (Exodus 15:5–6, NRSV). Indeed, Socha's sense of "the enemy" is shattered as he extends his hand to "the other."

Thus, after beginning *In Darkness* with intense darkness that overwhelms round flashlight beams, Holland ends the film with brilliant sunshine that overwhelms the dark manhole through which Jews climb to liberation. Illustrating "the gift" as explored a decade earlier by film theorist Kaja Silverman, Holland's film "lights up with a glittering radiance bodies long accustomed to a forced alignment with debased images."[42] Indeed, on the sunny street Wanda and Socha pass around food and drink as though celebrating their own salvation from images debased by an economy of exchange. As each Jew takes a small piece of cake off a common tray—cake broken to celebrate their salvation from the sewer—we are given an image of communion based on the gift; a gift that does not distinguish between Jew or Greek, slave or free, male or female; a gift that "dismantle[s] the binary opposition of ideality and abjection." This "active gift of love," as Silverman defines it, "provides the basis for conceptualizing … how we might put ourselves in a positive identificatory relation to bodies which we have been taught to abhor and repudiate."[43]

Derrida defines such a gift as "hospitality": "to receive another guest whom I am incapable of welcoming, to become capable of that which I am incapable of"—which aptly describes the anti-Semitic Socha. In Derrida's terms, the "Polish Moses" demonstrates "the exemplary experience of deconstruction itself. … Hospitality—this is a name or an example of deconstruction."[44] Note, however, that Socha does not abandon his religion; he merely opens it up, seeing what he was "taught to abhor and repudiate" as worthy of love. Derrida makes clear that deconstruction is not about the destruction of religion; it is about stripping religion of its reliance on economies of exchange, especially certitude about the exchange between cultural signifiers and the truths they attempt to signify. As philosopher Merold Westphal suggests, humility about our religious signifiers arises from the fact "that we are not God, that only God is absolute."[45]

Holland implies the same at the end of *In Darkness*. Not long after the Soviet liberation, Leopold Socha is killed by a careening Soviet truck while rescuing his daughter from its path. He thus ended his life as he eventually learned to live it: offering salvation that resonates with the founding doctrine of the religion with which he identifies, wherein the gift of salvation was made possible through the willing sacrifice of Jesus on the cross. Holland contrasts this doctrine with the attitude of Christians who reduce their faith to an economy of exchange. As film titles announce at its end, some church members suggested that God killed Socha in exchange for helping the Jews. After this chilling revelation, *In Darkness* closes with the following statement written on the screen: "As if we need God to punish each other."

The Gift of Religion and Film

Holland echoes Derrida, who encourages us to conceptualize religion in terms of "the gift" rather than according to an economy of exchange. How might this be done?

Different religions answer this question differently. Buddhism suggests that economies of exchange perpetuate the delusions of *samsara*, while the gift of enlightenment is an awakening from delusion. Unlike Buddhism and Hinduism, many religions theorize a Giver of the gift: a transcendent Source behind the unearned, unwarranted gifts of love, beauty, health, family, friendship, talent, if not of salvation itself. For those that posit a Source, usually in the form of a loving God, a new question then arises: are religious rituals and practices performed in thankful acknowledgment of gifts from the Giver, or are they merely enacted with hope of getting something in exchange? These questions might then apply to individuals' personal religious positions: what difference does gratitude to the Source make in the way they actually *see* others—especially those outside their religion? As Derrida puts it, "If I welcome only what I welcome, what I am ready to welcome, and that I recognize in advance because I expect the coming of the guest as invited, there is no hospitality."[46] Though an atheist, Derrida practiced what he preached, hospitably opening himself to the possibility of an "impossible" Source to "the gift"—what he started calling "God."

The principle of "the gift" should also influence how we as individuals respond to cinema. On the one hand, the act of seeing a film should generate thoughts about its source: is it constructed primarily to make money or does it offer gifts of beautiful artistry that exceed any sense of financial exchange? After all, the most lovingly constructed films often do not make the most money. On the other hand, film experiences should cause reflection about our own ritualized acts of seeing. Do we go to movies merely to get something that serves our own interests, exchanging the hours in front of the screen for mindless escape, for stimulating arousal, or even for religious insight? How might we instead see cinema as a gift in which devices of the medium speak without words, a gift that keeps on giving the more we think about the power of what we have seen? By regarding religion and film as gifts, viewers might be encouraged to follow the example of "the gift," responding to both religion and film with gifts of productive seeing that exceed economies of exchange.

Notes

1 In 1967 Derrida published three texts challenging structuralism. Originally written in French, they were later translated as *Writing and Difference*, *Speech and Phenomena*, and *Of Grammatology*.

2 Jacques Derrida, "'Le cinéma et ses fantômes', entretien avec Antoine de Baecque et Thierry Jousse," *Cahiers du cinéma* 556 (April 2001): 74–185. For the relevance of Derridean deconstruction to cinema studies, see Peter Brunette and David Wills, *Screen/Play: Derrida and Film Theory* (Princeton: Princeton University Press, 1989). Brunette and Wills note that the term "deconstruction," which Derrida borrowed from philosopher Martin Heidegger, was appropriated by ideology critics writing for *Cahiers du cinéma* (15).

3 Jacques Derrida, "The Spatial Arts: An Interview with Jacques Derrida," in Peter Brunette and David Wills, eds, *Deconstruction and the Visual Arts: Art, Media, Architecture* (Cambridge: Cambridge University Press, 1994), 9, 14.
4 Quoted in Tyler Roberts, "Sacrifice and Secularization: Derrida, de Vries, and the Future of Mourning," in *Derrida and Religion*, ed. Yvonne Sherwood and Kevin Hart (New York: Routledge, 2005), 274. For the continuing influence of deconstruction on religious studies, see the lucid work of John D. Caputo, who builds upon Derrida in *The Weakness of God: A Theology of the Event* (Bloomington: Indiana University Press, 2006), which was endowed with the 2007 American Academy of Religion Book Award for Excellence in Studies in Religion. Caputo deepens his deconstructive approach to religion in *The Insistence of God: A Theology of Perhaps* (Bloomington: Indiana University Press, 2013).
5 Ferdinand de Saussure, *Course in General Linguistics*, trans. Wade Baskin (New York: McGraw-Hill, 1959), 122.
6 Thomas Albert Sebeok, *Semiotics in the United States* (Bloomington: Indiana University Press, 1991), 79. Though Sebeok is describing the "consistent binarism" of Roman Jakobson, who coined the word *structuralism*, the phrase captures the structuralism of many others, most notably the anthropologist Claude Lévi-Strauss, whom Derrida challenged in his famous 1966 lecture at Johns Hopkins University: "Structure, Sign and Play in the Discourse of the Human Sciences."
7 Erin Runions takes a different approach to Derrida's both/and thinking in *How Hysterical: Identification and Resistance in the Bible and Film* (New York: Palgrave Macmillan, 2003), 69–71. Gregory Watkins challenges the oft-cited formalist/realist binary in "Religion, Film and Film Theory," *The Bloomsbury Companion to Religion and Film*, ed. William L. Blizek (New York: Bloomsbury, 2009), 80–8.
8 In 1949, Eisenstein encouraged deconstruction of a binary often attributed to him, descrying earlier "montage conceptions which presumed to supplant all other elements of film-expression. … Within normal limits these features enter, as elements, into any style of cinematography. But they are not opposed to nor can they replace other problems—for instance, the problem of *story*." Sergei Eisenstein, "Through Theater to Cinema," excerpted from *Film Form*, in *Theater and Film: A Comparative Anthology*, ed. Robert Knopf (New Haven: Yale University Press, 2005), 241, emphasis his.
9 William Rothman, "Against 'The System of the Suture,'" *Film Quarterly* 29.1 (Fall); reprinted in *Movies and Methods: An Anthology*, vol. 1, ed. Bill Nichols (Berkeley: University of California Press, 1982), 456, emphasis his.
10 Joanna Callaghan and Martin McQuillan, eds, *Love in the Post: From Plato to Derrida, The Screenplay and Commentary* (New York: Rowman & Littlefield, 2014). The comment I quote from Ellen Burt is repeated twice in the book, first in the filmmaker's "Reflections" (66), and second during the interview with Burt from which Callaghan quotes (155). Repeatedly mentioned in the book are two documentary films about Derrida—*Derrida d'ailleurs* (Fathy, 1999) and *Derrida* (Kofman and Dick, 2003)—as well as a narrative film in which Derrida appears: *Ghost Dance* (McMullen, 1983). A trailer for *Love in the Post*, that includes a shot of Derrida, can be accessed online at loveinthepost.co.uk/trailer/ (accessed June 24, 2015).
11 For Derrida's cinema-inspired name, see "Emmet Cole interviews John D. Caputo," *The Modern Word*. Available online at www.themodernword.com/features/interview_caputo.html (accessed February 18, 2014).
12 Mark C. Taylor, "What Derrida Really Meant," *New York Times*, 14 October 2004, A29.
13 Jacques Derrida, *Given Time: I. Counterfeit Money*, trans. Peggy Kamuf (Chicago: University of Chicago Press, 1994), 76.
14 For a good overview of psychological complexity in the first two *Godfather* films, see John C. Lyden, *Film as Religion: Myths, Morals, and Rituals* (New York: New York University Press, 2003), 156–63. Lyden notes the tension between vengeance and love in the films.

15 Lawrence S. Friedman, *The Cinema of Martin Scorsese* (New York: Continuum, 1997), 113; quoted in Christopher Deacy, *Faith in Film: Religious Themes in Contemporary Cinema* (Surrey: Ashgate, 2005), 73. Both were probably influenced by the Calvinist background of screenwriter Paul Schrader, who alluded to LaMotta's "redemption through physical pain" (quoted in Deacy, 79n. 17).
16 Jacques Derrida, *The Gift of Death* (Chicago: University of Chicago Press, 1995), 102.
17 Ibid., 102, 106. The translator uses the KJV, which I have changed to the NRSV.
18 Ibid., 106.
19 Anthropologist Marcel Mauss discusses religious notions of reciprocity in *The Gift: The Form and Reason for Exchange in Archaic Societies*, trans. W. D. Halls (New York: Norton, 1990). Not surprisingly, Derrida repeatedly challenges Mauss's constructs in *Given Time*.
20 "The gift" that defies exchangism is evident in *Babette's Feast*, a 1987 Danish film often discussed in books on religion and film.
21 John D. Caputo, *The Weakness of God: A Theology of the Event* (Bloomington: Indiana University Press, 2006), 175.
22 Information in this paragraph is taken from the following sources: Hubert Damisch, "A Cinema No Longer Silent" in *Cinema and the Shoah: An Art Confronts the Tragedy of the Twentieth Century*, ed. Jean-Michel Frodon, trans. Anna Harrison and Tom Mes (Albany: State University of New York Press, 2010), 45–6; Jean-Michel Frodon, "Referent Images," in ibid., 224, 230, 233, 234. Welles is quoted in Clinton Heylin, *Despite the System: Orson Welles versus the Hollywood Studios* (Chicago: Chicago Review Press, 2005), 163.
23 For a succinct overview of Holocaust films and controversies surrounding them, see Guy Matalon, "Holocaust Movies," *The Bloomsbury Companion to Religion and Film*, ed. William L. Blizek (London: Bloomsbury, 2009), 231–41.
24 Both the 1955 play and the 1959 film script were written by Frances Goodrich and Albert Hackett, based upon Anne Frank's diary published after the war.
25 Bruno Bettelheim, "The Ignored Lesson of Anne Frank," *Harper's Magazine*, November 1960, 45–6.
26 Theresa Sanders, *Celluloid Saints: Images of Sanctity in Film* (Macon: Mercer University Press, 2002), 142. Sanders is summarizing the response of documentary filmmaker Claude Lanzmann. Her Chapter on Holocaust films, "Saints and Auschwitz," provides a helpful summary of Vatican response to the Shoah, surveying films I do not discuss.
27 Judith E. Doneson, *The Holocaust in American Film*, 2nd edn (Syracuse: Syracuse University Press, 2002), 207.
28 Auschwitz survivor Primo Levi describes how "the concentration camp system ... had as its primary purpose shattering the adversaries' capacity to resist." See *The Drowned and the Saved*, trans. Raymond Rosenthal (New York: Summit, 1988), 38ff.
29 Ibid., 37.
30 Doneson, *The Holocaust in American Film*, 206. Though Doneson does not mention Derrida, and only briefly alludes to Primo Levi, she shares their concern with binary oppositions embedded in popular history (see 214).
31 We see and hear him play the abandoned instrument with passion, only to discover that he merely mimes the action, fingers above the keys. Polanski thus plays tricks with diegetic versus non-diegetic sound: what we thought we heard played on the piano was actually music in Szpilman's mind.
32 Caputo, *Weakness of God*, 212.
33 Derrida, *The Gift of Death*, 102. The translator bracketed Derrida's original French to foreground his pun. The phrase "counterfeit money" alludes to his earlier work, *Given Time* in which Derrida discusses a short narrative by French poet Charles Baudelaire called "Counterfeit Money."
34 Derrida, "The Spatial Arts," 26, 27–8.
35 Levi, *The Drowned and the Saved*, 42, 38.

36 Like most films based on historical incidents, *The Counterfeiters* counterfeits its narrative. While the real Burger was arrested for counterfeiting baptismal certificates to enable Jews to *stay* in Nazi-controlled territory, the film's Burger is arrested for printing anti-Nazi propaganda.
37 Quoted in "Dialogue with Jacques Derrida," in *Dialogues with Contemporary Continental Thinkers: The Phenomenological Heritage*, ed. Richard Kearney (Manchester: Manchester University Press, 1984), 124.
38 For this discussion of *In Darkness*, I have borrowed passages from Crystal Downing, "The Drowned and the Saved," *Books and Culture* 15 (Jan/Feb 2009): 24–5.
39 Levi, *The Drowned and the Saved*, 38.
40 Holland placed a very similar scene in *Angry Harvest* (West Germany 1985). Though she did not have a religious upbringing, many of her films allude to religious issues.
41 God's instructions about the Menorah appear in Exodus 25:31–40.
42 Kaja Silverman, *The Threshold of the Visible World* (New York: Routledge, 1996), 79.
43 Ibid., 4, 79. Silverman's phrase "the active gift of love" is appropriated from Lacan, who, she says, "is less than helpful" in explaining how the gift functions (*The Threshold of the Visible World*, 79), hence the importance of her work as well as that of Derrida, who was also familiar with Lacan.
44 Jacques Derrida, "Hostipitality," trans. Gil Anidjar, in Jacques Derrida, *Acts of Religion*, ed. Gil Anidjar (New York: Routledge, 2002), 364.
45 Merold Westphal, "Onto-Theology, Metanarrative, Perspectivism, and the Gospel," in *Christianity and the Postmodern Turn: Six Views*, ed. Myron B. Penner (Grand Rapids: Baker, 2005), 152.
46 Derrida, "Hostipitality," 362.

7 Seeing Cinema Differently
Salvation from Charles Sanders Peirce

In Roberto Rossellini's neorealist masterpiece, *Rome, Open City* (1945), an actress named Marina argues that her need for furniture and cigarettes justifies her promiscuity. Manfredi, her current lover and a leader of Communist resistance to the Nazi occupation, challenges her propensity to exchange sex for creature-comforts. Insulted by his chiding, Marina reveals Manfredi's location to Ingrid, a Nazi collaborator, receiving a fur coat in exchange. The captured and tortured Manfredi, however, refuses to give up the names of his co-conspirators in exchange for his life. Thus defying economies of exchange on several different levels, Manfredi offers what Derrida calls "the gift of death."[1]

To visually contrast Manfredi's gift of death with Marina's exchangist life, Rossellini maximizes the power of his black-and-white medium. Upon seeing Manfredi's disfigured corpse tied to a chair, Marina falls to the floor, such that her body stretches toward, without quite reaching, the threshold of the room that contains the corpse. The doorframe, matching the dark color of the fur coat on Marina's shoulders, provides a distinct separation between the high-key lighting on her death-like pose and the low-key grays inside the room containing an actual dead body. Rossellini thus visualizes, rather than verbalizes, the difficulty of crossing the threshold into sacrificial love. In the language of Jacques Lacan, Marina remains at "the threshold of the visible word": a place of self-serving narcissism that stymies "the active gift of love."[2]

Rossellini emphasizes Manfredi's "active gift of love" by creating a parallel for the film's last scene: a representative of Christ-like love, Father Pietro, is tied to a chair like Manfredi, shot to death for refusing to reveal the names of resistance fighters. This visual connection between Christian priest and Communist atheist confirms the "gift of death" as an active gift of love. Meanwhile, nestled between these shots of upright men tied to chairs—*upright* both literally and figuratively—appears a scene in which Ingrid approaches Marina's body splayed before the dark threshold. Bending low as though to lift the distraught actress upright to comfort her, Ingrid lifts the fur coat off Marina's shoulders instead, retrieving a token of exchange.

All too often exchangism wins out—not only in cinema but also in religion and theory. Indeed, even though Derrida deconstructed the exchangism of Saussure in the late 1960s, as discussed in Chapter 6, structuralist paradigms dominated film theory into the 1980s. Derrida, in fact, was often attacked for his views, paralleling Rossellini's Manfredi, both self-proclaimed atheists resisting those with power. Furthermore, just as Manfredi had a Christian compatriot in Father Pietro, Derrida had a compatriot who aligned himself with Christianity: Charles Sanders Peirce. Recognizing that Peirce's sign theory resisted the binary oppositions driving structuralism, Derrida suggested that Peirce "goes very far in the direction" of deconstruction.[3] This Chapter therefore explores the "semiotic" of Peirce, explaining how it has been appropriated by film theorists. It does so in order to argue for the importance of Peirce to the thesis of this book: that salvation is a matter of *seeing the medium* of salvation. Peirce, in other words, helps us cross the threshold of the visible world.

Semiotic Resistance: The Triadic Sign

As discussed in Chapter 5, apparatus theorists, having been influenced by psychoanalytic and Marxist structuralists, argue that film viewers are ideologically tethered to cinema seats by capitalist fascists—much as Manfredi and Pietro are tethered to chairs by Mussolini fascists. The difference, of course, is that Manfredi and Pietro fully comprehend the implications of their imprisonment, unlike movie spectators who fail to see how the capitalist apparatus manipulates their perceptions. Like prisoners in Plato's allegory of the cave, enthralled viewers naively believe that the imagery presented in movies realistically reflects truth about human psychology and values. Of course, Plato's answer was transcendence of the cave in search of Pure Truth, whereas apparatus theorists regarded ideological chains as inescapable.

In contrast, as Gérard Deledalle notes, C. S. Peirce

> was braver than Plato and was courageous enough to go back to the Cave and liberate his fellow-prisoners, not by helping them to escape, but by introducing into the Cave the freedom of reasoning and of analyzing Being into the categories of the Cave. ... Semiotics is the story of Plato back in the Cave.[4]

Though not referencing cinema, Deledalle's metaphor helps explain why several film theorists, even during the heyday of structuralism, gravitated toward the threshold-crossing semiotic of Peirce. In 1969, a mere two years after Derrida deconstructed Saussure, Peter Wollen's *Signs and Meaning in the Cinema* offered Peirce as an alternative to Saussure-inflected film theory. Rather than binary oppositions, as Wollen notes, Peirce offers a "trichotomy of the sign."[5]

In contrast to Saussure's signifier and signified, Peirce established three components to any visual sign: object, representamen, and interpretant.

Though his semiotic has "more to do with the constitution of reality than with a medium of expression," as Johannes Ehrat puts it, Peirce nevertheless provides guidelines for understanding the cinematic medium, inspiring Ehrat to publish *Cinema and Semiotic* in 2005.[6] Because it takes Ehrat over 150 pages to explain Peirce's philosophy before applying it to cinema, the following explanations and examples may strike specialists as highly simplified. But the goal of this Chapter is not to elucidate Peirce so much as to demonstrate how his foundational constructs might contribute to the field of religion and film. Rather than endorsing an economy of exchange, wherein cinematic signifiers are exchanged for religious signification, Peirce's triadic sign subverts binary oppositions. This makes possible a religious *approach* to cinema, encouraging what Kaja Silverman calls "an ethics of the field of vision."[7] It's about the way we *see*.

The Triadic Sign: Object

Saussure's followers were so fixated on mind-controlling signifier/signified dyads that they did not consider actual objects in the world, focusing instead on the linguistic system and/or cinematic apparatus that generated signifiers. In contrast, Peirce acknowledged that objects—like the Alps—do exist apart from their signifying power. Some scholars have therefore argued that the importance of "the object" to Peirce aligns with the film theory of André Bazin (see Chapter 5). Emphasizing the "realism" of mise-en-scène, Bazin writes, "The photographic image is the *object* itself, the *object* freed from the conditions of time and space that govern it."[8] Not coincidentally, a famous film theorist influenced by Peirce—Gilles Delueze—is sometimes paralleled with Bazin. However, while Bazin celebrates the "object freed from the conditions of time," Delueze regards the object as inseparable from time. For Delueze—who will be discussed more thoroughly in the next chapter—traditional film narration depends on the *movement* of "images as they themselves appear, as perceptible images in themselves."[9] Deleuze's terms *appear* and *perceptible* prepare us for the next component of Peirce's semiotic.

The Triadic Sign: Representamen

For Peirce, any "object itself," as Bazin calls it, is always mediated to viewers as a sign, what he calls a representamen. Because of this, Peirce identified the representamen as "First" in perception, whereas the object it represents is "the Second": we know an object exists because of its representamen. In other words, objects, though existing on their own, always represent something to their viewers. For instance, in most movies dogs are representamens of comforting, playful companions, but in some films they signal cultural decay, functioning as post-apocalyptic marauders.[10]

Even within the same film, dramatic effects can be achieved through change to an object's sign value. *Jaws* (Steven Spielberg) terrified millions of people in 1975 by undermining a common representamen. Early in the film, a comely female runs into a calm ocean, waters sparkling from the rising sun. Like a synchronized swimmer, she gracefully lifts her leg in the air to the non-diegetic accompaniment of a famous waltz, creating for most viewers a representamen of peaceful beauty. Suddenly, however, the girl gasps, pulled under and through the water by an unseen creature, resurfacing multiple times until she finally disappears. As people who attended the premiere of *Jaws* will attest, a representamen in their own world—sunrise over a calm ocean—suddenly signified something different than peacefulness, causing some to later hesitate before taking an ocean swim.

A similar change explains the power of Alfred Hitchcock's famous shower scene in *Psycho* (1960): a place of solitude, safety, and cleanliness suddenly became a representamen of terrifying vulnerability.[11] (Significantly, both *Jaws* and *Psycho* employ non-diegetic music to intensify the representamen change: a low-register Boom-ba Boom-ba Boom-ba in *Jaws* and a similarly repetitive high-register staccato in *Psycho*.) Horror movies, in fact, usually work by subverting representamens of comfort and safety, often to outrageous extremes.

Emphasis on the representamen aligns with neoformalist and cognitivist film theories, usually identified with Kristin Thompson, David Bordwell, and Noël Carroll.[12] These scholars assess how cinematic "schemata" and "cues" constructed by filmmakers elicit cognitive response, such that each spectator "*participates* in creating the illusion."[13] Their emphasis on viewer response, though often criticized, prepares us for the last component of Peirce's triadic sign.[14]

The Triadic Sign: Interpretant

The interpretant is the sign that registers in a film viewer's mind. For instance, a person who cannot swim might not actually *see* the sparkling ocean swim in *Jaws* as beautifully enticing the way others do. Interpretants, then, are about the ways we *see* representamens, not how we interpret them. And our interpretants are molded by what Peirce calls "collateral experience."[15] Interpretants, in other words, are shaped by experiences of the body, explaining why people of different genders, races, and sexualities often see signs differently.

Bodies are also affected by where and when they live. Cultural contexts inculcate what Peirce calls "habits" of perception "independent of the vagaries of me and you," as when many seventeenth-century people actually *saw* mountains as ugly.[16] Even within the same era, habits of perception differ from culture to culture. For example, while watching Hollywood comedies in Paris, Americans often laugh at entirely different sequences than do French audiences. Similarly, American viewers of award-winning Bollywood films, in which the entire Indian cast suddenly breaks into song and dance, may consider the scenarios as contrived—until, through the "collateral experience" of education, they learn that, in traditional Sanskrit theater, "there were no separate words for drama and dance," music and dance therefore "integrated into all forms of drama."[17] In sum, while Saussure's structuralism focuses almost entirely on mental manipulation, Peirce's semiotic considers the bodies of viewers: not simply where they are culturally situated but also what they have individually experienced.[18] This Peircean assumption has special meaning for feminist critics.

Peirce and Viewer Agency: Feminist Film Theory

In the early 1980s, two influential feminist theorists included Peirce in their assessment of the relation between cinema and female subjectivity. Lucidly summarizing various structuralist approaches, including that of Laura Mulvey (discussed in Chapter 3), Kaja Silverman applauds "the Peircean scheme, which offers a more satisfactory explanation of the role of the cognitive subject in the signifying process."[19]

Proving Silverman's point, Teresa De Lauretis explores how Peirce can enrich film theory. First she challenges various structuralist approaches to cinema, arguing that they place spectators in a passive position. As we have seen, for theorists influenced by Saussure, the cinematic apparatus generates and controls meaning, whether in the form of filmic codes or through the hegemonic signifiers of capitalist ideology. In contrast, De Lauretis argues, Peirce's triadic semiotic gives viewers agency, reinforcing that "each person goes to the movies with a semiotic history."[20]

By the twenty-first century, scholars were theorizing the body's relation to cinema in ways that exceed the sense of sight. In *The Skin of the Film*, and even more so in *Touch*, Laura U. Marks cites Peirce as she explores various ways cinema and other media arouse senses like touch, taste, and smell, illustrating how various senses are emphasized and filmed differently by different cultures. In *Carnal Thoughts*, Vivian Sobchack employs the language of semiotics to argue that cinema uses "sign-vehicles" to carry the body, itself a "precinct of signifiers," to sensations that it "makes sense of." The viewing body therefore engages with objects on the screen in a dynamic reciprocal relationship, giving and taking sensation and sense.[21]

The Passion of the Body: *The Passion of the Christ*

Though saying little about bodily senses other than vision, Peirce's work can nevertheless help unpack religious analyses of film. He implies that embodied interpretants situated in different religious backgrounds will actually *see* cinema differently. Take, for example, the radically different responses to Mel Gibson's *The Passion of the Christ* (2004).[22] Christians flocked to the film, despite what some identified as its Roman Catholic obsession with Christ's suffering, and what others descried as Gibson's anti-Semitism.[23] Rather than denouncing one or another of these various responses, we might attempt to understand them according to Peirce's semiotic, thus deconstructing binary oppositions like Jewish versus Christian, or Protestant versus Roman Catholic. Following the lead of Teresa de Lauretis, we should consider how "semiotic history" affects the way interpretants perceive representamens of objects on screen.

In *Signs and Meaning in the Cinema*, Peter Wollen outlines three ways an object on screen can function as representamen: what Peirce calls icon, index, and symbol. While an icon represents an object by its resemblance to it, an index points to the object that caused it.[24] For example, when a film cuts to a close-up on a heart-monitor that suddenly flat-lines, the filmmakers do not want viewers to see it as an icon of the hospital's technological prowess. The close-up instead *points to* the status of the object/person attached to the monitor: it is an index of life or death. Another common index in movies is vomiting, almost always pointing to emotional trauma in the afflicted character rather than functioning as an icon of gastric problems. In contrast to an icon or index, a symbol has meaning determined by cultural convention, as when Christians pray with folded hands while Muslims pray with open hands placed to the side of the face.

How viewers respond to *The Passion of the Christ*, then, depends on how their interpretants perceive various representamens. Those who regard the blood and gore as *icons* of excessively abusive torture are probably more disturbed than those who see the blood as an *index* of self-denying sacrifice, Jesus willing to undergo whatever it takes to atone for the sins of the world. Those who see the Pharisees and Sadducees as *icons* of Jewish resistance to "the truth" are certainly more disturbed than people who regard the leaders as *symbols* for all of humanity, the sins of which put Jesus to death. Of course, Mel Gibson would have done well to think of audience interpretants when he showered Los Angeles police with disgusting anti-Semitic slurs after being stopped for erratic driving two years after the film's release. Collateral experience gained through media reports of Gibson's offensive behavior helped legitimize interpretants that perceived anti-Semitism in the film.

However, to reduce *The Passion of the Christ* to either a "good film" or a "bad film" would perpetuate the binary thinking that Umberto Eco, influenced by Peirce, calls "the fundamentalist fallacy" discussed in Chapter 5.[25] Although many films do indeed deserve unstinting praise or disgusted dismissal, a movie that elicits diverse interpretants should be critiqued for both its strengths and weaknesses. And one strength of *The Passion of the Christ* is creative manipulation of the medium. For example, in the crucifixion scene Gibson used computer-generated imagery to simulate an aerial shot, in which the camera looks down on a scene from a crane or helicopter. Viewers are given a "bird's-eye view" as a huge ball of water drops from the sky over Jesus on the cross. The insertion of what seems to be a tear from heaven symbolizes not only God's sorrow at the violence generated by human sin, but also God's power to wash away sin's bloody consequences.[26] Rather than gratuitous, then, the film's antecedent gore intensifies the symbolic power of baptismal purification made available through the crucifixion. The representamen, as perceived by interpretants familiar with Christian symbolism, delivers the message.

Religion and Film: From Icon, Index, and Symbol to Habit Change

Peirce's second triad also helps explain the different approaches to cinema taken by theologians and religion scholars, as outlined in Chapter 1.[27] Pastors and professors who celebrate "story" regard films as parable-like *icons* of existence from which theological/religious insights might be extracted. Unfortunately, as Ehrat aptly notes in his book on Peirce, such treatment is usually a "relapse not into cinematic Iconicity but into narrative Iconicity." Failing to consider "the specificity of cinema *in se*," people taking this approach emphasize "messages or morals."[28]

Equally problematic, however, is scholarship that is solely indexical or primarily symbolic. Those who value experiences of transcendence seem to privilege any film that might "*point* beyond itself toward the transcendental dimension," as Michael Bird puts it: successful cinema as an *index* of spiritual enlightenment.[29] And those who focus on audience reception seem to regard cinema as *symbolic* of human thirst for "meaning-making." Scholars on all three paths are "gnostic" anytime they fail to assess *how* the representamen—whether icon, index, or symbol—*presents* its object.

Significantly, as noted by German semiotician Elisabeth Walther, Peirce sometimes substituted the word "medium" for "representamen."[30] And Deledalle, who suggested that Peirce can guide us around Plato's cave, asserts that "Peirce has proposed the best theory of signs which can fit McLuhan's theory of the media": a theory summarized with "the medium is the message."[31] Despite his potential to revolutionize religion and film, however, Peirce is little known and rarely studied, largely due to his opacity. As semiotician Jonathan Culler soberly notes, Peirce establishes "ten trichotomies by which signs can be classified ... yielding a possible 59,049 classes of sign."[32] Furthermore, among his 100,000+ pages of theory, most of it unpublished, Peirce sometimes changes the definitions of his already opaque terms, adding to the confusion. Nevertheless, his "trichotomy of the sign" lays the foundation for a triadic approach to narrative cinema, encouraging attention to three interdependent components in the analysis of any one film:

- diegetic *objects* that visualize story
- screen artistry shaping *representamens*
- the semiotic history of embodied *interpretants*.

All three are necessary for the medium to become message. Furthermore, Peirce provides a means for distinguishing artful movies from those that cynically pander to unreflective audiences.

Key to Peirce's semiotic is the idea of "semiosis," a word he coined to explain "habit-change," something he aligns with "acts of imagination" and the element of "surprise."[33] In the case of cinematic "acts of imagination," filmmakers concerned more about financial returns than about screen artistry usually employ generic representamens that appeal to generic habits of perception, surprising viewers merely by intensifying the clichés: making the violence more graphic; the sex and nudity more erotic; the chase-scenes more harrowing; the monsters more terrifying; the humor more crass; the sentimentality more saccharine.

One clichéd "surprise," for example, is to have gorgeous actors play roles in which they appear ugly. Such performances often generate accolades from viewers amazed that a sexy celebrity is dedicated enough to his or her craft to take on such a role. But the performance rarely generates "habit-change," for it merely reminds viewers of the star's usually stunning good-looks. Consider, for example, the emaciated figures of Matthew McConaughey and Jared Leto in *Dallas Buyers Club* (Jean-Marc Vallée, 2013). The left-leaning *Slant Magazine* went so far as to challenge Academy Award nominations for the movie, arguing that "The 'bravery' of actors losing weight has grossly overshadowed how toxic *Dallas Buyers Club* is for the culture at large." Putting the movie, instead, on a list of "The Ten Worst Films of 2013," *Slant* contributors essentially argued that the movie fails to generate habit-change in regard to signs about the AIDS crisis.[34]

The Wizardry of Firstness, Secondness, and Thirdness: From Kansas to Oz

Of course, habit-change relies not only on well-crafted representamens but also on the sophistication of interpretants, which, for Peirce, function at three different levels: Firstness, Secondness, and Thirdness. Though Peirce applies Firstness, Secondness, and Thirdness to every possible kind of signifying operation, explaining why he has 59,049 classes of sign, most helpful in this context is his distinction of an "immediate" from a "dynamic" and "final" interpretant. As Sean Cubitt notes in *The Cinema Effect*, these categories roughly correlate to "sensation, cognition, and comprehension" of the cinematic sign.[35]

Consider, for example, the sudden change from black and white to color in *The Wizard of Oz* (Victor Fleming, 1939). Initially viewers experience the *immediate* sensation of color, the interpretant not yet making sense of the sensation. Next comes the dynamic interpretant, in which cognition elicits emotional response: delight that Dorothy has escaped a black-and-white world for a more colorful realm. The final interpretant (thirdness) comprehends what this may mean: Dorothy has left behind a limited existence in Kansas to experience a realm of hope and possibility.

Or think of the scene when Dorothy and her companions discover that the Great Oz is merely an artificial projection generated by a bumbling "wizard." The revelation comes, of course, after Dorothy's dog Toto pulls away a curtain revealing a man manipulating buttons and levers inside a booth. The viewer first experiences an *immediate interpretant*: the initial sensation of distraction, the shot turning attention away from the Great Oz on his throne. The *dynamic interpretant* is the effect the image has on the viewer, which is often expressed physiologically, as in laughter, tensed muscles, or open-mouthed surprise. Third is the *final interpretant*, when the viewer comprehends the representamen: Toto has revealed the artifice of Oz.

Despite the term *final*, cognition does not end there. In Peirce's evolutionary semiosis, the *final interpretant* becomes a new sign, thus leading active minds through the same triadic process to a new *final interpretant*, perhaps about the apparent futility of Dorothy's trip to the Emerald City. And the process keeps going, eliciting multiple interpretations as people with different "semiotic histories" come to different conclusions about what they have seen. David C. Downing, for example, argues that *The Wizard of Oz* illustrates a demythologized view of religion: "Even though the god-figure is merely a human projection, all have found what they sought merely by believing him."[36]

The common moviegoer, of course, rarely moves beyond dynamic interpretants, explaining an apt comment by John May: "Movies are felt by the audience long before they are 'understood' *if indeed they are ever fully understood.*"[37] Hollywood, of course, counts on the failure of semiosis. Movies made merely for money appeal primarily to immediate and dynamic interpretants, their signs offering either cinematic clichés or outrageous scenarios that make little sense when analyzed.[38] Hence, in contrast to movies that primarily pander to economies of exchange, artistically significant films encourage the habit-change that arises from semiosis, often by drawing attention to the medium itself.

For Peirce, then, the triadic sign encourages gift-giving rather than an economy of exchange: the representamen makes a "gift" of the object to the interpretant. In contrast, "a dyadic, binary reduction of sense," as Ehrat explains, "cannot render the triadic operation *of giving.*"[39] A beautiful example of gift-giving appears in *The Politics of Iranian Cinema*. The author, Saeed Zeydabadi-Nejad, considers the "Islamization" of cinema after the Ayatollah Khomeini came to power, discussing organizations established to monitor cinematic portrayals of Islam. However, rather than denounce the resulting censorship of Iranian-made films, Zeydabadi-Nejad instead considers the semiotic history of both censors and spectators, interviewing Muslims about their viewing practices. And what he discovers is a triadic operation of giving, moviegoers watching for representamens of censorship in the medium itself: "Any slight jump in the picture often alerts them to the censors' scissors having been at work." Such viewers then gather to discuss what object the discarded representamen may have been offering, their final interpretants giving back to the filmmaker artistic freedom: "The pleasure that this activity gives the viewers is twofold; one in the 'discovery of oppositional messages' in the films or guessing what a censored message may have been. The other is the social pleasure of sharing what one has noticed with others."[40] Gifts of habit-changing semiosis have been offered on several different levels.

Semiosis and Habit-Change: *A Lonely Place to Die* and *The Wall*

While Iranian viewers make a gift of what they do not see on screen, moviegoers in other countries might learn from their hospitality, welcoming the unexpected gifts that artistic filmmakers explicitly offer. *A Lonely Place to Die* (Judy Gilbey, 2011), for example, plays with habitual understanding of cinematic devices to create thought-provoking "surprise." Early in the film, mountain climbers in Scotland discover a little girl who has been buried underground by kidnappers. After they develop plans to carry her to the nearest town, we see long shots of them hiking that are intercut with images of insidious-looking hunters in camouflage. Habitually used to POV shots, we assume that, every time we see the hunters aiming their rifles off-screen, followed by a long shot of the girl's rescuers, the hunters are aiming their guns at the rescuers. Trained to read film this way, our interpretants actually *see* the hunters as representamens of the girl's kidnappers, seeking to retrieve her for ransom. We are therefore confused when two new characters violently confront the hunters: are they good guys protecting the child? Or are they interlopers seeking to abscond with the ransom? After the newcomers kill the hunters, we are given another POV shot, this time through the scope of the dead hunter's rifle, which shows a herd of deer. Suddenly forced into a habit-change, we realize that what we originally regarded as POV shots were actually signs of crosscutting: the camera cutting back and forth between simultaneous actions of camouflaged hunters illegally stalking deer and rescuers hiking toward town. This habit-change, generated by semiotics of the medium itself, foreshadows the change in habit that culminates the film. We discover that the rescuers, most of whom die protecting the life of the child, unknowingly sacrificed their lives to satisfy the desires of a notorious Serbian war criminal, the child's father. Unlike classic Hollywood films that habitually reward rescuers, *A Lonely Place to Die* forces viewers to rethink their notion of heroism, to reassess notions of reward for meritorious action.

Another brilliant film encouraging habit-change is *The Wall* (Julian Pölsler, 2012), an Austrian-German adaptation of the 1963 Austrian novel *Die Wand*. It begins with an attractive middle-aged woman (Martina Gedeck) sitting in the backseat of a convertible as friends drive her along a beautiful mountain lake to their hunting cabin in the Austrian Alps. The shot cuts back and forth between close-ups on the woman seated against the side of the car and close-ups on a dog leaning out the other side of the backseat. By *not* putting the dog and woman together in the same shot, the filmmakers emphasize the distance between them, the woman warily glancing across the seat before the camera cuts to her point of view on the dog, Lynx. Later, when she first timidly attempts to pet Lynx, the dog growls and snaps at her hand. This prepares us for a habit-change later in the film, when Lynx will become her closest friend.

The change occurs due to a bizarre occurrence. After a night alone in the cabin, the unnamed woman searches for her friends, who failed to return from their evening stroll. As she follows their path along the lake, she suddenly runs up against an invisible, impenetrable wall. The scene is shot from the other side of the clear barrier as the woman faces it, such that when she places her hands on the wall, it looks to us as though she is placing her hands on our film screen, searching for a way out of the mise-en-scène that contains her. However, rather than breaking the fourth wall to draw attention to significance beyond the screen, the woman never looks into the camera, as though to signal that life on her side of the transparent screen is inescapable. *The Wall*, like the wall it contains, thus forces attentive viewers to think about the apparatus of cinema, challenging their habitual submission to cinematic illusion: the illusion that movie characters are free, choosing to do things viewers wish they could do, including breaking through the confining walls of everyday existence.

Thus undermining what is called "the reality-effect" of "classical Hollywood style,"[41] *The Wall* also relies heavily on voice-overs. For the most part, the classical style avoids voice-overs in order to sustain the illusion that the film screen is a "window" on the real world, a world in which it is impossible to hear others' thoughts. Throughout *The Wall*, in contrast, we hear the woman's ruminations on what the invisible wall means and how it affects her view of reality. *The Wall* thus draws attention to the changing interpretant of a character caught behind the plate-glass wall of the movie screen.

And viewer interpretants change in the process. As the film's protagonist explores Alpine territory hemmed in by the invisible wall, viewers start to view the Alpine scenery differently. Snow-capped peaks that we originally perceived as sublimely beautiful become representamens of imprisonment. As though creating a visual pun, a clear lens *capturing* Alpine vistas has *captured* the woman behind a clear wall. Thus *capturing* our attention as well, the film nudges us toward habit-change, like that of the woman *captured* both in and by the film. The dog, whom she first regards with apprehension, she comes to see with eyes of love. Originally disgusted with killing—even in order to eat—she ends up killing another human to protect animals she now considers her dearest friends. Viewers are thus encouraged to contemplate their own *views* about killing, as well as the distinction between animal and human that the woman discusses in voice-over.

The Wall thus illustrates "post-classical cinema" as defined by Eleftheria Thanouli. Unlike movies in the classical Hollywood style, which elicit for viewers the illusion of sitting "in front of a plate-glass window to the fictional world,"[42] *The Wall* draws attention to the illusion, encouraging attentive viewers to think about the plate-glass itself: how it is part of an apparatus that limits any film character to a camera-controlled mise-en-scène.[43] Characterized, in addition, by the use of voice-overs, post-classical film inculcates the self-reflexivity associated with avant-garde cinema, which usually disdains viewer reliance on entertaining stories. As Thanouli explains, self-reflexive films "refuse a transparent self-effacing cinematic language and opt for a 're-materialization of the filmic signifiers'"—as when *The Wall* re-materializes the transparent screen as a material barrier.[44] Thanouli, however, deconstructs the binary between the self-reflexive "aestheticism" of avant-garde films and the "realism" of classical Hollywood film by arguing that a post-classical film offers *both* an interesting story, accessibly rendered, *and* self-reflexive attention to the medium. A good example of post-classical cinema as Thanouli defines it is *Salmon Fishing in the Yemen* (Lasse Hallström, 2011), a film with intense religious significance.

Salmon Fishing in the Yemen: Catching the Medium

The novel *Salmon Fishing in the Yemen*, by Paul Torday, ends with a famous statement by the father of Latin Christianity, Tertullian (c. 160–c. 225 CE): *Credo, quia impossibile est*, or "I believe, because it is impossible."[45] In both the novel and the film, however, such belief is aligned with a Muslim, Sheikh Muhammad ibn Zaidi bani Tihama who wants to do something miraculous by bringing salmon fishing to his native Yemen. Significantly, while the novel's story line occasionally alludes to faith, the film creatively visualizes tensions about faith in the medium, making it a prime example of salvation from cinema.

In both the novel and the film, Sheikh Muhammad (Amr Waked) hires a London investment firm to oversee his "miracle." When the firm's consultant tries to recruit a fisheries expert, Dr. Alfred (Fred) Jones (Ewan McGregor) to coordinate the project, Fred scoffs at the plan, calling it "fundamentally unfeasible." The consultant therefore flies Fred to the sheikh's Scottish castle where the two men fly-fish in a stream, the film capturing Muhammad in his Yemeni robes and Fred in his British waders. At a candlelit dinner afterwards, the sheikh says of his plan "It would be a miracle of God if it were to happen," and Fred responds with skepticism: "I'm more a facts and figures man." Muhammad, however, subverts Fred's habits of perception by pointing out how much time Fred spends in streams waiting for a bite: "Is that a good use of your time? ... But you persist ... Why? ... Because you're a man of faith, Dr. Alfred." When Fred protests that "fishing and religion are hardly the same thing," the sheikh responds, "I have to disagree. ... A toast to faith and fish!"

And, sure enough, the outrageous plan works out, salmon eventually swimming upstream through a former Yemeni desert as Fred and Harriet (the consultant, played by Emily Blunt) fall in love. The film thus delivers a common cinematic sermon: in both life and love ya gotta have faith. Not much habit-change there. Furthermore, since the "miraculous" project is only made possible by the sheikh's fifty-million-pound investment, the message about "faith" would be gratuitous, based on an economy of exchange, if not for the *object–representamen* relation on the screen. Employing sly cinematic techniques, the medium of *Salmon Fishing* deepens the message, quite literally.

The film begins with a full-frame image of raging waters, the shot next cutting to under the water, the screen now filled with fish. After a montage of underwater shots, the camera then tilts up out of the water to the sky, so that for a moment the screen is split between the underwater realm and reality above it. This begins a visual motif that captures the essence of the film: the split between the empirical realm endorsed by Fred and the unseen mysteries of "faith and fish" that lie underneath.

The camera once again captures both realms when the sheikh and Fred go fishing. After the sheikh, a man of faith, catches a fish using a fly designed by Fred, a man of science, the screen is momentarily split, half the shot under water, the other half above. It is the very next scene, around a dinner table, in which the sermon about faith occurs. Fred, resistant to habit-change, adds to the sheikh's toast to "faith and fish," the phrase "and science." This division between the realm of faith and the realm of science, then, is anticipated by shots in which the screen is literally divided between realms of water—the location of unseen fish—and the air surrounding all that is seen above.

To reinforce this message of the medium, the dining-room scene is framed by Fred and Harriet walking down a hall toward the dining room and then walking back to their rooms via the same hall, giving the sense of a medieval triptych in which the central scene is the most significant. In the framing shots—on either side of the central "faith and fish" conversation—a large painting appears on the left wall, filling half the screen the first time, a third of the screen the second time. The image quite clearly alludes to multiple Renaissance depictions of St. Jerome translating the Bible into Latin. A long-bearded old man leans his head on one hand, looking discouraged, while the other hand holds a quill that he has apparently been applying to the open book behind his head.[46] It is an image of faith in the midst of a task many would consider "fundamentally unfeasible"—like salmon fishing in the Yemen.

The first time we see the Jerome painting, the screen appears split from side-to-side: the framed painting on the left (the realm of faith) with Fred on the right (the realm of science). But then, in the background of the shot, Harriet appears through a doorway where she stops to look at Fred. The heavy frame around the door makes Harriet look like another painting. And, indeed, it will be she that enables Fred to synthesize faith and science, foreshadowed when they return to their rooms after the toast about "faith and fish and science": they walk along the same hall, this time appearing together beside St. Jerome.

After the second Jerome shot, the film immediately cuts to another split image. This time the surface of a Scottish stream fills the lower half of the screen with a brightly lit sky above it, until the shot cuts to fish under the water. This prepares us for the moment when Fred, making a habit-change, finally commits to the "fundamentally unfeasible" salmon project. His turning point is visualized on the screen as a literal turning. We see him going with the flow along a crowded London sidewalk when he suddenly stops and turns around. A crane shot captures the turn from above, so that we see him walking alone against the flow of people, pushing and bumping against them—like a fish swimming upstream. Then, to later visualize the miracle's fulfillment in Yemen, we are given a graphic match of this scene: a shot underwater shows masses of salmon swimming in one direction until one turns around and swims against the flow to spawn upstream. The medium thus captures the miracle of faith in two senses: the miracle of Fred stepping out in faith to go against the flow of common sense, which results in the miracle of salmon going against the flow in the Yemen.

To reinforce Fred's habit-change—the watershed moment when he realizes how the plan might work—the camera once again captures the double realms of air and water. Fred stands by the koi pond in his backyard arguing with his wife, Mary, who contemptuously tells him it's in his DNA to stay married to her. At that moment the shot cuts, such that the lens is once again half under and half above water, as though we are getting a fish's perspective on Fred and Mary above. Once Mary leaves, a bubbling stream fills the screen and we hear a voice-over of Mary's statement: "It's in your DNA." Significantly, that *scientific concept* energizes Fred's *faith* in the project: he believes that even farm-raised salmon "will run" because it's in their DNA. When the sheikh hears of Fred's breakthrough, he responds by asking whether Fred's sudden support of the project is based on "new research." But rather than confirm a scientific perspective, Fred asserts, "I just know it!" After the devout sheikh comments, "I see ... Faith, Dr. Alfred?" Fred grumbles, "Yes ... Faith!"

To confirm the need for *both* faith *and* science, the film also visualizes the opposite side of the issue: what happens when faith refuses scientific advancement.

Before his DNA insight, Fred gives up on the project when the British fishing industry refuses to sell wild salmon to the Yemen. Asserting that farmed salmon won't work, Fred responds to Muhammad's words, "We must have faith, Dr. Alfred," with "You can't catch faith with a fishing rod." Immediately after this statement, which is delivered in the middle of the stream in Scotland, a Muslim fundamentalist tries to assassinate the Muslim sheikh because he is bringing "Western [scientific] ways to the land" of Yemen. Noticing the assassin's gun just in time, Fred casts his fish line at the would-be-murderer, hooking him so that his bullet misses the mark. We see, then, that one *can* "catch faith with a fishing rod." Hence, while scientific certitude nearly sabotages the salmon project in the first half of the film, religious certitude nearly sabotages the project in the second half of the film: the either/or thinking of binary oppositions. The point, of course, is that humans need to avoid such oppositions, allowing science to inform faith and faith to inform science. Both realms shape one's perspective on life—much as a camera lens might visualize underwater and above-water realms simultaneously.

To emphasize two realms viewed through one lens, director Lasse Hallström repeatedly visualizes the opposite: a severed split between perspectives. He does so using a split-screen technique, such that it looks like two separate projector lenses are throwing their different images side-by-side in the same frame. As though alluding to the problematic split between faith-based versus science-based fundamentalisms, Hallström literally splits the screen between people who try to impose their certitude on others. This happens most often in a subplot about a press secretary who seeks to control the news reported by media outlets, much as fundamentalists—both religious and scientific—try to control the way others interpret reality. We see her with a phone on one side of the screen as she harangues a person that appears on the other side of the screen. Hallström even puns on the "split-screen" technique by showing computer screens split with Skyped images of people arguing about fish (which, as the medium makes clear, represent the realm of faith). Significantly, the only time we see a radical failure of communication between Harriet and Fred is with a split-screen phone call, Fred appearing on the left side of our screen, Harriet refusing to answer the phone on the right. The technique, which always indicates physical distance between two representamens, here implies emotional distance as well. Like the screen, their relationship is severed at this point in the plot.

As in most films using the technique, the split-screening within *Salmon Fishing in the Yemen*, creates a *vertical* line of separation between images shot with separate lenses. In contrast, all the splits between the realms of water and air are *horizontal*, shot with one camera lens. The medium, then, is the message: a constellation of multiple split-screen images signal the need to synthesize, rather than sever, the seemingly disparate realms of faith and science. Another way to put it is in the language of Peirce-endorser Jacques Derrida: *Salmon Fishing in the Yemen* deconstructs the binary oppositions between faith and empiricism, religion and science, cultural traditionalism and habit-changing progress. Rather than looking at each half of a binary through the separate lenses of a split screen, deconstruction encourages viewers to use one lens, one that visualizes the interdependence of different realms of discourse. *Salmon Fishing* thus captures, as from waters on its screen, Derrida's sense that "the most theoretical act of any scientific community ... appeals to an act of faith."[47]

Acts of Faith in Religion and Film

Describing deconstruction as "openness toward the other,"[48] Derrida recognizes that C. S. Peirce fishes from the same stream. Encouraging habit-change, Peirce challenges dogmatism in both faith and science, calling it "the fixation of belief."[49] (Significantly, Umberto Eco, who coined "Fundamentalist Fallacy," was a Peirce scholar.) More importantly, Peirce makes "the other" part of the sign itself.

As we have seen, Peirce's triadic sign resists the binary oppositions that have plagued film theory, from Bazin's "long-standing opposition between realism and aestheticism on the screen" to the "consistent binarism" of theorists who attribute cinematic effects to some kind of autonomous power, whether that of auteurs, of genres, or of signifiers.[50] While Metz and apparatus theorists put all the power in the hands of ideologically manipulated (and manipulating) filmmakers, Peirce gives power back to the viewer. An *object* visualized on screen, no matter how creatively presented as *representamen*, has creative power only by way of the *interpretant*. At the same time, the triadic sign precludes one-sided discussions of audience reception that have infiltrated the field of religion and film. Each component of the sign needs *the other*. As Peirce appreciator M. Gail Hamner argues in her aptly titled *Imaging Religion in Film*,

> religion lies not in the film itself, nor in the viewer's mind or act of interpretation, but rather in the *movement* between construction and connotation or between the film's material composition and presentation, and the viewer's creative reception of them.[51]

Without creative reception, even experimental and post-classical films fail to generate habit-change. At the same time, a "classical Hollywood style" movie, one easily dismissed by avant-garde elitists, can both illustrate and encourage habit-change—at least for those attentive to the medium itself.[52] This does not mean that well-crafted films should cause people to change their beliefs. Habit-change refers, instead, to changes in the way people of faith (including those with faith in science or Marxism or capitalism) *see* and *understand* their beliefs.

Encouraging openness to the other—whether divine or human, transcendent or immanent—religion, for Peirce, echoes the "Relational events in the Sign" that ground perception. As he put it in the gendered language of 1902, "To believe in a god at all, is not that to believe that man's reason is allied to the originating principle of the universe?" Furthermore, as he argues a year later, that very "universe is a vast representamen, a great symbol of God's purpose, working out its conclusions in living realities."[53] The parallel with cinema is clear: every well-made film is an extended representamen (what Peirce calls a *medium*), a great symbol of its filmmakers' purpose, working out its conclusions in living realities projected by the cinematic apparatus. But it takes a creative interpretant, what I earlier called a "beautiful mind," to recognize the constellation-like patterns that take shape on the canvas of the screen.

Notes

1. Jacques Derrida, *The Gift of Death* (Chicago: University of Chicago Press, 1995).
2. Jacques Lacan, "The Mirror Stage as Formative of the Function of the 'I' as Revealed in Psychoanalytic Experience," in *Écrits: A Selection*, trans. Alan Sheridan (New York: Norton, 1977), 3; Jacques Lacan, *The Seminar of Jacques Lacan, Book I: Freud's Papers on Technique, 1953–54*, trans. John Forrester (Cambridge: Cambridge University Press, 1988), 276.
3. Derrida, "Circumfession," in Geoffrey Bennington and Jacques Derrida, eds, *Jacques Derrida*, trans. Geoffrey Bennington (Chicago: University of Chicago Press, 1993), 155. Using the ambiguous phrase "I rightly pass for an atheist," Derrida deconstructed certitude about his atheism. Since Peirce felt similar ambivalence about his own Christianity, the phrase "rightly pass" applies to him as well.
4. Gérard Deledalle, "Media between Balnibarbi and Plato's Cave," in *Semiotics of the Media: State of the Art, Projects, and Perspectives*, ed. Winfried Nöth (Berlin & New York: Mouton de Gruyter, 1997), 55.
5. Peter Wollen, *Signs and Meaning in the Cinema* (Bloomington: Indiana University Press, 1969), 136. Craig Detweiler briefly introduces Wollen's appropriation of Peirce in "Seeing and Believing: Film Theory as a Window into a Visual Faith," in *Reframing Theology and Film: New Focus for an Emerging Discipline*, Robert K. Johnston, ed. (Grand Rapids: Baker Academic, 2007), 44–5. Detweiler, however, quickly transitions into the Eastern Orthodox understanding of icons, which, though fascinating, has little to do with Peirce's employment of the term.
6. Johannes Ehrat, *Cinema and Semiotic: Peirce and Film Aesthetics, Narration, and Representation* (Toronto: University of Toronto Press, 2005), 11. If I had not already read scores upon scores of works by and about Peirce, I would have been baffled by explanations like this: "'Once upon a time' functions semiosically as an 'uncoupling' de-Dicent, 'de-Indexizer'; it quite literally disorients spatiotemporally and constructs a new universe with a Symbolic, Legisign Interpretant: the plot" (Ehrat, 134). Since my goal is to illuminate religious approaches to cinema more than Peirce's philosophy, I have skipped over most of Peirce's coinages, inevitably sacrificing nuance in the process.
7. Kaja Silverman, *The Threshold of the Visible World* (New York: Routledge, 1996), 2.
8. André Bazin, "The Ontology of the Photographic Image," *What Is Cinema?*, vol. 1, translated Hugh Gray (Berkeley: University of California Press, 1967), 14, emphasis mine. Bazin repeatedly uses the word "realism" in his work.
9. Gilles Deleuze, *Cinema 1: The Movement-Image*, trans. Hugh Tomlinson and Barbara Habberjam (Minneapolis: University of Minnesota Press, 1986), 58. The second Deleuze quotation, taken from *Cinéma 2: L'image-temps* (Paris: Éditions de Minuit, 1985), is translated by and quoted in D. N. Rodowick, *Gilles Deleuze's Time Machine* (Durham: Duke University Press, 1997), 41. Rodowick parallels Deleuze with Bazin on p. 44.
10. This differs dramatically from the way Deleuze discusses Peirce. Interested primarily in perceptions of movement and time in cinema, Deleuze appropriates Peirce's concepts of Firstness, Secondness, and Thirdness to discuss the philosophic implications of perception itself, almost entirely ignoring the visual medium. As Rodowick

laments, Deleuze rarely illustrates his difficult theory with tangible examples (xiv). Furthermore, "What Deleuze calls an image or a sign can vary to a dizzying degree, and Deleuze's definition of the sign clearly differs from Peirce's in many respects" (Rodowick, *Gilles Deleuze's Time Machine*, 58).

11 For a helpful discussion of cinematic technique in *Psycho*, see Larry E. Grimes, "Shall These Bones Live? The Problem of Bodies in Alfred Hitchcock's *Psycho* and Joel Coen's *Blood Simple*," in *Screening the Sacred: Religion, Myth, and Ideology in Popular American Film*, ed. Joel W. Martin and Conrad E. Ostwalt Jr. (Boulder: Westview, 1995), 19–25.

12 Kristin Thompson, *Breaking the Glass Armor: Neoformalist Film Analysis* (Princeton: Princeton University Press, 1988); David Bordwell, *Making Meaning: Inference and Rhetoric in the Interpretation of Cinema* (Cambridge: Harvard University Press, 1989); David Bordwell and Noël Carroll, eds, *Post-Theory: Reconstructing Film Studies* (Madison: University of Wisconsin Press, 1996).

13 David Bordwell, Janet Staiger, and Kristin Thompson, *The Classical Hollywood Cinema: Film Style and Mode of Production to 1960* (New York: Columbia University Press, 1985), 7.

14 Peirce's tripartite interpretant reinforces the role of emotions in cognitivist film theory, which is well summarized in Mitch Avila, "From Film Emotion to Normative Criticism," *Reframing Theology and Film*, 219–37.

15 Peirce scholars tend not to discuss "collateral experience," a phrase (along with "collateral observation" and "collateral acquaintance") that Peirce employs several times in his papers. Kaja Silverman is one of the few who refer to "collateral acquaintance," in *The Subject of Semiotics* (New York: Oxford University Press, 1983), 22. She, like most scholars who value Peirce, cites his papers (CP) by volume and paragraph number, as will I. See The *Collected Papers of Charles Sanders Peirce*, vols 1–6, ed. Charles Hartshorne and Paul Weiss; vols 7 & 8 ed. Arthur W. Burkes (Cambridge: Harvard University Press, 1931–58). Peirce refers to collateral experience, observation, or acquaintance in CP 6.338; 8.178, 179, 183, 314.

16 C. S. Peirce, "Some Consequences of Four Incapacities," in *Philosophical Writings of Peirce*, ed. Justus Buchler (New York: Dover, 1955), 247.

17 Martha P. Nochimson, *World on Film: An Introduction* (Malden: Wiley-Blackwell, 2010), 245.

18 Ehrat summarizes this Peircean perception with, "any knowledge participates in all other knowledge and can be traced back to experiences, be they direct or stored in language" (*Cinema and Semiotic*, 105).

19 Silverman, *The Subject of Semiotics*, 22.

20 Teresa De Lauretis, *Alice Doesn't: Feminism, Semiotics, Cinema* (Bloomington: Indiana University Press, 1984), 145. Some material in this book had been published several years earlier, but De Lauretis's intervention in semiotics, inspired by the work of Peirce scholar Umberto Eco, first appears in this volume. De Lauretis discusses Peirce's emphasis on "the physical world and empirical reality" at greater depth in *Technologies of Gender: Essays on Theory, Film, and Fiction* (Bloomington: Indiana University Press, 1987), 38–41.

21 Laura U. Marks, *The Skin of the Film: Intercultural Cinema, Embodiment, and the Senses* (Durham: Duke University Press, 2000); Laura U. Marks, *Touch: Sensuous Theory and Multisensory Media* (Minneapolis: University of Minnesota Press, 2002); Vivian Sobchack, *Carnal Thoughts: Embodiment and Moving Image Culture* (Berkeley: University of California Press, 2004), 74, 75, 83. Sobchack borrows "sign-vehicle" from Umberto Eco and "precinct of signifiers" from phenomenologist Alphonso Lingis.

22 For overviews of conflicting responses to Gibson's controversial film, see Christopher Deacy, *Faith in Film: Religious Themes in Contemporary Cinema* (Burlington: Ashgate, 2005), 106–26; Sheila J. Nayar, *The Sacred and the Cinema: Reconfiguring the*

"Genuinely" Religious Film (London: Continuum, 2012), 138–41; and the Epilogue to *Cinéma Divinité: Religion, Theology and the Bible in Film*, ed. Eric S. Christianson, Peter Francis, and William R. Telford (London: SCM Press, 2005), 311–30.

23 For a brief discussion of accusations about anti-Semitism and violence in Gibson's film, see James Abbott, "Following His True Passion: Mel Gibson and *The Passion of the Christ*," in *Through a Catholic Lens: Religious Perspectives of Nineteen Film Directors from around the World*, ed. Peter Malone (Lanham: Rowman & Littlefield, 2007), 231–2.

24 Wollen, *Signs and Meaning in the Cinema*, 121–6. Like Wollen, other film scholars tend to reduce Peirce's contribution to cinema studies to the icon–index–symbol trichotomy, discussed in vol. 2 of *CP*, ignoring Peirce's far more fundamental, and helpful, distinction between object, representamen, and interpretant.

25 Umberto Eco, "Semiotics and the Philosophy of Language," in *Reading Eco: An Anthology*, ed. Rocco Capozzi (Bloomington: Indiana University Press, 1997), 7.

26 William R. Telford briefly mentions this technique in "Epilogue: Table Talk: Reflections on *The Passion of the Christ*," in *Cinéma Divinité*, attributing the tear to God's "sadness or judgement" (313).

27 Narrowing the distinction between icon and index to characteristics of the photographic image itself, scholars often discuss whether Bazin regarded photographed objects as icons or indices. See, for example, Tom Gunning, "Moving Away from the Index: Cinema and the Impression of Reality," in Marc Furstenau, ed. *The Film Theory Reader: Debates and Arguments* (New York: Routledge, 2010), 255–60. Paul Coates cites Peirce to establish cinematic images as "'indexical' imprints of the reality they represent" (*Cinema, Religion and the Romantic Legacy* [Burlington: Ashgate, 2003], 45), whereas Kaja Silverman regards all cinematic images as "iconic," arguing that editing generates signifiers that are "indexical" (*Subject of Semiotics*, 22–3).

28 Ehrat, *Cinema and Semiotic*, 146.

29 Michael Bird, "Film as Hierophany," in John R. May and Michael Bird, eds, *Religion in Film* (Knoxville: University of Tennessee Press, 1982), 3–4, emphasis mine.

30 Elisabeth Walther, "The Sign as Medium, the Medium Relation as the Foundation of the Sign" in *Semiotics of the Media*, 79.

31 Deledalle, "Media between Balnibarbi and Plato's Cave," 59.

32 Jonathan Culler, *The Pursuit of Signs: Semiotics, Literature, Deconstruction: An Augmented Edition with a New Preface by the Author* (Ithaca: Cornell University Press, 2002), 23.

33 Peirce, "Pragmatism in Retrospect: A Last Formulation," in *Philosophical Writings*, 278–9.

34 Ed Gonzales and R. Kurt Osenlund, "The 10 Worst Films of 2013," *Slant*, December 27, 2013.

35 Sean Cubitt, *The Cinema Effect* (Cambridge: MIT Press, 2004), 3. See also 48–9, and Ehrat, *Cinema and Semiotic*, 207–8. In his earlier work, Peirce used the less helpful terms *emotional*, *energetic*, and *logical* ("Pragmatism," 277).

36 David C. Downing, "Waiting for Godoz: Deconstructing *The Wizard of Oz*," *Christianity and Literature* (Winter 1984): 28–30. See also J. Scott Cochrane, "*The Wizard of Oz* and Other Mythic Rites of Passage" in *Image and Likeness: Religious Vision in American Film Classics*, ed. John R. May (New York: Paulist, 1992), 79–86.

37 John R. May, ed., paraphrasing Roger Angell, in *Image and Likeness*, 3, emphasis his.

38 Note Ehrat: "Only in its final result is the Aesthetic habit the foundation of a cognitive habit, which might eventually be expressed as an abstract concept" (*Cinema and Semiotic*, 483). On the evolution of semiosis, see Peirce, "Evolutionary Love," *Philosophical Writings*, 364–5.

39 Ehrat, *Cinema and Semiotic*, 122, emphasis mine.

40 Saeed Zeydabadi-Nejad, *The Politics of Iranian Cinema: Film and Society in the Islamic Republic* (New York: Routledge, 2010), 38, 163, 103.

162 Salvation from Film Theory

41 Charles Affron, *Cinema and Sentiment* (Chicago: University of Chicago Press, 1982), 133. The phrase "reality-effect" comes from Roland Barthes's 1968 essay "The Reality Effect," republished in *The Rustle of Language*, trans. Richard Howard (Oxford: Blackwell, 1986), 141–8.
42 Eleftheria Thanouli, *Post-Classical Cinema: An International Poetics of Film Narration* (London: Wallflower, 2009), 72.
43 Thanouli aligns breaking the fourth wall with post-classical cinema, giving the examples of *Run Lola Run* (1998), *Amélie* (2001), *Trainspotting* (1996), and *Fight Club* (1999). *The Wall*, of course, goes one step further, playing with the impossibility of breaking the wall.
44 Thanouli quotes film theorist Thomas Elsaessert (Thanouli, 141). Another element of post-classical cinema reflected in *The Wall* is what Thanouli calls "mediated time" (118). The film jumps back and forth in time as we see images of the woman in the hunting lodge writing down her earlier experiences interspersed with visualizations of those experiences. Lighting techniques help to distinguish the later time of reflection, always shot in low-key lighting, with the earlier experiences, usually shot in high-key lighting.
45 Paul Torday, *Salmon Fishing in the Yemen* (New York: Harvest, 2007), 325.
46 See, for example, *St. Jerome in his Study* by Domenico Ghirlandaio (1480) and *St. Jerome* (1632) by Jacques Blanchard.
47 Jacques Derrida, "Above All, No Journalists!" in *Religion and Media*, ed. Hent de Vries and Samuel Weber (Stanford: Stanford University Press, 2001), 63. Several paragraphs later Derrida says "the pure 'relation to the other,' there where the alterity of the *alter ego* deprives me forever of proof and originary intuition, is faith" (64, emphasis his).
48 "Dialogue with Jacques Derrida," in *Dialogues with Contemporary Continental Thinkers: The Phenomenological Heritage*, ed. Richard Kearney (Manchester: Manchester University Press, 1984), 124.
49 C. S. Peirce, "The Fixation of Belief," in *Philosophical Writings*, 5–22.
50 André Bazin, *What Is Cinema?*, vol. 2, translated Hugh Gray (Berkeley: University of California Press, 1971), 16; Thomas Albert Sebeok, *Semiotics in the United States* (Bloomington: Indiana University Press, 1991), 79.
51 M. Gail Hamner, *Imaging Religion in Film: The Politics of Nostalgia* (New York: Palgrave Macmillan, 2011), 5. Hamner invokes Peirce repeatedly in her book, largely due to his appropriation by Gilles Deleuze, who will be discussed in the next chapter.
52 David Bordwell argues that the "classical style" still dominates Hollywood filmmaking. Directors merely integrate into their classical style techniques developed by avant-garde and foreign filmmakers, demonstrating what Bordwell calls "stylistic assimilation." See David Bordwell, Janet Staiger, and Kristin Thompson, *The Classical Hollywood Cinema: Film Style and Mode of Production to 1960* (New York: Routledge, 1985), 373.
53 CP 2, 24; C. S. Peirce, *Pragmatism as a Principle and Method of Right Thinking: The 1903 Harvard "Lectures on Pragmatism,"* ed. Patricia Ann Turrisi (Albany: State University of New York Press, 1997), 201.

8 From Delusion to Deleuzean Cinema
Salvation from Hugo

In *The Varieties of Religious Experience* (1902), William James explores psychological states that differ from everyday rational consciousness: "parted from it by the filmiest of screens, there lie potential forms of consciousness entirely different."[1] Though James does not refer here to cinema screens, his diction has prophetic undertones. In less than seventy years, scholars would be discussing cinema as the filmiest form of religious consciousness. *Salvation from Cinema* differs in its emphasis, of course, encouraging religion and film scholars to recognize the artistry of the cinematic medium rather than simply to employ it as a content delivery system or as a variety of religious experience.

William James is nonetheless relevant to this project, for he was powerfully influenced by C. S. Peirce, the philosopher discussed in the preceding chapter. In 1897 James dedicated *The Will to Believe* to Peirce, who later returned the favor by invoking James in an essay explaining the interpretant and habit-change, constructs important to multiple film scholars.[2] Furthermore, in *The Varieties of Religious Experience*, James infuses with religious meaning a concept that he attributes to Peirce: *pragmatism*.[3] Exercising a will to believe in Peirce's genius, James almost single-handedly kept Peirce solvent, not only through lectures about him but also by organizing paid lectureships for him.[4]

William James contributed to film theory in yet another oblique way. In 1892 he arranged for German psychologist Hugo Münsterberg to teach at Harvard University. Dedicating to James his 1900 book *Basics of Psychology*, Münsterberg went on to publish what some describe as the first scholarly work of film theory: *The Photoplay: A Psychological Study* (1916). A structuralist would consider it no coincidence that Münsterberg's psychological analysis came out not long after students of Ferdinand de Saussure published his lectures about the psychological effects of signs (*Course in General Linguistics*, 1915): both professors from Europe, they reflected similar langues. Unfortunately, as we have seen, theorists who appropriated Saussure's structuralist semiology believed that perceptions of reality are merely delusions perpetuated by language. This view, as discussed in Chapter 5, dominated film theory for many years, reinforcing problematic either/or binaries that drowned out the more nuanced both/and thinking of Münsterberg. Not only does Münsterberg consider both popular and professional responses to cinema, he also assesses both psychological and aesthetic effects of film, valuing the medium as well as the spectator. Discussing cinematic devices like close-ups and crosscutting, Münsterberg celebrates film as "a new form of true beauty" that energizes "the free and joyful play of the mind."[5]

In honor of Hugo Münsterberg's both/and thinking, making him "the spiritual father of a number of currents within film theory,"[6] this book concludes with another significant Hugo: the habit-changing protagonist of Martin Scorsese's *Hugo* (2011). Based on a children's novel, *Hugo* provides an accessible lens through which the montage of *Salvation from Cinema* might be viewed as a unified whole. Winning five Oscars (and nominated for six more), *Hugo* is a *tour de force*: not only does it recount a delightful fictional story, but it embeds within that fiction historically accurate details about the history of narrative cinema. And, as this chapter will demonstrate, *Hugo* also encapsulates the thesis of *Salvation from Cinema*.

Like a conclusion, then, this chapter pulls together threads woven throughout the book, showing how they are tied together in *Hugo*. Unlike a conclusion, however, this chapter inserts a new thread: the film theory of Gilles Deleuze. In reaction to Grand Theory's structuralist emphasis on the delusions of cinema, Deleuze instigated an approach to cinema that reinforces the paradigms of Derrida and Peirce, as discussed in Chapters 6 and 7. Both a conclusion and not a conclusion, this chapter practices the both/and thinking encouraged by *Salvation from Cinema*.

The Adaptation of Martin Scorsese: From *Mean Streets* to *Hugo*

Creating its own framing device, *Salvation from Cinema* ends by focusing on the director with which it began: the creator of *Raging Bull* (Introduction) and *The Last Temptation of Christ* (Chapter 1). Martin Scorsese illustrates Peirce's habit-change by repeatedly challenging his own propensity to make darkly violent films like *Mean Streets* (1973), the title of which could summarize them all.[7] Though earning accolades and awards for this auteur-like habit, Scorsese has taken the risk to attempt many different kinds of genre: a musical with *New York, New York* (1977); a satire with *The King of Comedy* (1983); a Jesus film with *The Last Temptation of Christ* (1988); a literary costume drama with *The Age of Innocence* (1993); an Asian biopic with *Kundun* (1997); a historical epic with *The Gangs of New York* (2002); a black comedy with *The Wolf of Wall Street* (2013); and multiple documentaries. One might argue, however, that *Hugo* was the greatest risk of all, for not only had Scorsese never before adapted a children's book, it was also his first attempt at 3D projection.

Scorsese adapted *Hugo* from Brian Selznick's *The Invention of Hugo Cabret* (2007), which won the Caldecott Medal in 2008 for "the most distinguished American picture book for children."[8] Significantly, many of the book's 284 illustrations are photographs from the early days of cinema. The eponymous protagonist is a twelve-year-old boy living in the walls of a Parisian railway station in 1931. Placed there by a dissolute uncle, the orphaned Hugo has adapted to his dismal circumstances by taking over his absent uncle's job: winding up and maintaining the huge station clocks. From his lonely position behind the walls, Hugo watches people who work in the railway station as though he were watching a serialized movie. Significantly, by aligning Hugo's watching with the winding of clocks, Selznick implies a pun on the word "watch": Hugo, who "always had clockworks in his pockets," often heard "blood beating hard in his ears, like the rhythm of a clock."[9]

Scorsese visualizes this pun on "watch" in several ways, giving repeated close-ups on Hugo's eyes watching from behind the mechanized realm where he sustains the clocks, usually looking through transparencies or apertures in the clocks themselves. The director also provides multiple shots of Hugo's pocket watch, highlighting it in one scene as the boy retires for the evening. After a close-up on the watch as Hugo (Asa Butterfield) winds it, we see him hang it on a pillar at the foot of his bed. Scorsese then gives a shot/reverse shot of the two faces watching each other: the face of Hugo cuts to the face of the watch, before cutting back to Hugo staring at it. A rack focus then blurs out the boy, such that the watch in the foreground dominates the mise-en-scène. The medium thus suggests that *Hugo* is about the watching of time.[10]

The Adaptation of Georges Méliès

Hugo spends much of his time watching a grouchy old man (Ben Kingsley) who maintains a toy booth in the train station. The first time Scorsese gives us a close-up on the old man, it is an eyeline match cut from Hugo's point of view. As the camera moves closer to the old man, we see reflected in his eyeball the station clock through which Hugo peers, as though to say the toy-seller sees only the message of time and not the medium that sustains time. Later we realize the symbolism of this shot. For we discover that the man behind the toy counter is an aging Georges Méliès (1861–1938): the French stage designer and magician who "recognized the vast illusionist possibilities" of the cinematic medium after attending a Lumière screening.[11] Wanting to adapt the new medium for his magic shows, Méliès built his own camera and cinema studio, where he produced over five-hundred films. In 1913, the studio went bankrupt, reducing Méliès to the limited space of a kiosk in a Paris train station.

Scorsese's film suggests that the Great War (1914–18) contributed to Méliès's demise. Having experienced horrors in the trenches, soldiers were "bored" by the magician's fanciful films. Unable to pay his actors, Méliès burned his studio and props in despair.[12] Showing us how Méliès's film footage was melted down to use the chemicals for boot heels, Scorsese does not comment on the historical irony: Méliès was born into a family that operated a boot factory, such that his earliest childhood memories were shaped by shoes. The magician's celluloid medium, melted into shoes, returns him to the powerlessness of a child, symbolized by the fact he sits all day among toys—which, in his childhood, were often made of celluloid.[13]

It is therefore appropriate that the novel creates a fictional scenario in which the medium of salvation for Méliès is a child: a child who, like Méliès, is a mechanical wizard. In fact, the two meet when Hugo steals mechanisms and tools from the old man's booth in order to fix a robot-like automaton. While Selznick has Hugo find the automaton in a burned-down museum, Scorsese adds flashbacks of Hugo remembering his father (Jude Law) trying to fix the automaton, which he rescued from the museum. Hugo therefore believes that his father, before he died, programmed the automaton to write a special message to him. Only later does Hugo discover that *the medium* is the message.

Aiding Hugo in his discovery is another orphaned child invented by Selznick: Isabelle, who lives with her godparents. When Hugo discovers a heart-shaped key hanging from Isabelle's neck, he realizes that it might fit a keyhole in his automaton. While Selznick has Hugo steal the key, injuring Isabelle in the process, Scorsese shows Isabelle (Chloë Grace Moretz) eagerly helping Hugo, the automaton beginning to move after they turn the key. Hugo's jubilation turns to despair, however, when the automaton stops writing after making only a few random lines and squiggles. Then, after a long melancholy moment, the gears start turning again and the automaton's pen, instead of writing a message, draws a picture of a cartoon-like moon with a huge bullet in its eye. As Hugo and Isabelle stare in bafflement, the automaton signs the picture "Georges Méliès." Astounded, Isabelle reveals that Méliès is her godfather's name. Though Hugo knew the cranky toy-shopkeeper was Isabelle's godfather, up until that moment she had only called him "Papa Georges." Even she, however, did not know her godfather once made movies.

Hugo's much anticipated message from his father, then, is about the medium of film, the automaton's sketch capturing an iconic moment in cinema history. In his famous *A Trip to the Moon*—produced the same year William James published *Varieties of Religious Experience* (1902)—Méliès has characters shoot a rocket toward a lunar smiley face, cheese oozing into its mouth after impact from the rocket. Looking like a huge bullet stuck in the moon's eye, the famous representamen anticipates the gun aimed at viewer eyes in the closing "shot" of *The Great Train Robbery* (1903), a shot Scorsese inserts later in *Hugo*. Like Méliès, Edwin S. Porter, who directed *The Great Train Robbery* (see Chapter 4), was an early pioneer of narrative cinema. Both, then, gesture toward the relationship between medium and the "eye" of the spectator: what Peirce calls the relations among object, representamen and interpretant.

Hugo gestures toward spectatorship—watching movies—in other ways as well. Unlike the novel, Isabelle tells Hugo she has never seen a movie, her Papa Georges banning all cinema.[14] Hugo therefore sneaks Isabelle into a theater, where we see them watching *Safety Last!* (1923), including a scene famous in film history: Harold Lloyd hangs from the hands of a tower clock high above the ground until the face pulls away from its stone frame. The shot connects to both the past and future of the film that contains it. Not only are we reminded of Hugo's life maintaining the mechanisms of train station clocks, but later we will see Hugo copy this trick from *Safety Last!* in order to escape from hardhearted Station Inspector Gustave (Sacha Baron Cohen), who wants to put him in an orphanage, Hugo hangs from the hands of one of his clocks high above the ground: an incident not in the novel. By inserting this scene, Scorsese implies that film can help people *see* how to cope with the difficulties of existence—a message he also includes in *Raging Bull*. As noted in the introduction, *Raging Bull* closes with Jake LaMotta, returned to health, reciting a speech from *On the Waterfront*. *Raging Bull* then ends with words about seeing: "once I was blind and now I can see."

Hugo alludes to a similar kind of miracle, adumbrated by the return to life of the automaton. Attempting to uncover the secret behind the moon drawing, Hugo and Isabelle search her house, where they find a trove of hidden Méliès drawings. When the former filmmaker discovers the children surrounded by his images, he sighs "Back from the dead" before describing himself as "a broken wind-up toy." Like the once broken automaton, Méliès needs fixing. And, like the automaton, Méliès can be fixed only by bringing "back from the dead" the medium of his films: salvation from cinema.

To effect the salvation of Méliès, the children go to the Film Academy Library in Paris, where they peruse a book on the history of cinema. Scorsese interpolates actual historical clips to illustrate what the children are reading about: Lumière *actualités*; the final shot of *The Great Train Robbery* (1903); *The Cabinet of Dr. Caligari* (1920); works by Charlie Chaplin, Buster Keaton, and more. He even includes the "founding myth" of cinema by inserting a clip of audiences jumping away from the train they see approaching in the *Arrival of a Train at a Station* (1895).[15] When the book's fictional author, René Tabard (Michael Stuhlbarg), sees the children reading his history of cinema, he approaches them, only to be told of an error, the book reporting that Méliès was killed in the Great War. The children thus bring the famous filmmaker "back from the dead" for Tabard, who learns that the war had killed the spirit of Méliès rather than his body.

Significantly, after reading Tabard's cinema history, called *The Invention of Dreams*, and listening to Tabard describe Méliès's studio as a place "where dreams come from," Hugo has two dreams, both of which allude to the history of film. First Hugo dreams of being on train tracks, the approaching engine exactly like the one in the Lumières' *Arrival of a Train*. Running over him, the speeding train jumps the tracks and smashes through the wall of the station, its engine dangling out the wall onto the ground a story below. Significantly, this latter event is historical, occurring October 22, 1895, two months before the Lumières screened their *Arrival of a Train*. A famous photograph of the accident, included in Selznick's novel, helps explain "the founding myth" of cinema. Since a train had recently broken through a station wall, it makes sense that viewers might imagine a train breaking through the fourth wall of the movie screen.

In his second dream, Hugo imagines himself turning into a "mechanical man," his limbs, chest, and face duplicating those of his automaton. The relevance to cinema of this particular dream will become apparent later. For now, we need only consider what Christian Metz (see Chapter 5) calls the "kinship relations" between film and dream.[16] It is no coincidence that when Steven Spielberg, Jeffrey Katzenberg, and David Geffen formed their own studio in 1994 they called it DreamWorks.

Salvation from the Dream Work

In "Film and Dream: Perception and Hallucination," Metz discusses viewer tendency "to perceive as true and external the events and the heroes of the fiction" they watch on screen. It is "a tendency, in short, to perceive as real the represented and not the representer." Metz's word *representer*, like Peirce's word *representamen*, refers to the "*medium* of the representation." As Metz continues to lament, all too many moviegoers "pass over" the medium "without seeing it for what it is"; they "press on blindly."[17] In other words, rather than proclaiming "once I was blind and now I can see," as Scorsese does at the end of *Raging Bull*, all too many spectators remain contented with their blindness, preferring the dream-like escapism of cinema.

In *Hugo*, therefore, Scorsese explicitly encourages viewers to *see* the medium. After giving us a brief history of cinema before 1931, he has Tabard, author of *The Invention of Dreams*, bring to the Méliès home a copy of *A Trip to the Moon* to screen for the children. Hearing the projector, Méliès storms into the room, but upon seeing the children he suppresses his anger in order to recount his life story. Significantly, after telling Hugo, "Just like you, I loved to fix things," Ben Kingsley's Méliès breaks the fourth wall. As discussed in Chapter 4, this technique signals recognition that, for the world to have any meaning, something must exist beyond the frame of life as a character experiences it. By breaking the fourth wall in *Hugo*, then, Scorsese implies that the meaning of Méliès's life exceeds the tiny frame of his broken-toy-booth existence. Meaning, for Méliès, comes from the films he produced before his bankruptcy. Indeed, after having Kingsley break the fourth wall, Scorsese inserts a visual history of Méliès, including dramatizations of his magic acts and film projects. At one point in this biographical flashback, an extreme close-up of a much younger Méliès breaks the fourth wall again, looking out at us to say "I am ready." We then discover that the camera he looks into is located at his studio, for we next see him turn his back on it in order to direct a scene. Thus connecting the shrunken old man with his exuberant younger self, Scorsese (and screenwriter John Logan) reinforce that the medium of film is the message.[18] To put it another way, while the older Méliès seeks to save himself and his goddaughter from the delusion of cinema, the only way he can be saved from hopeless despair is through the artistic power of his movies, one definition of "salvation from cinema" being replaced by another.

Significantly, during the biographical flashback, Méliès narrates that he put his "heart and soul" into building an automaton for a magical act, donating it to a museum after he burned his studio and props. Suddenly realizing that Méliès's automaton must be the one that his father rescued from the museum, Hugo runs out of the house to retrieve it from his hideout. However, as he walks through the station with the automaton cradled in his arms, Inspector Gustave starts to chase him, causing the apparatus to fly out of Hugo's arms and land on the train track: a change from Selznick's novel, which has Hugo break the "mechanical man" inside his hideout. As Hugo jumps onto the tracks to rescue the automaton, Scorsese inserts a POV shot that captures an approaching train from Hugo's point of view, duplicating what the boy saw in his dream.[19] By twice aligning Hugo's perspective with the founding myth of cinema, Scorsese implies that the salvation of Hugo from a train alludes to the salvation of cinema. Indeed, soon after Inspector Gustave pulls Hugo to safety, Méliès runs into the station yelling "He belongs to me." Assuming that Méliès refers to his automaton, Hugo shows him the battered machine, apologizing, "I'm sorry he's broken." But Méliès responds "No, he's not. He worked perfectly." The implication, of course, is that the automaton, with its dead mechanisms revived, drew attention to the medium of film. And by exploring this medium, Hugo and Isabelle energized new life in Méliès, through resurrection of a medium he had once renounced.

Indeed, in the next scene we see a ceremony in honor of Méliès. After being introduced by Tabard, Méliès looks out into the audience in order to thank Hugo, describing him as a boy "who saw a broken machine and fixed it." Méliès, of course, refers not only to the automaton but also to himself. Scorsese then allows us to revel in actual clips from some of the eighty Méliès films that have survived—immediately after the filmmaker says "Come and dream with me." Eyeline match cuts from Hugo and Isabelle in the audience to the enchanting Méliès clips suggest that salvation from cinema—like the "fixing" of the automaton and Méliès—depends on the power of sight.

A Theory of Adaptation

Some might consider it ironic that Scorsese adapts a novel in order to focus on salvation from cinema. But perhaps this is the point. By adapting an accessible, award-winning novel filled with stills from cinema history, Scorsese can highlight differences between the two mediums. After all, the seeing of cinema is different from the seeing of still pictures—explaining why *Salvation from Cinema* does not include stills. Cinema, as *Hugo* implies, is about the seeing of *movement through time*: an issue *key* to adaptation studies.

Early in his watershed essay "A Certain Tendency in French Cinema" (discussed in Chapter 5), Truffaut quotes a statement from French filmmaker Carlo Rim: "An honest adaptation is a betrayal." Because Truffaut believed that auteurs write films with their cameras, he was dismissive of film adaptation, and hence relegated Rim's statement to an "audacious aphorism."[20] But people who specialize in adaptation studies recognize the insight of Rim's statement. When filmmakers attempt to create "honest" adaptations by meticulously transferring elements of literary texts—characters, settings, descriptions, conversations, chronology—they *betray* the distinctiveness of the cinematic medium. Furthermore, since cinema communicates differently than does a written text, a filmmaker must *betray* narrative elements in a play or novel in order to honestly capture its message.[21] We saw this demonstrated not only in Chapter 2 with *A Streetcar Named Desire* and *A Raisin in the Sun*, but also in Chapter 7 with *Salmon Fishing in the Yemen*. And the "betrayal" of the medium was made explicit in Chapter 3, not only in *A Room with a View*, but also through discussion of *Girl with a Pearl*

170 *Salvation from Film Theory*

Earring. We should therefore take special note of Scorsese's "betrayal" of his source text in order to adapt it to the screen.

For example, Scorsese changes the way Isabelle sees and is seen, as though in recognition of cinema's problematic focus on the female body, as discussed in Chapter 3. Rather than have her fight and injure Hugo, as in Selznick, Scorsese provides Isabelle with mental rather than physical prowess. In addition to impressing viewers with Isabelle's sophisticated vocabulary and apt literary allusions, Scorsese gives her the last word in the film. While Selznick closes with Hugo programming a new automaton to write the book we have just read, Scorsese delivers a voice-over from a seated Isabelle who, pen in hand, begins to write the narrative we have just seen. He then closes *Hugo* with a shot that dollies in to a room containing the seated automaton, pen in hand, thus aligning transformative vision with a female mind.

To ground this vision, Scorsese establishes that Isabelle's mind has been shaped by books. Comforting the weeping Hugo by telling him literary heroes like Sydney Carton and Heathcliff both cry, she introduces Hugo to a bookstore lined floor to ceiling with gorgeous leather-bound, gilt-edged volumes.[22] The enchantment of the place, emphasized with high-angle and low-angle shots, lies in the beauty of the books rather than merely in the stories they tell. Like Marshall McLuhan, then, Scorsese alludes to the power of the visual medium—as much as to its contents—to shape perception and behavior. In fact, he adds a scene that encompasses other kinds of artistic media, like painting and music. In a brief pan of the station café early in *Hugo*, Scorsese adds short takes of novelist James Joyce (1882–1941), painter Salvador Dalí (1904–1989), and jazz guitarist Django Reinhardt (1910–1963)—all of whom are listed as characters in the film credits. Furthermore, he places on walls of the train station posters echoing post-war Dadaism: a movement that not only influenced Salvador Dalí but also produced a *Mechanical Head* (by Raoul Hausmann, c. 1920), looking very much like Hugo's "mechanical man," as Selznick repeatedly calls the automaton. By the end of *Hugo*, we realize that Scorsese gestures toward film's ability to synthesize the best of all these media: story presented not only through inscription, as when Isabelle writes it down, but also through painterly physicality on the screen, with the added enhancement of music. Scorsese thus visualizes Sergei Eisenstein's belief that "the cinema is able, more than any other art, to disclose the process that goes on microscopically in all other arts."[23]

Scorsese's most radical "betrayal," however, is a story he develops around Station Inspector Gustave, adding a subplot not in Selznick's novel. Like Méliès, Scorsese's Gustave has experienced loss due to the Great War, his left leg permanently encased in a metal brace. Viewers actually feel sorry for the otherwise humorously despicable Gustave at a moment when he tries to approach a lovely flower-seller (Emily Mortimer). His brace locks with a loud metallic squeak, causing him to turn away in shame. More significant is the fact that the metal leg brace looks strikingly similar to the metal legs of Hugo's automaton. Scorsese gives us close-ups on both, his graphic match establishing a visual pun: the dastardly inspector, who wants to put every parentless child into an orphanage, is an emotional robot who will not move toward the good until someone finds the key to his heart.

Hence, Scorsese has Gustave lapse into acrimonious accusations after saving Hugo from being hit by the approaching train, only to soften his tone when he notices the lovely flower-seller watching him. As the subject of the gaze, she becomes the heart-shaped key to the flesh-and-blood robot—at a moment when Hugo is holding his robotic automaton. Significantly, at a party after Tabard's tribute to Méliès, we see that Hugo has also fixed Inspector Gustave, replacing his clunky brace with watch-like gears, cogs, levers, and rods that make him walk like new, the flower-seller on his arm. Hugo, of course, knew how to fix the brace because he lived inside a medium filled with gears, cogs, levers, and rods, where he turned cranks just like the cranks on the cameras in Méliès's studio.[24] The apparatuses of clocks, cameras, and automatons thus generate a message of salvation that is mediated through time: once I was dead but now I live; once I was blind but now I see. Though ostensibly a children's film, *Hugo* thus visualizes issues important to the philosopher who echoes Derrida and Peirce: Gilles Deleuze.

The Medium of Time: Gilles Deleuze through the Lens of Scorsese

Seeking salvation from the delusions of Grand Theory, Gilles Deleuze established cinema as a medium of time. At first flush this seems obvious: images move on the screen, a narrative achieving its end(s) through time. Deleuze, however, is more interested in how movies enable viewers to *see time itself*. He therefore celebrates what he calls the "time-image," which he contrasts to the more conventional "movement-image."[25]

According to Deleuze, the movement-image, usually identified with "classical cinema," draws attention to temporal change through continuity editing, such that one action succeeds another in a logically coherent manner. Even flashbacks and dream insertions in classical cinema obey certain "sensory-motor" schemas that do not confuse viewers. In contrast, the time-image is disorienting, because it "subordinates" temporal movement to time as "it appears in itself." For example, when the screen remains "black or white" for an uncomfortably long time in the middle of a movie, some spectators become so aware of the time lapse that they wonder if the projector is broken. Similarly, long takes of deep-focus shots create discomfort, viewers questioning what they are supposed to be seeing, a question that elicits from Deleuze a succinct answer: "the thought of the image, the thought in the image." He especially celebrates "irrational cuts" that juxtapose totally unrelated shots, because they undermine viewers' sense of visual contiguity and hence of narrative continuity. Drawing attention to the time between shots, these inexplicable "gaps" trigger what C. S. Peirce calls "habit-change." Not coincidentally, Deleuze draws upon Peirce as he considers how signs on the screen can destabilize a "commonsense" understanding of the world.[26]

Deleuze's time-image might help explain the scandal generated by Scorsese's *Last Temptation of Christ*, discussed in Chapter 1. People horrified by images of a sexually active Jesus failed to notice what Deleuze calls a "fragmentation of linearity" in the medium. Habituated to conventional movement-images, naive spectators thought they were viewing temporal continuity: Jesus getting down off the cross to sire children. Instead, through disjunctions in sound and strange gaps in the mise-en-scène, Scorsese drew attention to the perception of Jesus—which is the perception of time and its possibilities. For Deleuze, "a character ... SEES so that the viewer's problem becomes 'What is there to see in the image?' (and not now 'What are we going to see in the next image?')." What we see in the image, of course, is not only time as Jesus thinks he could have experienced it—virtual time—but also the time on the cross: the time of temptation. Deleuze could almost be describing Scorsese's Jesus when he writes, "We are in the situation of an actual image *and* its own virtual image, to the extent that there is no longer any linkage of the real with the imaginary, but *indiscernibility of the two*, a perpetual exchange."[27] Deleuze's diction is reminiscent of the *indiscernibility* between the two natures of Christ, a perpetual exchange of human and divine, wherein Jesus was tempted like every human even as he simultaneously performed as God: the hypostatic union declared at Chalcedon in 451 CE. *The Last Temptation*, then, shocked attentive viewers into seeing the time of thought on the cross, thus generating habit-change by subverting conventional gnostic notions about Jesus.

Deleuze aligns habit-change with historical changes to signs in the medium itself. Whereas the movement-image dominated cinema before World War II, post-war Italian neorealism and the French New Wave helped initiate the time-image: "we see the birth of a race of charming, moving characters who are hardly concerned by the events that happen to them ... [They] experience and act out obscure events which are as poorly linked as the portion of the any-space-whatever which they traverse."[28] This should remind us of Truffaut's *400 Blows*, discussed in Chapter 5: the film inexplicably cuts from boys randomly wandering the streets to different boys traversing another seemingly random space. These irrational cuts set free the interpretant from the control of narrative, such that "the power of thought [gives] way," as Deleuze puts it, "to an unthought in thought."[29] For Deleuze, effective cinema is not about story; it is about igniting thought.

Significantly, Selznick lists *400 Blows* as one of the "three films that were very influential" as he wrote *The Invention of Hugo Cabret*.[30] Indeed, like Antoine, Truffaut's movie-loving protagonist, the movie-loving Hugo absconds with items aligned with writing. Whereas Antoine steals a pen and typewriter, Hugo steals devices to get his automaton to write. And, as a result of misbehavior, both boys are forced into similar-looking jail cages. Selznick also creates Truffaut-like discontinuities, suddenly interrupting his verbal narrative with a series of drawings that imitate continuity editing in film. The drawings and photographs usually do not illustrate the written narrative; instead they *take over* the narrative. Selznick thus calls attention to different views of narrative time: the time taken to read words on the page, versus the time taken to look at a series of connected pictures. In other words, he does for children what Marshall McLuhan and Quentin Fiore did for adults in *The Medium is the Massage: An Inventory of Effects*, as discussed in the Introduction.

Because an honest adaptation is a betrayal, Scorsese signals time quite differently than Selznick. Avoiding citations of Truffaut's time-image—discontinuities that would baffle *Hugo*'s intended audience—Scorsese gives, instead, repeated close-ups on the faces and internal mechanisms of clocks. While Selznick's novel opens with an image of the moon, Scorsese's opening shot fills the mise-en-scène with the multiple gears, cogs, levers and rods that keep the train station clocks running. This, of course, gives new meaning to Scorsese's first shot of Méliès, where a clock is reflected in his iris. While the Lumières merely projected moving images in single shots, Méliès envisioned the temporality of film in an entirely new way, essentially "inventing" the movement-image of narrative cinema. Scorsese, then, to signal his own contribution to narrative cinema inserts himself into *Hugo*—just as Truffaut inserted his body into *400 Blows*. Whereas Truffaut rides a cinema-like apparatus with Antoine, Scorsese plays a photographer capturing the cinema apparatus built by Méliès.

Méliès, then, who repudiated the movement-image when he stopped making movies, is succeeded by Hugo, who is literally embedded in images of time. When Hugo first appears in the film, we see only his eyes peering through the aperture of a clock. The camera then follows his body as he runs behind and through giant gears as he hastens to maintain the apparatus of multiple clocks. Hugo thus sustains time by manipulating the mechanisms behind the station walls, where he also works to fix the automaton: a medium whose gears, cogs, levers, and rods mimic those of the station clocks. More importantly, the cranks on both clocks and automaton mimic the cranks we see turned on movie cameras and projectors repeatedly in the film. This reflects how, as Gaby Wood notes, "automata gave birth to the movies," Méliès having constructed his first camera using spare parts from a magician who employed automata in his shows.[31]

Deleuze and the Spiritual Automaton

Even more significant is the fact that Deleuze aligns the representation of time in cinema with the "automaton" as theorized by Baruch Spinoza (1632–77), a philosopher who, like Jacques Derrida, had Sephardic Jewish roots. In a lecture on Spinoza, Deleuze explains,

> we are, he says, spiritual automata, that is to say it is less we who have the ideas than the ideas which are affirmed in us. … As such spiritual automata, within us there is the whole time of ideas which succeed one another, and in according with this succession of ideas, our power of acting or force of existing is increased or diminished in a continuous manner, on a continuous line, and this is what we call affectus, it's what we call existing.[32]

Though Spinoza lived centuries before the invention of cinema, he seems to have conceptualized thought cinematically, ideas succeeding one another like images on celluloid. Deleuze therefore appropriates Spinoza's idea of the "automaton" for the habit-change ignited by cinema.

If, as Spinoza suggests, "spiritual automata" generate "what we call existing," we have a new way to think about Hugo's automaton bringing Méliès "back from the dead." Indeed, Deleuze suggests that modern cinema energizes the brain's "capacity to 'resume a resurrection from the dead.'" Such salvation from cinema occurs as viewer thoughts connect with thoughts on the screen: "The spiritual automaton is in the psychic situation of the seer, who sees better and further than he can react, that is, think."[33] We are reminded of Hugo, who sees better and further than he can react as he spies through apertures in clocks: a seeing *through time* that Scorsese often accompanies with flickering lights reminiscent of old-fashioned film projectors. Whether Scorsese intended to allude to Deleuze or not is beside the point. As suggested in Chapter 5, structuralists were at their best when they challenged modernist ideas of originality and influence, arguing that perception, as of Alpine beauty, is inevitably shaped by the discursive practices of *the time* in which individuals are embedded. Scorsese, then, by making award-winning films at the same time Deleuze was writing about cinema, seems to have grappled with cinema in ways that parallel Deleuze.[34] Indeed, Deleuze references a film by Scorsese—*Taxi Driver* (1976)—to illustrate the "any-space-whatever" of the time-image. And when Deleuze states that "*Automatic movement* gives rise to a *spiritual automaton* in us," he cites earlier film theorists that Scorsese surely encountered in graduate school.[35]

We should pay attention, then, when Scorsese invents a subplot in which humans mimic the automaton that Hugo resurrects. When Inspector Gustave's automaton-like leg freezes to a squeaking halt, he becomes paralyzed like Méliès, who sits in his toy booth as inertly as the automaton that sits in Hugo's hiding place. In fact, in one of Scorsese's early shots of Méliès, the seller of mechanical toys sits paralyzed in the exact same pose as Hugo's automaton, his motionless hands resting on a counter with his right index finger elevated. This graphic match, not pictured in the novel, visualizes a point made by Deleuze: "The spiritual automaton has become the Mummy, this dismantled, paralysed, petrified, frozen instance which testifies to 'the impossibility of thinking that is thought.'"[36] Both Gustav and Méliès are "trapped" in what Deleuze calls "the permanent state of a daily banality": one in a tiny toy booth, the other by his mechanical brace, both looking like Hugo's "mechanical man," a term used also used by Deleuze.[37] In Scorsese's film, Hugo seems to fear the same for himself, dreaming that his limbs freeze into the same form as his mechanical man (a dream not in the novel). However, by energizing his automaton with a key that comes from *outside* his imprisonment in time, Hugo receives a wholly unexpected message about the power of cinema itself, as though in fulfillment of Deleuze's words:

> It is the material automatism of images which produces from the outside a thought which it imposes, as the unthinkable in our intellectual automatism. ... The automaton is cut off from the outside world, but there is a more profound outside which will animate it.[38]

The "outside world" in Hugo is represented by Isabella, who holds the key that will animate mechanical men: both Hugo's automaton and her Papa Georges. By helping to ignite change in both, she becomes the "conduit for triggers that can un-stick us": Gail Hamner's delightful phrase for a Deleuze-inspired approach to cinema.[39] Indeed, Deleuze sees people "trapped" in their view of the world—much as Hugo is trapped behind station walls, Méliès is stuck in a tiny booth, and Gustav is halted by his automaton-like brace. Escape, for Deleuze, is "the impossible, the unthinkable, which none the less cannot but be thought."[40]

Placing hope in "the impossible," Deleuze brings us back to Jacques Derrida. As discussed in Chapter 6, Derrida uses the term *impossible* to describe a "pure" gift: something unearned and wholly unanticipated; an event that changes one's perception of reality. Significantly, after Hugo sneaks Isabella into a theater to see her first movie, she tells him "it was a gift."[41] Indeed, the experience exposes Isabella to a medium unlike any she has ever before experienced: a medium of time, as signaled by Harold Lloyd hanging from a clock face. But Isabelle's most life-changing habit-change comes after the melancholy moment when Hugo's automaton stops drawing. The awareness of time generated during this gap in the automaton's movement opens up thought to the unthinkable: Papa Georges, inert in a toy booth, was once a master of the movement-image. Isabella has thus experienced the "spiritual automaton" that Deleuze aligns with the "time-image" of cinema. Indeed, Deleuze scholar Ronald Bogue describes the powers of time-images with language redolent of the moment when Hugo's automaton gets unstuck: they are "powers of becoming, dynamic change, metamorphosis, and transformation, and hence powers that undermine fixed identities, thereby falsifying established truths and generating new forms."[42]

The Impossible Made Possible

Derrida once admitted to a "nearly total affinity" with Deleuze, despite their different strategies and emphases.[43] While Deleuze celebrates how cinema is "capable of restoring our belief in the world," Derrida places his hope in a "messianic" impossible that exceeds the "messianisms" of the known world.[44] Nevertheless, both encourage openness to the "other," to that which is "outside" the known of thought. Related to Peirce's concept of semiosis, such openness can "apply to all religions," as noted by religion scholar Carl Raschke.[45] Hence, for Deleuze, it is a matter of faith: "We need an ethic or a faith, which makes fools laugh." Similarly for Derrida, as John Caputo summarizes, it "comes down to an affirmation or hope or invocation which is a certain *faith* ... in something that pushes us beyond the sphere of the same, of the believable, into the unbelievable, that which exceeds the horizon of our pedestrian beliefs and probabilities."[46]

This, as well, has been the goal of *Salvation from Cinema*: to push scholarship about religion and film beyond the sphere of the same. Employing a shocking analogy—the hypostatic union of human and divine in Jesus Christ—it encourages spectators to consider how the hypostatic union of medium and message exceeds the horizon of pedestrian beliefs and probabilities. It encourages, in other words, *metanoia*, a word that recurs in the Greek New Testament. As noted by a contemporary of C. S. Peirce and William James, *metanoia* means "change of Mind, a change in the trend and action of the whole inner nature, intellectual, affectional and moral."[47] In other words, just as multiple religions encourage *metanoia*, so also does *Salvation from Cinema*, which seeks to ignite a creative return to the beauty of cinema—not as a substitute for the message of story but as an endorsement of the "hypostatic" relations within cinematic signs themselves. As Peirce scholar Johannes Ehrat aptly summarizes, "Beauty is not a thing, nor is it a transcendental idea. The aestheticizing process always involves an apprehending subject that is the condition of its possibility."[48] Like Hugo Münsterberg energizing film theory and Hugo Cabret energizing his automaton, cinema can energize the spiritual automaton in each of us, but only if we have eyes to see.

Notes

1 William James, *The Varieties of Religious Experience: A Study in Human Nature* (Hazelton: The Electronic Classics Series, 2002–13), 373. For scholars who regard film as a variety of religious experience, see the first several pages of my introduction.
2 Charles Sanders Peirce, "Pragmatism in Retrospect: A Last Formulation" (c. 1906), in *Philosophical Writings of Peirce*, ed. Justus Buchler (New York: Dover, 1955), 269, 280.
3 James, *Varieties*, 430–1. Though James asserts that Peirce coined *pragmatism* (430), the OED shows earlier usage (in 1860), though not with Peirce's meaning. In 1905 Peirce coined a new term—*pragmaticism*—in order to distinguish his thought from that of James. See "The Essentials of Pragmatism," in *Philosophical Writings*, 255.
4 Louis Menand, *The Metaphysical Club: A Story of Ideas in America* (New York: Farrar, Straus and Giroux, 2001), 349–50.
5 Hugo Münsterberg, *The Photoplay: A Psychological Study* (New York: Appleton, 1916), 140–1, 233. Noël Carroll critiques the way Münsterberg parallels cinematic devices with mental processes, aligning him with theorists he dismisses, like Metz and Baudry. In a footnote, however, Carroll acknowledges there are other ways to read Münsterberg. See Noël Carroll, *Theorizing the Moving Image* (Cambridge: Cambridge University Press, 1996), 293–304.
6 Robert Stam, *Film Theory: An Introduction* (Malden: Blackwell, 2000), 31.
7 In his book on Antiochene Christ-figures in film noir, Christopher Deacy discusses "redemption through suffering" in multiple Scorsese films. See *Screen Christologies: Redemption and the Medium of Film* (Cardiff: University of Wales Press, 2001), 104–37.
8 See the Caldecott website: www.ala.org/alsc (accessed 24 June 2015).
9 Brian Selznick, *The Invention of Hugo Cabret: A Novel in Words and Pictures* (New York: Scholastic Press, 2007), 146, 124.
10 Though Selznick includes drawings that focus on people's eyes, he has no images of Hugo's watch.
11 David A. Cook, *A History of Narrative Film*, 2nd edn (New York: Norton, 1990), 14. Cook notes that some biographical details reported by Méliès in his *Mémoires* have since been discredited (50n.).
12 Selznick, in contrast, has Méliès say "the war came, and afterward there was too much competition, and everything was lost" (*The Invention of Hugo Cabret*, 405).
13 Kyle Meikle, "Rematerializing Adaptation Theory," *Literature/Film Quarterly* 41.3 (July 2013): 178.
14 Selznick makes Isabelle more familiar with movies than is Hugo.
15 As discussed in Chapter 5, the Lumières' fifty-second film "is supposed to have been met with gasps and shrieks, and there are stories of spectators even leaping out of the

way of the oncoming train, and rushing for the exits." Marc Furstenau, "Introduction," *The Film Theory Reader: Debates and Arguments* (New York: Routledge, 2010), 15–16, n. 4. Selznick recounts the myth as fact (*The Invention of Hugo Cabret*, 347).

16 Three essays under the title "Film and Dream" have been republished in Christian Metz, *The Imaginary Signifier: Psychoanalysis and the Cinema,* trans. Celia Britton, Annwyl Williams, Ben Brewster, and Alfred Guzzetti (Bloomington: Indiana University Press, 1977), 101–28. The quotations are from 123 and 125.

17 Ibid., 115, emphasis mine.

18 Playwright John Logan, who wrote the screenplay for Scorsese's film *The Aviator* (2004), did the adaptation for *Hugo*. Since Scorsese was both co-producer and director for the film, I use his name as a synecdoche for all the talented contributors to the script and cinematography.

19 In addition to having Hugo break the automaton in his hideout (*The Invention of Hugo Cabret*, 412), Selznick later has Hugo fall onto the tracks without the automaton (450).

20 François Truffaut, "A Certain Tendency in French Cinema," in *The French New Wave: Critical Landmarks*, ed. Peter Graham with Ginette Vincendeau (New York: Palgrave Macmillan, 2009), 41.

21 See John M. Desmond and Peter Hawkes, *Adaptation: Studying Film and Literature* (New York: McGraw Hill, 2006), 34–48.

22 In the novel, Hugo enters the bookstore on his own. Carton, from *A Tale of Two Cities* by Charles Dickens (1859), and Heathcliff, from *Wuthering Heights* by Emily Brontë (1847), are not mentioned in the novel.

23 Sergei Eisenstein, "Through Theater to Cinema," excerpted from *Film Form*, in *Theater and Film: A Comparative Anthology,* trans. Jay Leyda and Paya Haskelson (New Haven: Yale University Press, 2005), 241. For the religious implications of cinematic music, see Kutter Callaway, *Scoring Transcendence: Contemporary Film Music as Religious Experience* (Waco: Baylor University Press, 2013).

24 Selznick's inspector does not have a leg brace. I have borrowed passages in this analysis of *Hugo* from Crystal Downing, "3-D-Light-ful Hugo," *Books and Culture* (December 2011). Available online at www.booksandculture.com/articles/ webexclusives/2011/december/3dlight.html (accessed 24 June 2015).

25 Gilles Deleuze, *Cinema 1: The Movement-Image*, trans. Hugh Tomlinson and Barbara Habberjam (Minneapolis: University of Minnesota Press, 1986); Gilles Deleuze, *Cinema 2: The Time-Image*, trans. Hugh Tomlinson and Robert Galeta (Minneapolis: University of Minnesota Press, 1989). Sylvain De Bleeckere parallels Deleuze's interest in time with that of filmmaker Andrei Tarkovsky, author of *Sculpting in Time*. See "The Religious Dimension of Cinematic Consciousness in Postmodern Culture," in *New Image of Religious Film*, ed. John R. May (Kansas City: Sheed & Ward, 1997), 105.

26 Deleuze, *Cinema 2*, 213, 126, 271, xi, 200, 174, 173, 183. Considering Peirce's "classification of signs [as] the richest and the most numerous that has ever been established," Deleuze nevertheless uses Peirce only as the scaffolding for his own construction of cinematic signs, changing Peirce's vocabulary in the process (*Cinema 1*, 69, 98).

27 Deleuze, *Cinema 2*, 272, 273, emphasis his.

28 Deleuze, *Cinema 1*, 213.

29 Deleuze, *Cinema 2*, 181.

30 Selznick, *The Invention of Hugo Cabret*, 533.

31 Gaby Wood, *Edison's Eve: A Magical History of the Quest for Mechanical Life* (New York: Knopf, 2002), 183.

32 See http://deleuzelectures.blogspot.com/2007/02/on-spinoza.html (accessed 24 June 2015).

33 Deleuze, *Cinema 2*, 170.

34 For more about the problematic notion of "intention," see W. K. Wimsatt Jr. and Monroe C. Beardsley, "The Intentional Fallacy," in *The Verbal Icon*, ed. W. K. Wimsatt Jr. (New York: Farrar, Straus, 1964), 3–18. Deleuze is not mentioned by any of the contributors to *The Philosophy of Martin Scorsese*, ed. Mark T. Conard (Lexington: University Press of Kentucky, 2007).

35 Deleuze, *Cinema 1*, 207–8; *Cinema 2*, 156, emphasis his. Deleuze cites a 1934 essay about "material automatism" by Élie Faure called "Introduction à la mystique du cinéma," as well as Jean Epstein's work from *Écrits sur le cinéma, 1921–1953*. Scorsese was certainly familiar with the image that opens Jean-Luc Godard's film *Pierrot le Fou* (1965), wherein a character reads from Faure's *Histoire de l'art* (1919–21).

36 Deleuze, *Cinema 2*, 166. To this end, perhaps motivated by petrified busts Selznick places in his drawing of the bookstore, Scorsese gives shots of statues throughout the film, adding huge paralyzed figures to tombstones in a cemetery across from the Méliès home.

37 Ibid., 170, 169.

38 Ibid., 178–9.

39 M. Gail Hamner, *Imaging Religion in Film: The Politics of Nostalgia* (New York: Palgrave Macmillan, 2011), 148. Hamner employs the phrase not to summarize Deleuze but to capture her theory of transcendence generated by filmic technique, a theory profoundly influenced by Deleuze (and Peirce).

40 Deleuze, *Cinema 2*, 170.

41 It was not a "pure" gift, in Derrida's terms, because Isabella first said "Thank you for the movie": a sign of exchange.

42 Ronald Bogue, "Gilles Deleuze," in *The Routledge Companion to Philosophy and Film*, ed. Paisley Livingston and Carl Plantinga (New York: Routledge, 2009), 374. For Bogue's discussion of Deleuze's spiritual automaton, see his book *Deleuze on Cinema* (New York: Routledge, 2003), 177–82.

43 Jacques Derrida, "I'm Going to Have to Wander All Alone," trans. Leonard Lawlor, in *The Work of Mourning*, trans. and ed. Pascale-Anne Brault and Michael Naas (Chicago: University of Chicago Press, 2001), 192. For an overview of parallels and differences between the two philosophers, see *Between Deleuze and Derrida*, ed. Paul Patton and John Protevi (London: Continuum, 2003).

44 Deleuze, *Cinema 2*, 181; Jacques Derrida, "Hostipitality," trans. Gil Anidjar, in Jacques Derrida, *Acts of Religion*, ed. Gil Anidjar (New York: Routledge, 2002), 362.

45 Carl Raschke, *Postmodernism and the Revolution in Religious Theory: Toward a Semiotics of the Event* (Charlottesville: University of Virginia Press, 2012), 200.

46 Deleuze, *Cinema 2*, 173; John D. Caputo, *The Prayers and Tears of Jacques Derrida: Religion Without Religion* (Bloomington: Indiana UP, 1997), 64, emphasis his.

47 Treadwell Walden, *The Great Meaning of the Word Metanoia: Lost in the Old Version, Unrecovered in the New* (New York: Thomas Whittaker, 1896), 4. Walden notes that *metanoia* in the Bible is often mistranslated as "repentance."

48 Johannes Ehrat, *Cinema and Semiotic: Peirce and Film Aesthetics, Narration, and Representation* (Toronto: University of Toronto Press, 2005), 459. Ehrat also talks about "a Hypostatic Abstraction of Relational events in the Sign" (127), borrowing the word *hypostatic* from Douglas Greenlee, "Peirce's Hypostatic and Factorial Categories," *Transactions of the Charles S. Peirce Society*, 4.1 (Winter 1965): 49–58.

Bibliography

Abbott, James. "Following His True Passion: Mel Gibson and *The Passion of the Christ*." In *Through a Catholic Lens: Religious Perspectives of Nineteen Film Directors from around the World*, edited by Peter Malone, 225–38. Lanham: Rowman & Littlefield, 2007.

Abramson, Ronald. "Structure and Meaning in the Cinema." In *Movies and Methods: An Anthology*, vol. 1, edited by Bill Nichols, 558–67. Berkeley: University of California Press, 1982.

Acker, Ally. *Reel Women: Pioneers of the Cinema, 1896 to the Present*. New York: Continuum, 1991.

Adorno, Theodor W., and Hanns Eisler. *Composing for the Films*. Oxford: Oxford University Press, 1969.

Affron, Charles. *Cinema and Sentiment*. Chicago: University of Chicago Press, 1982.

Aichele, George, and Richard G. Walsh, eds. *Screening Scripture: Intertextual Connections between Scripture and Film*. Harrisburg: Trinity Press International, 2002.

Anker, Roy. *Catching the Light: Looking for God in the Movies*. Grand Rapids: Eerdmans, 2004.

Avila, Mitch. "From Film Emotion to Normative Criticism." In *Reframing Theology and Film*, edited by Robert K. Johnston, 219–37. Grand Rapids: Baker Academic, 2007.

Babington, Bruce, and Peter Williams Evans. *Biblical Epics: Sacred Narrative in the Hollywood Cinema*. New York: Manchester University Press, 1993.

Balthasar, Hans Urs, von. *The Scandal of the Incarnation: Irenaeus against the Heresies*. Translated by John Saward. San Francisco: Ignatius Press, 1981.

Barthes, Roland. *Image—Music—Text*. Translated by Stephen Heath. London: Fontana, 1977.

———. *Mythologies*. Translated by Annette Lavers. New York: Hill & Wang, 1972.

———. "The Reality Effect." Translated by Richard Howard. In *The Rustle of Language*, 141–8. Oxford: Blackwell, 1986.

———. "Towards a Semiotics of Cinema." Interview with Michel Delahaye and Jacques Rivette (September 1963). Translated by Annwyl Williams. In *Cahiers du Cinéma, Volume 2, 1960–1968: New Wave, New Cinema, Reevaluating Hollywood*, edited by Jim Hillier, 276–83. Cambridge: Harvard University Press, 1986.

Baudry, Jean-Louis. "The Apparatus: Metapsychological Approaches to the Impression of Reality in Cinema." In *Film Theory and Criticism: Introductory Readings*, 6th edn, edited by Leo Braudy and Marshall Cohen, 206–23. New York: Oxford University Press, 2004.

———. "Ideological Effects of the Basic Cinematographic Apparatus." Translated by Alan Williams. *Film Quarterly* 28.2 (Winter 1974–5): 39–47.

Baugh, Lloyd. *Imaging the Divine: Jesus and Christ-Figures in Film*. Kansas City: Sheed & Ward, 1997.

Bazin, André. *What Is Cinema?* 2 volumes. Translated and edited by Hugh Gray. Berkeley: University of California Press, 1967 & 1974.

Benjamin, Walter. "The Work of Art in the Age of Its Technological Reproducibility." In *The Norton Anthology of Theory and Criticism*, edited by Vincent B. Leitch et al., 1051–71. New York: Norton, 2010.

Benne, Robert. *Seeing is Believing: Visions of Life through Film*. Lanham: University Press of America, 1998.

Bettelheim, Bruno. "The Ignored Lesson of Anne Frank." *Harper's Magazine*, November 1960.

Bird, Michael S. "Film as Hierophany." In *Religion in Film*, edited by John R. May and Michael S. Bird, 3–22. Knoxville: University of Tennessee Press, 1982.

Björkman, Stig. *Woody Allen on Woody Allen*. London: Faber & Faber, 1995.

Blake, Richard A. *Afterimage: The Indelible Catholic Imagination of Six American Filmmakers*. Chicago: Loyola Press, 2000.

Bloom, Harold. *The American Religion: The Emergence of the Post-Christian Nation*. New York: Simon & Schuster, 1992.

Blandford, Steve, Barry D. Grant, and Jim Hillier. *The Film Studies Dictionary*. London: Arnold, 2001.

Bogue, Ronald. *Deleuze on Cinema*. New York: Routledge, 2003.

———. "Gilles Deleuze." In *The Routledge Companion to Philosophy and Film*, edited by Paisley Livingston and Carl Plantinga, 368–77. New York: Routledge, 2009.

Bordwell, David. "Contemporary Film Studies and the Vicissitudes of Grand Theory." In *Post-Theory: Reconstructing Film Studies*, edited by David Bordwell and Noël Carroll, 3–37. Madison: University of Wisconsin Press, 1996.

———. *Making Meaning: Inferences and Rhetoric in the Interpretation of Cinema*. Cambridge: Harvard University Press, 1989.

Bordwell, David, Janet Stiger, and Kristin Thompson. *The Classical Hollywood Cinema: Film Style and Mode of Production to 1960*. New York: Columbia University Press, 1985.

Bottomore, Stephen. "The Panicking Audience? Early Cinema and the 'Train Effect'." *Historical Journal of Film, Radio and Television* 19.2 (1999): 177–216.

Bray, Christopher. "The Cat in Catatonia." *Times Literary Supplement*, November 13, 2009.

Brintnall, Kent. "Psychoanalysis." In *The Routledge Companion to Religion and Film*, edited by John Lyden, 292–309. London: Routledge, 2009.

Brooks, Cleanth. *The Well Wrought Urn: Studies in the Structure of Poetry*. New York: Harcourt, Brace & Co., 1947.

Brunette, Peter, and David Wills. *Screen/Play: Derrida and Film Theory*. Princeton: Princeton University Press, 1989.

Buckland, Warren. *The Cognitive Semiotics of Film*. Cambridge: Cambridge University Press, 2000.

Callaghan, Joanna, and Martin McQuillan, eds. *Love in the Post: From Plato to Derrida, The Screenplay and Commentary*. New York: Rowman & Littlefield, 2014.

Callaway, Kutter. *Scoring Transcendence: Contemporary Film Music as Religious Experience*. Waco: Baylor University Press, 2013.

Caputo, John D. *The Insistence of God: A Theology of Perhaps*. Bloomington: Indiana University Press, 2013.

———. *The Prayers and Tears of Jacques Derrida: Religion without Religion*. Bloomington: Indiana University Press, 1997.

———. *The Weakness of God: A Theology of the Event*. Bloomington: Indiana University Press, 2006.

Carr, Nicholas G. *The Shallows: What the Internet is Doing to our Brains*. New York: W. W. Norton, 2010.

Carroll, Noël. *Engaging the Moving Image*. New Haven: Yale University Press, 2003.

———. *Philosophy of Film and Motion Pictures: An Anthology*. Malden: Blackwell, 2006.

———. "Prospects for Film Theory: A Personal Assessment." In *Post-Theory: Reconstructing Film Studies*, edited by David Bordwell and Noël Carroll, 37–68. Madison: University of Wisconsin Press, 1996.

———. *Theorizing the Moving Image*. Cambridge: Cambridge University Press, 1996.

Chevalier, Tracy. *Girl with a Pearl Earring*. New York: Penguin, 2001.

Cho, Francisca. "Buddhism, Film, and Religious Knowing: Challenging the Literary Approach to Film." In *Teaching Religion and Film*, edited by Gregory J. Watkins, 117–28. New York: Oxford University Press, 2008.

———. "Imagining Nothing and Imagining Otherness in Buddhist Film." In *The Religion and Film Reader*, edited by Jolyon Mitchell and S. Brent Plate, 398–406. New York: Routledge, 2007.

Christianson, Eric S., Peter Francis, and William R. Telford, eds. *Cinéma Divinité: Religion, Theology and the Bible in Film*. London: SCM Press, 2005.

Clarke, Anthony J., and Paul S. Fiddes, eds. *Flickering Images: Theology and Film in Dialogue*. Macon: Smyth & Helwys, 2005.

Coates, Paul. *Cinema, Religion and the Romantic Legacy*. Burlington: Ashgate, 2003.

Cochrane, Scott J. "*The Wizard of Oz* and Other Mythic Rites of Passage." In *Image and Likeness: Religious Vision in American Film Classics*, edited by John R. May, 79–86. New York: Paulist, 1992.

Colebrook, Claire. *Gilles Deleuze*. London: Routledge, 2002.

Conrad, Mark T., ed. *The Philosophy of Martin Scorsese*. Lexington: University Press of Kentucky, 2007.

Constandinides, Costas. *From Film Adaptation to Post-Celluloid Adaptation: Rethinking the Transition of Popular Narrative and Characters across Old and New Media*. New York: Continuum, 2010.

Cook, David A. *A History of Narrative Film*. New York: Norton, 1990.

Cubitt, Sean. *The Cinema Effect*. Cambridge: MIT Press, 2004.

Culler, Jonathan. *The Pursuit of Signs: Semiotics, Literature, Deconstruction: An Augmented Edition with a New Preface by the Author*. Ithaca: Cornell University Press, 2002.

Damisch, Hubert. "A Cinema No Longer Silent." In *Cinema and the Shoah: An Art Confronts the Tragedy of the Twentieth Century*, edited by Jean-Michel Frodon, translated by Anna Harrison and Tom Mes, 43–54. Albany: State University of New York Press, 2010.

Dayan, Daniel. "The Tutor-Code of Classical Cinema." In *Film Theory and Criticism: Introductory Readings*, 6th edn, edited by Leo Braudy and Marshall Cohen, 106–17. New York: Oxford University Press, 2004.

Deacy, Christopher. *Faith in Film: Religious Themes in Contemporary Cinema*. Farnham: Ashgate, 2005.

———. "From Bultmann to Burton, Demythologizing the Big Fish: The Contribution of Modern Christian Theologians to the Theology–Film Conversation." In *Reframing Theology and Film: New Focus for an Emerging Discipline*, edited by Robert K. Johnston, 238–60. Grand Rapids: Baker Academic, 2007.

———. *Screen Christologies: Redemption and the Medium of Film*. Cardiff: University of Wales Press, 2001.

Deacy, Christopher, and Gaye Williams Ortiz. *Theology and Film: Challenging the Sacred/Secular Divide*. Malden: Blackwell, 2008.

De Bleeckere, Sylvain. "The Religious Dimension of Cinematic Consciousness in Postmodern Culture." In *New Image of Religious Film*, edited by John R. May, 95–110. Kansas City: Sheed & Ward, 1997.

De Lauretis, Teresa. *Alice Doesn't: Feminism, Semiotics, Cinema*. Bloomington: Indiana University Press, 1984.

———. *Technologies of Gender: Essays on Theory, Film, and Fiction*. Bloomington: Indiana University Press, 1987.

Deledalle, Gérard. "Media between Balnibarbi and Plato's Cave." In *Semiotics of the Media: State of the Art, Projects, and Perspective*, edited by Winfried Nöth, 49–60. Berlin: Mouton de Gruyter, 1997.

Deleuze, Gilles. *Cinema 1: The Movement-Image*. Translated by Hugh Tomlinson and Barbara Habberjam. Minneapolis: University of Minnesota Press, 1986.

———. *Cinema 2: The Time-Image*. Translated by Hugh Tomlinson and Robert Galeta. Minneapolis: University of Minnesota Press, 1989.

———. "I'm Going to Have to Wander All Alone." Translated by Leonard Lawlor. In *The Work of Mourning*, edited by Pascale-Anne Brault and Michael Naas, 189–96. Chicago: University of Chicago Press, 2001.

Derrida, Jacques. "Above All, No Journalists!" In *Religion and Media*, edited by Hent de Vries and Samuel Weber, 56–93. Stanford: Stanford University Press, 2001.

———. "'Le cinéma et ses fantômes', entretien avec Antoine de Baecque et Thierry Jousse," *Cahiers du cinéma* 556 (April 2001): 47–185.

———. "Circumfession: Fifty-nine Periods and Periphrases." Translated by Geoffry Bennington. In *Jacques Derrida*, edited by Geoffrey Bennington and Jacques Derrida, 3–315. Chicago: University of Chicago Press, 1993.

———."Dialogue with Jacques Derrida." In *Dialogues with Contemporary Continental Thinkers: The Phenomenological Heritage*, edited by Richard Kearney, 105–26. Manchester: Manchester University Press, 1984.

———. *The Gift of Death*. Translated by David Wills. Chicago: University of Chicago Press, 1995.

———. *Given Time: 1. Counterfeit Money*. Translated by Peggy Kamuf. Chicago: University of Chicago Press, 1994.

———. "Hostipitality." In *Acts of Religion*, translated and edited by Gil Anidjar, 356–420. New York: Routledge, 2002.

———. *Of Grammatology*. Translated by Gayatri Chakravorty Spivak. Baltimore: Johns Hopkins University Press, 1976.

———. "The Spatial Arts: An Interview with Jacques Derrida." In *Deconstruction and the Visual Arts: Art, Media, Architecture*, edited by Peter Brunette and David Wills, 9–32. Cambridge: Cambridge University Press, 1994.

———. *Speech and Phenomena and Other Essays on Husserl's Theory of Signs*. Translated by David B. Allison. Evanston: Northwestern University Press, 1973.

———. *Writing and Difference*. Translated by Alan Bass. Chicago: University of Chicago Press, 1978.

Detweiler, Craig. *Into the Dark: Seeing the Sacred in the Top Films of the 21st Century*. Grand Rapids: Baker, 2008.

———. "Seeing and Believing: Film Theory as a Window into a Visual Faith." In *Reframing Theology and Film: New Focus for an Emerging Discipline*, edited by Robert K. Johnston, 29–50. Grand Rapids: Baker Academic, 2007.

Doane, Mary Ann. *Femmes Fatales*. New York: Routledge, 1991.

Doneson, Judith E. *The Holocaust in American Film*. Syracuse: Syracuse University Press, 2002.

Dorsky, Nathaniel. *Devotional Cinema*. 2nd edn. Berkeley: Tuumba, 2005.
Downing, Crystal. "Broadway Roses: Woody Allen's Romantic Inheritance." *Literature/Film Quarterly* 17.1 (1989): 13–17.
———. *Changing Signs of Truth: A Christian Introduction to the Semiotics of Communication*. Downers Grove: IVP Academic, 2012.
———. "Woody Allen's Blindness and Insight: The Palimpsests of *Crimes and Misdemeanors*." *Religion and the Arts* 1 (1997): 73–92.
Downing, David C. "Waiting for Godoz: Deconstructing *The Wizard of Oz*." *Christianity and Literature* 33.2 (March 1984): 28–30.
Dyer, Richard, and Paul McDonald. *Stars*. 2nd edn. London: British Film Institute, 1998.
Eco, Umberto. "Semiotics and the Philosophy of Language." In *Reading Eco: An Anthology*, edited by Rocco Capozzi, 1–13. Bloomington: Indiana University Press, 1997.
———. *Travels in Hyperreality: Essays*. San Diego: Harcourt Brace Jovanovich, 1986.
Ehrat, Johannes. *Cinema and Semiotic: Peirce and Film Aesthetics, Narration, and Representation*. Toronto: University of Toronto Press, 2005.
Eisenstein, Sergei. *The Film Sense*. New York: Harcourt, Brace, 1941.
———. "Through Theater to Cinema." In *Theater and Film: A Comparative Anthology*, edited by Robert Knopf, 239–50. New Haven: Yale University Press, 2005.
Faber, Alyda. "Redeeming Sexual Violence? A Feminist Reading of *Breaking the Waves*." *Literature and Theology* 17.1 (March 2003): 59–75.
Farahmand, Azadeh. "Disentangling the International Festival Circuit: Genre and Iranian Cinema." In *Global Art Cinema: New Theories and Histories*, edited by Rosalind Galt and Karl Schoonover, 263–81. Oxford: Oxford University Press, 2010.
Ferlita, Ernest. "Film and the Quest for Meaning." In *Religion in Film*, edited by John R. May and Michael S. Bird, 115–32. Knoxville: University of Tennessee Press, 1982.
Ferlita, Ernest, and John R. May. *Film Odyssey: The Art of Film as Search for Meaning*. New York: Paulist, 1976.
Forster, E. M. *A Room with a View*. New York: Dover, 1995.
Forshey, Gerald E. *American Religious and Biblical Spectaculars*. Westport: Praeger, 1992.
Foucault, Michel. *The Archaeology of Knowledge and the Discourse on Language*. Translated by A. M. Sheridan Smith. New York: Pantheon, 1972.
Fraser, Peter. *Images of the Passion: The Sacramental Mode in Film*. Westport: Praeger, 1998.
Fraser, Peter, and Vernon Edwin Neal. *ReViewing the Movies: A Christian Response to Contemporary Film*. Wheaton: Crossway, 2000.
Friedman, Lawrence S. *The Cinema of Martin Scorsese*. New York: Continuum, 1997.
Furstenau, Marc. "Film Theory: A History of Debates." In *The Film Theory Reader: Debates and Arguments*, edited by Marc Furstenau, 1–20. New York: Routledge, 2010.
Gabara, Rachel. "Abderrahmane Sissako: Second and Third Cinema in the First Person." In *Global Art Cinema*, edited by Rosalind Galt and Karl Schoonover, 321–32. New York: Oxford University Press, 2010.
Gaer, Joseph. *What the Great Religions Believe*. New York: Signet, 1963.
Grace, Pamela. *The Religious Film: Christianity and the Hagiopic*. Malden: Wiley-Blackwell, 2009.
Grimes, Larry E. "Shall these Bones Live? The Problem of Bodies in Alfred Hitchcock's *Psycho* and Joel Coen's *Blood Simple*." In *Screening the Sacred: Religion, Myth, and Ideology in Popular American Film*, edited by Joel W. Martin and Conrad E. Ostwalt Jr., 19–29. Boulder: Westview, 1995.
Gunning, Tom. "Moving Away from the Index: Cinema and the Impression of Reality." In *The Film Theory Reader: Debates and Arguments*, edited by Marc Furstenau, 255–69. New York: Routledge, 2010.

Hamner, M. Gail. *Imaging Religion in Film: The Politics of Nostalgia*. New York: Palgrave Macmillan, 2011.
Heath, Stephen. "Introduction: Questions of Emphasis." *Screen* 14 (Spring/Summer 1973): 9–14.
———. *Questions of Cinema*. Bloomington: Indiana University Press, 1981.
Heylin, Clinton. *Despite the System: Orson Welles versus the Hollywood Studios*. Chicago: Chicago Review Press, 2005.
Hill, Geoffrey. *Illuminating Shadows: The Mythic Power of Film*. Boston: Shambhala, 1992.
Hinson, Hal. "The Last Temptation of Christ." *Washington Post*, August 12, 1988.
Hoberman, J. *Film After Film: Or, What Became of 21st Century Cinema?* New York: Verso, 2012.
Hogan, James. *Reel Parables: Life Lessons from Popular Films*. Mahwah: Paulist, 2007.
Hollows, Joanne, Peter Hutchings, and Mark Jancovich, eds. "Genre Criticism." In *The Film Studies Reader*, 83–8. New York: Oxford University Press, 2000.
Horkheimer, Max, and Theodor W. Adorno. *Dialectic of Enlightenment*. Translated by John Cumming. New York: Continuum, 1972.
Horner, Grant. *Meaning at the Movies: Becoming a Discerning Viewer*. Wheaton: Crossway, 2010.
Humphreys, Christmas. *Buddhism*. Harmondsworth: Pelican, 1951.
Humphries-Brooks, Stephenson. *Cinematic Savior: Hollywood's Making of the American Christ*. Westport: Praeger, 2006.
Hurley, Neil. *Theology through Film*. New York: Harper & Row, 1970.
Jackson, Kevin, ed. *Schrader on Schrader*. London: Faber & Faber, 1990.
Jacobs, Lewis. *The Rise of the American Film: A Critical History*. New York: Harcourt, Brace and Company, 1947.
Jakobson, Roman. "Is the Film in Decline?" In *Selected Writings: Poetry of Grammar and Grammar of Poetry*, vol. 3, 732–7. Berlin: Walter de Gruyter, 1981.
James, William. *The Varieties of Religious Experience: A Study in Human Nature*. Hazelton: Penn State University Electronic Classics, 2002. Available online at http://hermetic.com/93beast.fea.st/files/section1/James%20%20Varieties%20of%20Religious%20Experience.pdf (accessed June 24, 2015).
Jameson, Fredric. *Signatures of the Visible*. New York: Routledge, 1990.
Jewett, Robert. *Saint Paul at the Movies: The Apostle's Dialogue with American Culture*. Louisville: Westminster/John Knox Press, 1993.
Johnston, Robert K. *Reel Spirituality: Theology and Film in Dialogue*. Grand Rapids: Baker Academic, 2006.
Kaplan, E. Ann. "Is the Gaze Male?" In *The Film Theory Reader: Debates and Arguments*, edited by Marc Furstenau, 209–21. New York: Routledge, 2010.
Kelso, Julie. "Gazing at Impotence in Henry King's *David and Bathsheba*." In *Screening Scripture: Intertextual Connections between Scripture and Film*, edited by George Aichele and Richard Walsh, 155–88. Harrisburg: Trinity, 2002.
Keuss, Jeffrey F. "Reading Stanley Kubrick: A Theological Odyssey." In *Cinéma Divinité: Religion, Theology and the Bible in Film*, edited by Eric S. Christianson, Peter Francis, and William R. Telford, 78–93. London: SCM Press, 2005.
Kinnard, Roy, and Tim Davis. *Divine Images: A History of Jesus on the Screen*. New York: Citadel, 1992.
Kravitz, Leonard, and Kerry M. Olitzky, eds. *Pirke Avot: A Modern Commentary on Jewish Ethics*. New York: UAHC Press, 1993.

Kreitzer, L. Joseph. *Gospel Images in Fiction and Film: On Reversing the Hermeneutical Flow.* Sheffield: Sheffield Academic Press, 2002.

———. *The Old Testament in Fiction and Film: On Reversing the Hermeneutical Flow.* Sheffield: Sheffield Adacemic Press, 1994.

———. *Pauline Images in Fiction and Film: On Reversing the Hermeneutical Flow.* Sheffield: Sheffield Academic Press, 1999.

Kristeva, Julia. "Women's Time." In *Critical Theory since 1965*, edited by Hazard Adams and Leroy Searle, 469–84. Tallahassee: Florida State University Press, 1986.

Lacan, Jacques. *The Four Fundamental Concepts of Psycho-Analysis.* Translated by Alan Sheridan. New York: Norton, 1978.

———. "The Mirror Stage as Formative of the Function of the 'I' as Revealed in Psychoanalytic Experience." In *Écrits: A Selection*, translated by Alan Sheridan, 1–9. New York: Norton, 1997.

———. *The Seminar of Jacques Lacan, Book I: Freud's Papers on Technique, 1953–54.* Translated by John Forrester. Cambridge: Cambridge University Press, 1988.

Lang, J. Stephen. *The Bible on the Big Screen: A Guide from Silent Films to Today's Movies.* Grand Rapids: Baker, 2007.

Leonard, Richard, SJ. *Movies that Matter: Reading Film through the Lens of Faith.* Chicago: Loyola Press, 2006.

Levi, Primo. *The Drowned and the Saved.* Translated by Raymond Rosenthal. New York: Summit, 1988.

Lewis, C. S. *An Experiment in Criticism.* Cambridge: Cambridge University Press, 1965.

Lindvall, Terry. *Sanctuary Cinema: Origins of the Christian Film Industry.* New York: New York University Press, 2007.

Livaneli, O. Z. *Bliss.* Translated by C. A. Fromm. New York: St. Martin's Griffin, 2006.

Loiperdinger, Martin. "Lumière's *Arrival of the Train*: Cinema's Founding Myth." *The Moving Image* 4.1 (2004): 89–118.

Loughlin, Gerard. *Alien Sex: The Body and Desire in Cinema and Theology.* Malden: Blackwell, 2004.

Lowenstein, Adam. "Interactive Art Cinema: Between 'Old' and 'New' Media with *Un Chien Andalou* and *eXistenZ*." In *Global Art Cinema: New Theories and Histories*, edited by Rosalind Galt and Karl Schoonover, 92–105. New York: Oxford University Press, 2010.

Lyden, John C. *Film as Religion: Myths, Morals, and Rituals.* New York: New York University Press, 2003.

Lynch, Gordon. "Cultural Theory and Cultural Studies." In *The Routledge Companion to Religion and Film*, edited by John Lyden, 275–91. London: Routledge, 2009.

MacCullough, Diarmaid. *Christianity: The First Three Thousand Years.* New York: Viking, 2010.

McCann, Graham. New Introduction to *Composing for the Films*, by Theodor Adorno and Hanns Eisler, xxx–xxxi. New York: Continuum, 2007.

McLuhan, Marshall. *The Gutenberg Galaxy; The Making of Typographic Man.* Toronto: University of Toronto Press, 1962.

———. *Understanding Media: The Extensions of Man.* New York: McGraw-Hill, 1964.

McLuhan, Marshall, and Quentin Fiore. *The Medium is the Massage: An Inventory of Effects.* Berkeley: Ginko Press, 2005.

Maisto, Maria Consuelo. "Cinematic Communion? *Babette's Feast*, Transcendental Style, and Interdisciplinarity." In *Imag(in)ing Otherness: Filmic Visions of Living Together*, edited by S. Brent Plate and David Jasper, 83–9. Atlanta: Scholars Press, 1999.

Makarushka, Irena. "Women Spoken For: Images of Displaced Desire." In *Screening the Sacred: Religion, Myth, and Ideology in Popular American Film*, edited by Joel W. Martin and Conrad E. Ostwalt Jr, 142–51. Boulder: Westview Press, 1995.

Malone, Peter. *Screen Jesus: Portrayals of Christ in Television and Film*. Lanham: Scarecrow, 2012.

Malraux, André. "Outlines of a Psychology of Cinema." Translated by Stuart Gilbert. *Verve* 8 (1940): 69–73.

Mann, William J. *How to Be a Movie Star: Elizabeth Taylor in Hollywood*. London: Faber & Faber 2009.

Marks, Laura U. *The Skin of the Film: Intercultural Cinema, Embodiment, and the Senses*. Durham: Duke University Press, 2000.

———. *Touch: Sensuous Theory and Multisensory Media*. Minneapolis: University of Minnesota Press, 2002.

Marsh, Clive. *Cinema and Sentiment: Film's Challenge to Theology*. Milton Keynes: Paternoster Press, 2004.

———. *Theology Goes to the Movies: An Introduction to Critical Christian Thinking*. London: Routledge, 2007.

Martin, Joel W., and Conrad E. Ostwalt Jr., eds. *Screening the Sacred: Religion, Myth, and Ideology in Popular American Film*. Boulder: Westview Press, 1995.

Marty, Joseph. "Toward a Theological Interpretation and Reading of Film: Incarnation of the Word of God—Relation, Image, Word." In *New Image of Religious Film*, edited by John R. May, 131–50. Kansas City: Sheed & Ward, 1997.

Matalon, Guy. "Holocaust Movies." In *The Bloomsbury Companion to Religion and Film*, edited by William L. Blizek, 231–41. London: Bloomsbury, 2009.

Mauss, Marcel. *The Gift: The Form and Reason for Exchange in Archaic Societies*. Translated by W. D. Halls. New York: Norton, 1990.

May, John. Preface to *Religion in Film*, edited by John R. May and Michael S. Bird, vii–xi. Knoxville: University of Tennessee Press, 1982.

———. "Visual Story and the Religious Interpretation of Film." In *Religion in Film*, edited by John R. May and Michael S. Bird, 23–43. Knoxville: University of Tennessee Press, 1982.

Meikle, Kyle. "Rematerializing Adaptation Theory." *Literature/Film Quarterly* 41.3 (July 2013): 174–83.

Menand, Louis. *The Metaphysical Club: A Story of Ideas in America*. New York: Farrar, Straus and Giroux, 2001.

Metz, Christian. *Film Language: A Semiotics of the Cinema*. Translated by Michael Taylor. Chicago: University of Chicago Press, 1974.

———. *The Imaginary Signifier: Psychoanalysis and the Cinema*. Translated by Celia Britton, Annwyl Williams, Ben Brewster, and Alfred Guzzetti. Bloomington: Indiana University Press, 1982.

———. *Language and Cinema*. Translated by Donna Jean Umiker-Sebeok. The Hague: Mouton, 1974.

Miles, Margaret R. *Seeing and Believing: Religion and Values in the Movies*. Boston: Beacon, 1996.

Mimura, Glen M. *Ghostlife of Third Cinema: Asian American Film and Video*. Minneapolis: University of Minnesota Press, 2009.

Mitry, Jean. *Semiotics and the Analysis of Film*. Translated by Christopher King. London: Athlone, 2000.

Monaco, James. *How to Read a Film: The Art, Technology, Language, History, and Theory of Film and Media*. New York: Oxford University Press, 1981.

Morgan, Daniel. "Rethinking Bazin: Ontology and Realist Aesthetics," *Critical Inquiry* 32 (Spring 2006): 443–81.
Mulvey, Laura. "Looking at the Past from the Present: Rethinking Feminist Film Theory of the 1970s." *Signs: Journal of Women in Culture and Society* 30.1 (2004): 1288–9.
———. *Visual and Other Pleasures*. Bloomington: Indiana University Press, 1989.
Münsterberg, Hugo. *The Photoplay: A Psychological Study*. New York: Appleton, 1916.
Nayar, Sheila J. *The Sacred and the Cinema: Reconfiguring the "Genuinely" Religious Film*. London: Continuum, 2012.
Nicholson, Marjorie Hope. *Mountain Gloom and Mountain Glory: The Development of the Aesthetics of the Infinite*. New York: Norton, 1963.
Nochimson, Martha P. *World on Film: An Introduction*. Malden: Wiley-Blackwell, 2010.
Nolan, Steve. *Film, Lacan and the Subject of Religion: A Psychoanalytic Approach to Religious Film Analysis*. London: Continuum, 2009.
———. "Understanding Films: Reading in the Gaps." In *Flickering Images: Theology and Film in Dialogue*, edited by Anthony J. Clarke and Paul S. Fiddes, 25–48. Macon: Smyth & Helwys, 2005.
Ortiz, Gaye Williams. "Feminism." In *The Routledge Companion to Religion and Film*, edited by John Lyden, 237–54. New York: Routledge, 2009.
Pagels, Elaine. *The Gnostic Gospels*. New York: Random House, 1979.
Patton, Paul, and John Protevi, eds. *Between Deleuze and Derrida*. London: Continuum, 2003.
Peirce, Charles Sanders. *Collected Papers of Charles Sanders Peirce*. Volumes 1–6 edited by Charles Hartshorne and Paul Weiss. Volumes 7–8 edited by Arthur W. Burkes. Cambridge: Harvard University Press, 1931–58.
———. "The Essentials of Pragmatism." In *Philosophical Writings of Peirce*, edited by Justus Buchler, 251–68. New York: Dover, 1955.
———. "Evolutionary Love." In *Philosophical Writings of Peirce*, edited by Justus Buchler, 361–74. New York: Dover, 1955.
———. "The Fixation of Belief." In *Philosophical Writings of Peirce*, edited by Justus Buchler, 5–22. New York: Dover, 1955.
———. *Pragmatism as a Principle and Method of Right Thinking: The 1903 Harvard "Lectures on Pragmatism."* Edited by Patricia Ann Turrisi. Albany: State University of New York Press, 1997.
———. "Pragmatism in Retrospect: A Last Formulation." In *Philosophical Writings of Peirce*, edited by Justus Buchler, 269–89. New York: Dover, 1955.
———. "Some Consequences of Four Incapacities." In *Philosophical Writings of Peirce*, edited by Justus Buchler, 228–50. New York: Dover, 1955.
Perkins, Victor F. *Film as Film: Understanding and Judging Movies*. New York: Penguin, 1972.
Plate, S. Brent. *Religion and Film: Cinema and the Re-Creation of the World*. London: Wallflower, 2008.
———. Introduction to *Representing Religion in World Cinema: Filmmaking, Mythmaking, Culture Making*, edited by S. Brent Plate, 1–18. New York: Palgrave Macmillan, 2003.
Plato. "The Republic." Translated by Benjamin Jowett. In *Dialogues of Plato*, edited by J. D. Kaplan, 235–386. New York: Washington Square Press, 1967.
Raschke, Carl. *Postmodernism and the Revolution in Religious Theory: Towards a Semiotics of the Event*. Charlottesville: University of Virginia Press, 2012.
Reinhartz, Adele. *Scripture on the Silver Screen*. Louisville: Westminster John Knox, 2003.

Roberts, Tyler. "Sacrifice and Secularization: Derrida, de Vries, and the Future of Mourning." In *Derrida and Religion: Other Testaments*, edited by Yvonne Sherwood and Kevin Hart, 263–82. New York: Routledge, 2005.

Rodowick, D. N. *Gilles Delueze's Time Machine*. Durham: Duke University Press, 1997.

Romanowski, William D. *Reforming Hollywood: How American Protestants Fought for Freedom at the Movies*. New York: Oxford University Press, 2012.

Rosen, Philip. "Notes on Art Cinema and the Emergence of Sub-Saharan Film." In *Global Art Cinema: New Theories and Histories*, edited by Rosalind Galt and Karl Schoonover, 252–62. New York: Oxford University Press, 2010.

Rothman, William. "Against 'The System of the Suture.'" In *Movies and Methods: An Anthology*, vol. 1, edited by Bill Nichols, 451–68. Berkeley: University of California Press, 1982.

Runions, Erin. *How Hysterical: Identification and Resistance in the Bible and Film*. New York: Palgrave Macmillan, 2003.

Sanders, Theresa. *Celluloid Saints: Images of Sanctity in Film*. Macon: Mercer University Press, 2002.

Sarris, Andrew. "Notes on the *Auteur* Theory in 1962." In *The Film Studies Reader*, edited by Joanne Hollows, Peter Hutchings, and Mark Jancovich, 68–71. New York: Oxford University Press, 2000.

Saussure, Ferdinand de. *Course in General Linguistics*. Translated by Wade Baskin. New York: McGraw-Hill, 1959.

Schatz, Thomas. *Hollywood Genres: Formulas, Filmmaking, and the Studio System*. Philadelphia: Temple University Press, 1981.

Schrader, Paul. *Transcendental Style in Film: Ozu, Bresson, Dreyer*. Berkeley: University of California Press, 1972.

Scott, Bernard Brandon. *Hollywood Dreams and Biblical Stories*. Minneapolis: Fortress, 1994.

Sebeok, Thomas Albert. *Semiotics in the United States*. Bloomington: Indiana University Press, 1991.

Selznick, Brian. *The Invention of Hugo Cabret: A Novel in Words and Pictures*. New York: Scholastic Press, 2007.

Sherwood, Yvonne, and Kevin Hart, eds. *Derrida and Religion: Other Testaments*. New York: Routledge, 2005.

Shohat, Ella. "Post Third-Worldist Culture: Gender, Nation, and the Cinema." In *Rethinking Third Cinema*, edited by Anthony R. Guneratne and Wimal Dissanayake, 51–78. New York: Routledge, 2003.

Shohat, Ella, and Robert Stam. *Unthinking Eurocentrism: Multiculturalism and the Media*. London: Routledge, 1994.

Silverman, Kaja. *The Subject of Semiotics*. New York: Oxford University Press, 1983.

———. *The Threshold of the Visible World*. New York: Routledge, 1996.

Sinnerbrink, Robert. *New Philosophies of Film: Thinking Images*. New York: Continuum International, 2011.

Sison, Antonio D. "Perfumed Nightmare: Religion and the Philippine Postcolonial Struggle in Third Cinema." In *Representing Religion in World Cinema: Filmmaking, Mythmaking, Culture Making*, edited by S. Brent Plate, 181–96. New York: Palgrave Macmillan, 2003.

Smith, Huston. *The Religions of Man*. New York: Harper & Row, 1965.

Sobchack, Vivian. *Carnal Thoughts: Embodiment and Moving Image Culture*. Berkeley: University of California Press, 2004.

Solanas, Fernando, and Ottavio Getino. "Towards a Third Cinema: Notes and Experiences for the Development of a Cinema of Liberation in the Third World." In *Twenty-five Years of the New Latin American Cinema*, translated and edited by Michael Chanan, 17–27. London: British Film Institute, 1983.
Spiegel, James S. Introduction to *Faith, Film and Philosophy: Big Ideas on the Big Screen*, edited by R. Douglas Geivett and James S. Spiegel, 9–20. Downers Grove: IVP Academic, 2007.
Stahlman, Mark K. "The Place of Marshall McLuhan in the Learning of his Times." *Renascence: Essays on Values in Literature* 64.1 (2011): 5–18.
Staley, Jeffrey L., and Richard Walsh. *Jesus, the Gospels, and Cinematic Imagination: A Handbook to Jesus on DVD*. Louisville: Westminster John Knox, 2007.
Stam, Robert. *Film Theory: An Introduction*. Malden: Blackwell, 2000.
Stern, Richard C., Clayton N. Jefford, and Guerric DeBona. *Savior on the Silver Screen*. New York: Paulist Press, 1999.
Stewart, Garrett. *Framed Time: Toward a Postfilmic Cinema*. Chicago: University of Chicago Press, 2007.
Stone, Bryan. *Faith and Film: Theological Themes at the Cinema*. St. Louis: Chalice, 2000.
Tatum, W. Barnes. *Jesus at the Movies: A Guide to the First Hundred Years*. Santa Rosa: Polebridge, 1997.
Taylor, Mark C. "What Derrida Really Meant." *New York Times*, October 14, 2004.
Thanouli, Eleftheria. *Post-Classical Cinema: An International Poetics of Film Narration*. London: Wallflower, 2009.
Thompson, Kristin. *Breaking the Glass Armor: Neoformalist Film Analysis*. Princeton: Princeton University Press, 1988.
Tillich, Paul. *The Protestant Era*. Abridged edition. Chicago: University of Chicago Press, 1957.
Torday, Paul. *Salmon Fishing in the Yemen*. New York: Harvest, 2007.
Trier, Lars, von with Christian Braad Thomsen. "Trier on von Trier." In *The Religion and Film Reader*, edited by Jolyon Mitchell and S. Brent Plate, 230–2. New York: Routledge, 2007.
Truffaut, François. "A Certain Tendency of the French Cinema." In *The Film Studies Reader*, edited by Joanne Hollows, Peter Hutchings, and Mark Jancovich, 58–63. New York: Oxford University Press, 2000.
Vincendeau, Ginette. "Fifty Years of the French New Wave: From Hysteria to Nostalgia." In *The French New Wave: Critical Landmarks*, edited by Peter Graham, 1–29. New York: Palgrave Macmillan, 2009.
Vries, Hent, de. *Philosophy and the Turn to Religion*. Baltimore: Johns Hopkins University Press, 1999.
Vollmer, Ulrike. *Seeing Film and Reading Feminist Theology: A Dialogue*. New York: Palgrave Macmillan, 2007.
Walden, Treadwell. *The Great Meaning of the Word Metanoia: Lost in the Old Version, Unrecovered in the New*. New York: Thomas Whittaker, 1896.
Wall, James M. "Paradoxical Goodness." *The Christian Century* 114.5 (February 1997): 115.
Walsh, Richard G. *Finding St. Paul in Film*. New York: T&T Clark International, 2005.
———. *Reading the Gospels in the Dark: Portrayals of Jesus in Film*. Harrisburg: Trinity Press International, 2007.
Walther, Elisabeth. "The Sign as Medium, the Medium Relation as the Foundation of the Sign." In *Semiotics of the Media: State of the Art, Projects, and Perspective*, edited by Winfried Nöth, 79–86. Berlin: Mouton de Gruyter, 1997.

Watkins, Gregory. "Religion, Film and Film Theory." In *The Bloomsbury Companion to Religion and Film*, edited by William L. Blizek, 80–8. New York: Bloomsbury, 2009.

———. "Seeing and Being Seen: Distinctively Filmic and Religious Elements in Film." *Journal of Religion and Film* 3.2 (October 1999). Available online at www.unomaha.edu/jrf/ (accessed June 24, 2015).

Westphal, Merold. "Onto-Theology, Metanarrative, Perspectivism, and the Gospel." In *Christianity and the Postmodern Turn: Six Views*, edited by Myron B. Penner, 141–56. Grand Rapids: Baker, 2005.

Williams, Raymond. *Television: Technology and Cultural Form*. London: Routledge Classics, 2003.

Wimsatt, W. K. Jr., and Monroe C. Beardsley. "The Intentional Fallacy." In *The Verbal Icon*, edited by W. K. Wimsatt Jr., 3–20. New York: Farrar, Straus, 1964.

Wolfe, Tom. "Snob's Progress." *New York Times*, June 15, 1986.

Wollen, Peter. *Signs and Meaning in the Cinema*. Bloomington: Indiana University Press, 1969.

Wood, Gaby. *Edison's Eve: A Magical History of the Quest for Mechanical Life*. New York: Knopf, 2002.

Wright, Melanie J. *Religion and Film: An Introduction*. New York: I.B.Tauris, 2007.

Žižek, Slavoj. *The Sublime Object of Ideology*. New York: Verso, 1989.

Index

Chapter endnotes are indicated by a letter n between page number and note number; a solidus is used to separate references to multiple notes on the same page.

12 Years a Slave 82, 83
400 Blows, The 100–2, 172, 173

Abbot, James 161n23
Acker, Ally 64
adaptation studies 40–2, 55, 57, 58–63, 169–70, 154–5
Adorno, Theodore W. 4–5, 97
aerial shots 111, 149
Affron, Charles 7, 116n19
Agel, Henri 32n19
Allen, Woody 75–8, 83–91, see also *Annie Hall*, *Purple Rose of Cairo*, *Whatever Works*
Althusser, Louis 112–13, 114
Anker, Roy 92n13
Annie Hall 75–6, 77–8, 83, 84
apparatus theory 25, 112, 113, 145, 158
Aristotle 23
Arnheim, Rudolf 38
Arnoux, Alexander 96
Arrival of a Train at a Station 96, 167, 115n5
Astruc, Alexandre 100
Augustine 6, 83
auteur cinema/theory 100–3, 105–7, 117n39
Avila, Mitch 160n14

Babette's Feast 142n20
Babington, Bruce 35n65, 36n69/72
Balanta 79
Balthasar, Hans Urs von 23
Bamako 104–5
Barthes, Roland 105, 106–7, 162n41
Battleship Potemkin 98, 108, 127
Baudry, Jean-Louis 25
Baugh, Lloyd 36n66/67/69/72/76
Bazin, André 3, 24, 31n8, 32n30, 99–102, 105–6, 108, 146, 158
Beasts of the Southern Wild 50–52
Beautiful Mind, A 39
Benjamin, Walter 116n7
Benne, Robert 33n39
Bergman, Ingmar 78
Bettelheim, Bruno 127–8
Bian Lian see *King of Masks*
Bible books cited: Acts 137; Deuteronomy 30n1; Exodus 19, 137, 138–9; Genesis 17, 30, 89; Hebrews 29; Isaiah 4; Jeremiah 30n1; Job 38; John 10; Matthew 125; 2 Peter 4; Psalms 38, 52–3; Revelation 4
binary oppositions: defined 58; in film theory 103, 105, 107–9, 119n56/62, 123, 154, 158, 163; in movies 124, 128, 131–2, 136, 138–9, 149; in religion 122, 157; in Saussure's structuralism 105, 121, 123, 145–6, 152
Bird, Michael 21, 22, 150
black-and-white film 8–9, 40, 87–8, 90, 127, 144, 151
Blade Runner 72n17
Blake, Richard A. 33n32
Bliss 42–3
Bloom, Harold 20, 30
bodhisattva 5, 125, see also *King of Masks*
Bogart, Humphrey 77, 123
Bogue, Ronald 175
Bollywood 147
Booth, Herbert 2
Bordwell, David 24, 91n6, 114, 147, 162n52

Index

Bottomore, Stephen 96
breaking the fourth wall: as comic effect 76–7; defined 76; religious significance 80, 82, 83, 85–6, 88–90, 111; as self-referential 77, 79, 162n43, 168
Breaking the Waves 110–12, 113
Breathless 77, 79, 102
Bresson, Robert 22, 23
Brintnall, Kent 112
Brooks, Cleanth 24, 27
Buckland, Warren 115
Buddhism 6, 10, 20, 54n11, 111, 114, 125, 140; see also *King of Masks*
Burt, Ellen S. 122–3
Butch Cassidy and the Sundance Kid 102
Butler, The 108–9

Cahiers du cinéma 99, 100, 121, 140n2, 73n27
Callaghan, Joanna 123
Callaway, Kutter 1, 23, 177n23
camera obscuro 63
caméra stylo 100
Cameron, James 112–13
canted shots: defined 109
Caputo, John D. 126, 130, 175
Carr, Nicholas 3
Carroll, Noël 4, 13n7, 114–15, 147, 176n5
Chaplin, Charlie 99, 123, 167
Chevalier, Tracy 59, 63
chiaroscuro effects 8, 9, 109
chick flicks 57–8
Cho, Francisca 10
Christ-figures in film 39, 111, 113
Christianity 1, 126; medium of salvation 6, 10; as presented in film 52, 87, 144–5, 137–9, 156; see also Augustine, Ecumenical Councils, hypostatic union, Jesus, Tertullian
Circle of Deceit 73n25
Citizen Kane 9
Coates, Paul 161n27
cognitivism 114–15, 147
Coixet, Isabel 69–71
Colebrook, Claire 11
continuity editing 98, 171, 172
Coppola, Francis Ford 123–4
Counterfeiters, The 131–5
crane shots 42–3, 58, 106, 156
Crimes and Misdemeanors 87, 92n16
Cronenberg, David 79, 80
crosscutting 108–9, 153, 164
Cubitt, Sean 151
Culler, Jonathan 150

Dallas Buyers Club 151
Dayan, Daniel 73n27
De Bleeckere, Sylvain 59, 177n25
De Bona, Guerric 35n58, 36n69
De Lauretis, Teresa 148
Deacy, Christopher 6, 31n7, 32n22, 34n54, 35n65, 36n76, 53n4, 117n40, 125, 176n7
deconstruction 6, 72n14, 154; defined 58, 121–3; as hospitality 139–40; illustrated in film 124, 130–4, 136–9, 157–8; in C. S. Peirce 145, 148; see also Derrida, "the gift"
deep focus 9, 99, 171
Deledalle, Gérard 150, 145
Deleuze, Gilles 11, 24, 37n79, 146, 159n10; movement-image/time-image 171–3; spiritual automaton 173–5
Derrida, Jacques 6, 115, 121, 134, 144, 145, 157, 164, 173; see also deconstruction, exchangism, "the gift"
Detweiler, Craig 13n21, 34n52, 115n2, 159n5
Diary of Anne Frank, The 127
Diary of a Country Priest 22
Dickson, William 18
diegetic/nondiegetic sound 29, 39, 142n31, 146
dissolves 39, 40–1, 46, 47, 54n7, 132
Doane, Mary Ann 72n13
dogmatism 114–15
Don't Look Now 64
Doneson, Judith E. 127, 142n30
Dorsky, Nathaniel 30
Downing, David C. 151–12
Duhamel, Georges 97
Dulac, Germaine 24
Dutch shot 109
Dyer, Richard 3, 31n6

Eco, Umberto 114, 149, 158
Ecumenical Councils 10, 28, 36n76; Chacedon 26, 29, 30, 34n55, 35n56, 36n71, 172; Ephesus 26, 34n55; Nicaea 30, 36n74
Edison, Thomas 17–18, 95
Ehrat, Johannes 39, 145–6, 149–50, 152, 176
Eisenstein, Sergei 24, 98–9, 108, 127, 141n8, 170
Eisler, Hanns 97, 99
Elegy 69–71
Erin Brockovich 105
Evans, Peter Williams 35n65, 36n69/72

exchangism 123–4, 126, 128, 138, 144–5, 146; in religion 125–6, 130, 137, 139–40
eXistenZ 79–81
eyeline match cuts 42, 46, 60, 68, 70, 165, 169; defined 28

Faber, Alyda 111
feminist theory 56, 58, 71n3, 72n5, 104, 107, 111, 147–8
Ferlita, Ernest 21, 26–7
film noir 20, 36n76, 107, 123, 176n7
Fiore, Quentin 4, 172
Ford, John 126, 127
Forgiveness of Blood, The 124–5
Forshey, Gerald 36n67
Foucault, Michel 2, 73n27
framing devices 10, 43–5, 67–8, 82, 86, 134–5, 155
Fraser, Peter 35n60/63, 36n76, 92n13
free will vs. determinism 88–9, 153
French New Wave 24, 77, 99–101, 105, 116n22, 172
Freud, Sigmund 3, 56
Friedman, Laurence 125
fundamentalist fallacy 114, 123, 149, 157
Furstenau, Marc 10

Gaer, Joseph 96
Gance, Abel 96
genre criticism 107
German expressionism 99
Getino, Octavio 103
Gibson, Mel 148–9
"gift, the": and Derrida 125–6, 130–1, 139, 144, 175; in Lacan 111–12, 143n43, 144; in Peirce 152; in religion 140; in Silverman 139
Girl with a Pearl Earring 59–64
Glover, Danny 104
gnosticism 20–1, 23, 25, 122, 128, 150; in *The Last Temptation of Christ* 27–30
Godard, Jean-Luc 77, 79, 91n5, 102, 117n38
Godfather movies 123–4
Gorky, Maxim 115n5
Grace, Pamela 30
Grand Theory 114–15, 121, 123, 164, 171
graphic matches 36n73, 52, 67, 132, 156, 170, 174; defined 41
graphic motifs 40–3, 50–2, 60, 65, 155; defined 41
Great Train Robbery, The 79, 166, 167
Grimes, Larry 160n11

Hallström, Lasse 154, 157
Hamner, M. Gail 31n14, 158, 175
Hannah and Her Sisters 85
Heath, Stephen 62, 63, 91n4, 113, 118n47
Her Screen Idol 19
high-angle shots 29, 43, 124, 170
Hinduism 45, 52, 111, 140
Hiroshima, mon amour 11
history of cinema 17–20, 95–100, 117n27, 165–6; founding myth 96, 167, 169
Hitchcock, Alfred 101, 109, 147
Hitler, Adolf 97, 106, 126
Hogan, James 33n37
Holland, Agnieszka 135, 138, 143n40
Hollywood: classical style 77, 99, 103, 104, 153, 154, 158, 162n52, 171; Golden Age 126; materialism 18–20, 103; New Hollywood directors 79, 91n8
Holocaust in film 126–40
Horkheimer, Max 4–5, 97
Horner, Grant 31n14
horror movies 147
Horse Feathers 77
Hugo 164–75
Humphries-Brooks, Stephenson 36n69
Hurley, Neil 21
hypostatic union 26, 27, 28, 36n76, 172, 175

I Confess 109
In Darkness 135–9
Islam 43, 111, 114, 125, 149, 152; see also *Salmon Fishing in the Yemen*
Italian neorealism 24, 99, 144, 172

Jacobs, Lewis 18
Jakobson, Roman 105
James Bond movies 57
James, William 163, 166
Jameson, Fredric 113
Jaws 146, 147
Jazz Singer, The 38
Jefford, Clayton N. 35n58, 36n69
Jesus: crucifixion/resurrection 26, 29, 149; in Derrida's work 125; healing the blind 7, 10; as Jew 136–7; as medium of salvation 6, 29, 137–9; in Woody Allen films 83, 85, 87, 88; see also hypostatic union
Jesus films 20, 27; see also *The Last Temptation of Christ*, *The Passion of the Christ*
Jewett, Robert 33n37
John Rabe 106

Index

Johnston, Robert K. 31n9, 33n33/39, 35n60, 116n6
Judaism 105, 111, 114, 125, 137

Kaplan, E. Ann 58
Kazantzakis, Nikos 28
Keaton, Buster 167
Kelso, Julie 34n48, 72n5, 120n77
Keuss, Jeffrey F. 31n10
Kiarostami, Abbas 24
Kinetograph/Kinetoscope 18, 95–6
King of Masks, The 45–9
Koyaanisqatsi 39
Kristeva, Julia 111

Lacan, Jacques 34n50, 73n28, 110–13, 114, 143n43
Last Temptation of Christ, The 27–30, 36n73/76, 171–2
Latham Loop 96
Leonardo da Vinci 5, 57, 59, 70
Levi, Primo 128, 131, 136, 142n28
Lewis, C. S. 27
liberation theology 104, 107
Life Is Beautiful 127
lighting, high-key/low-key 8, 9, 29, 81, 109, 144, 162n44, *see also* chiaroscuro effects
Lindvall, Terry 2
Little Moth 43–5
Livaneli, O. Z. 54n8/9
Loiperdinger, Martin 96
Lonely Place to Die, A 152–4
long shots 28, 48, 65, 66, 100, 103, 109, 136, 152; defined 42
long takes 43, 44, 46, 59, 60, 83, 102, 171; defined 99
Loughlin, Gerard 32n15
Love in the Post 123
low-angle shots 9, 47, 48, 52, 67, 170; defined 42
Lowenstein, Adam 80
Lumière, Auguste and Louis 95–6, 165, 167
Lyden, John C. 1, 32n23, 34n42, 39, 141n14
Lynch, Gordon 120n81

MacCullough, Diamond 35n55/56
McLuhan, Marshall 2–4, 6, 7, 17, 38, 56, 74–6, 91, 97, 150, 170, 172
Mafia films 123
Maisto, Maria Consuelo 24
Makarushka, Irena 72n14
male gaze, the 56–8, 65, 69–70, 72n13

Malone, Peter 36n70
Malraux, André 99
Manichaean tendency 20, 128, 129, 131, 132, 134, 135, 136
Marks, Laura U. 25, 148
Marsh, Clive 1, 34n52, 53n3
Martin, Joel W. 120n76
Marty, Joseph 21
Marx Brothers 77
Marx, Karl 3, 56, 83, 98
Marxist theory 3, 4, 97, 104, 112–13, 145
Matalon, Guy 142n23
Mauss, Marcel 142n19
May, John R. 26–7, 35n57, 152
Méliès, Georges 165, 166
Merchant Ivory Productions 55, 71n2
Metz, Christian 24, 27, 158; alternating syntagma 108–9; semiotic theory 39–40, 54n7, 107, 118n54, 119n61; spectator psychology 109–10, 119n62, 167–8
Miles, Margaret R. 34n42, 92n13
mise-en-scène: defined 29, 40; technical employment 51, 59, 66, 68, 69, 70, 81, 129, 136, 153–4, 165; theorized 99, 100, 102–3, 106, 108, 146
Mission, The 81–2
Mitry, Jean 120n83
Monaco, James 10
montage: exemplified 7, 9, 46, 88, 129–30, 136, 155; theorized 98–9, 103, 108, 116n19, 119n65, 122, 141n8
Mulvey, Laura 55, 56, 62, 69, 107, 110, 148; to-be-looked-at-ness 57, 60, 61, 70; *see also* the male gaze
Münsterberg, Hugo 163–4
Mutluluk see *Bliss*
My Week with Marilyn 65

Narcissus trance 3, 75, 80, 87, 90, 97, 99, 102
Nayar, Sheila 32n19/25, 33n32, 160n22
Nazism 106, 126, 144, *see also* Holocaust in film
Neal, Vernon 35n60
neoformalism 11, 147
Nestorius 26–7, 30, 34n55
Nirvana 45, 48, 111, 125
Nolan, Steve 14n36, 24, 25, 70, 119n65
Nouvelle Vague see French New Wave
nudity in film 55, 56, 61, 64–7, 69–70

On the Waterfront 7–8, 9, 167
Ortiz, Gaye Williams 71n3

Ostwalt, Jr., Conrad E. 120n76
Oudart, Jean-Pierre 70

Pagels, Elaine 20
paintings in movies 57, 69, 71, 170; *Battle of San Romano* (Paolo Uccello) 58–9; *The Concert* (Johannes Vermeer) 62; Dadaist 170; Dutch Realist 59; *Girl with a Pearl Earring* (Johannes Vermeer) 59, 61, 62; by Francisco Goya 70, 73n30; *Las Meninas* (Diego Velasquez) 70–1; Quattrocento 59; of St. Jerome 156; *Young Woman with a Water Jug* (Johannes Vermeer) 62–3
Paramount Studios 19
Passion of Anna, The 78
Passion of the Christ, The 91n9, 148–9
Peirce, Charles Sanders 120n86, 145, 163; habits of perception and habit-change 147, 150–6, 158, 164, 172, 175; *see also* triadic signs
Perlasca: the Courage of a Just Man 130–1
Pianist, The 128–30
Pickford, Mary 19
Plate, S. Brent 1, 11, 12n8, 22, 31n14
Plato 32n29, 122; allegory of the cave 20–3, 25–6, 56, 112, 145
point of view (POV) shots 47, 50–1, 101, 139, 152–3, 168–9
Polley, Sarah 65
Pope, Robert 32n24
Porter, Edwin S. 79, 166
post-classical cinema 154, 162n44
post-structuralism 121
post-theory 114–15
Psycho 147
psychoanalytic film theory 25, 110–14, 145
Purple Rose of Cairo, The 87–90

Radio Days 90
Raging Bull 5–10, 13n31, 27, 53, 125, 167, 168
Raisin in the Sun, A 40–1, 169
Raschke, Carl 175
reception studies 113
Resnais, Alain 11
Rim, Carlo 169
Road to Bali, The 77
Rodowick, D. N. 159n10
Romanowski, William D. 2, 31n5, 36n67
romantic comedies 77–8, 84, 85, 89, 107
Rome, Open City 122
Room with a View, A 55–9, 70
Rossellini, Roberto 116n20, 144

Rothman, William 122
Runions, Erin 141n7
Ruzowitzky, Stefan 131, 133

Safety Last! 166
Salmon Fishing in the Yemen 154–7
Sanders, Theresa 142n26
Sarris, Andrew 103
Saussure, Ferdinand de 105, 110, 114, 145, 146, *see also* structuralism
Schindler's List 127–8
Schrader, Paul 13n29, 22, 27, 142n15
scopophilia 56, 61, 62, 64, 66, 69, 71
Scorsese, Martin 6, 36n66/71, 79, 124, 164, *see also Hugo, The Last Temptation of Christ, Raging Bull*
Scott, Bernard Brandon 33n35
Scott, Ridley 72n17, 79
Selznick, Brian 164–5, 166, 167, 168, 170, 172, 173
semiology 105, 108, 110
semiosis 150–2
semiotics 105–6, 113–15, 122; of Metz 107–110, 118n53; of Peirce 145–53
Sennett, Mack 19
sex on screen 64, 66–9
shot/reverse shot 52, 71, 79, 165; defined and theorized 60, 119n65
Siddhartha 45
silent film 24, 38, 79
Silverman, Kaja 60, 139, 146, 148, 161n27
Singer, Irving 92n20
Sinnerbrink, Robert 4
Sison, Antonio 117n40
Sissako, Abderrahmane 104
Skyfall 57, 72n10
slavery/human trafficking 43–4, 48, 82–3, 92n14
Smith, Brian 30n1
Smith, Huston 45–6
Sobchack, Vivian 73n31, 148
socialist realism 98
Solanas, Fernando 103
spectator theory 25, *see also* psychoanalytic film theory
Spielberg, Steven 127, 167
Spinoza, Baruch 173–4
split-screen device 157
Staley, Jeffrey L. 28, 35n58
Stam, Robert 25, 72n5, 95, 99, 120n81
Stern, Richard C. 35n58, 36n69
Stevens, George 126, 127
Stone, Bryon 36n70
Stranger, The 127

196 Index

Streetcar Named Desire, A 41–2, 169
structuralism 24, 119n62, 105–8, 121–3, 144–5, 147–8, 163, 164, *see also* Althusser, Barthes, Lacan, Metz
suture theory 70, 73n28, 91n4, 119n65

Take This Waltz 65–9
tanha 45, 49
Tao, Peng 43, 45
Tarkovsky, Andrei 177n25
Taste of Cherry 24
Tatum, Barnes W. 36n67/72
Taxi Driver 174
Taylor, Mark C. 123
Telford, William R. 161n26
Tertullian 6, 154
Thanouli, Eleftheria 154
Thelma and Louise 102
Third Cinema 103–5, 107
Thompson, Kristin 11, 147
Tillich, Paul 22
Titanic 112–13
tolerance, religious 6, 114, 139–40
Top Hat 90
tracking shots 102, 124, 125
transcendence through film 21–3, 25–7, 81, 87, 91, 95, 114, 125, 128, 145, 150
triadic sign, the 145–8; icon/index/symbol 148–50; immediate/dynamic/final interpretant 151–2; *see also* Peirce
Trier, Lars von 110

Trip to the Moon, A 166, 168
Truffaut, François 24, 100, 107, 117n26, 121, 169, see also *The 400 Blows*

Vermeer, Johannes see *Girl with a Pearl Earring*, paintings in film
voice-overs 60, 72n17, 81, 153–4
Vollmer, Ulrike 31n14
voyeurism 58, 61–5, 70

Wall, The 153–4
Walsh, Richard 28, 35n58/64
Walther, Elisabeth 150
Watkins, Gregory 12n6, 120n74, 141n7
Welles, Orson 9, 127
Westerns 104, 107
Westphal, Merold 139
Wetzel, Michael 6
Whatever Works 83–6
wide shots 99, 103
Wilder, Billy 126
Wizard of Oz, The 151
Wolfe, Tom 97
Wollen, Peter 145, 148
Wood, Gaby 173
Wright, Melanie J. 1, 21, 27, 30n2, 31n14, 34n54
Wu, Tianming 45, 49

Zizek, Slavoj 119n71